THE FINNS IN NORTH AMERICA

A Social Symposium

THE FINNS IN
NORTH AMERICA

A Social Symposium

Edited by Ralph J. Jalkanen

Published by
MICHIGAN STATE UNIVERSITY PRESS

for

SUOMI COLLEGE

Hancock, Michigan
1969

E
184
·F5
F513

★ ★
★
★ ★
★

FOREWORD

According to Martin Buber, there are "two kinds of epochs in the history of the human spirit: epochs of habitation and epochs of homelessness. In the former man lives in the world as in a house, as in a home. In the latter he looks out upon an open field, and there are not even four pegs with which to set up a tent." The emigrant must feel that he lives his life in an epoch of homelessness no matter how much other men remain safely at home and discover themselves in a time of habitation. Buber appears to intuit something about the connection, which only now is becoming a problem for research, between an environment and man's sense of security.

The chief component of the emigrant's attitude toward his past is undoubtedly a longing for the remembered security of early days. No matter how hazardous life may be nor how miserable the conditions of existence, the four walls of home still mean food and shelter to the young, and familiar sights reassure the adventurer that he has not lost his way in a world he cannot cope with. Apparently this confidence becomes firmly associated with the shapes and patterns of the surroundings in which a man develops, so that similar shapes and patterns will ever after be reminders of the sense of asylum enjoyed during earlier days or in a different part of the earth. Thus, the greater the changes in the world of the emigrant, the less remains of the stimuli which restore the sense of security gained in childhood.

It was an extremely rare immigrant who did not remember with nostalgia the land of his childhood, even if that land had been wretched. The immigrant's search for, discovery of, and migration to areas reminiscent of his homeland helped to lessen his anxieties and his sense of alienation. So it was for the Finn in North America.

The *raison d'etre* for this book lies in several different directions.

v

The seventy-fifth anniversary of the only institution of higher education founded by Finno-Americans is merely the historical occasion. The modesty of the work is the result. Another reason for the inception of this work was the abortive attempt by the Finnish Evangelical Lutheran Church to produce a history of that body before its merger into the Lutheran Church in America in 1963. Thence came the sections dealing with the Finnish religious communities in America.

However, no sooner were these plans realized than it became apparent that to provide the proper perspective it would be necessary to include material on the land from which the immigrants had come. This realization led to the contributions, not only on immigration, but on the history of Finland and its national awakening involving the *Kalevala* and music.

A book on the Finns in America would be incomplete without some discussion of the immigrant communities in the new land. An investigation of the process of Americanization led naturally to an attempt to treat the second- and third-generation immigrant. The remainder of the contributions are intended, insofar as the scope of the work allows, to complete the picture of the Finnish-American experience.

The present work does not purport to give an altogether adequate or complete picture of any phase of that experience. Certain lacunae are immediately evident. However, they must be filled at another time or by other individuals.

Although a topic was suggested to each, the contributors were given latitude to write on any subject within the general area covered by the volume. No careful documentation was required. Someone has said, "Give a small boy a hammer and he will find everything he encounters needs pounding." It should be no surprise that each author formulates the problem in a way which requires those techniques in which he himself is especially skilled. Each author selected his own point of view and was free to present the facts as he saw them and to make whatever interpretations he desired.

Translations of almost all the Finnish essays, as well as Thomas A. Sebeok's article which appeared originally in Finnish, are by the editor.

Each author is hereby extended our appreciation. I must also thank my colleagues at Suomi College, some of whom read and commented on the first drafts of the contributions. The members of the Board of Directors of Suomi College who served on the seventy-fifth anniversary publications committee—Dr. Raymond W. Wargelin, Dr. Milton J. Hagelberg, Dr. Vaino A. Hoover, Judge Charles Madsen and Mr. Russell Parta—provided much helpful guidance.

A special note of thanks is due Dr. Lyle Blair, the director of Michigan State University Press, East Lansing, whose decision it was to publish the book under the auspices of that Press; Mrs. Jean Busfield, associate director; and Mrs. Lark Cowling, editorial assistant.

The Board of College Education and Church Vocations of the Lutheran Church in America, located in New York, through the good offices of Dr. Francis E. Gamelin, former Executive Secretary, provided a research and creativity grant to help defray some of the costs involved. Without the generous contribution of Dr. Vaino A. Hoover, the work might never have been completed.

A final word to those who will immediately make the judgment that this book ought to be seen as a small immigrant minority's search for identity. It has served its purpose well if it helps one man to understand *mitä miehiä olemme* (who we are), and, especially, if it helps the descendants of the Finns to understand their origins, goals, and loyalties. If some of the discontinuities between our immigrant forebearers and their children and children's children are hereby erased, and life can be seen once again as a continuation from generation to generation, this book will have achieved its purpose.

This leaves us only to recapitulate the intent of any history in the words of George Santayana: "those who cannot remember the past are condemned to repeat it."

> "For men are homesick in their homes,
> And strangers under the sun;
> And lay their heads in a foreign land
> Whenever day is done."

RALPH J. JALKANEN
November 6, 1968
Suomi College
Hancock, Michigan

TABLE OF CONTENTS

ix

A LONG PAST,
A SHORT HISTORY

Aulis J. Joki

❖ THE RIDDLE OF FINNISH ORIGINS

AT THE BEGINNING OF the eighteenth century in accordance with the "linguistic" theories of Rudbeck and his followers, there was a serious attempt to prove that the Finns were related to the Greeks and to the inhabitants of the Holy Land. Such fantastic boasting of "holy forefathers" prevailed, however, only in a very narrow circle of scholars and churchmen and was quietly forgotten when Indo-European comparative linguistics developed in the beginning of the nineteenth century.

One of the great figures of this period was the renowned traveler and gifted linguist, Matias Alexander Castren. On his far-reaching and arduous journeys in Northern Russia and Siberia (1841–44 and 1845–49), he studied fourteen languages, some of them Uralic, i.e., Fenno-Ugric and Samoyed, and others Altaic, i.e., Turkish, Mongolian, and Tungus. Castren had, accordingly, a broader knowledge of the North-Eurasian languages than anyone before him. A nationalistic romantic, Castren had set for himself the goal of proving scientifically that the despised Finnish people was not some trifling splinter of a swamp-tribe but a race akin to at least a sixth of the world's population.

From his studies Castren drew the following conclusion: "Our language-family (the Fenno-Ugric) is closest to the Samoyed and to the

3

Turkish languages, but in addition has a definite relationship to the Mongolian and Tungus languages." The original home of all these languages he judged to have been in the Altai mountains, from whence during the course of millennia different tribes had scattered out in all directions to their present locations. Although a few earlier scholars, especially the noted German, W. Schott, had considered the Uralic and Altaic language-families to be originally of near relationship, only Castren gave this Uralic-Altaic hypothesis a firm basis. However, he was careful in the formulation of his theory and did not claim final validity for it.

This theory of an original relationship between the Uralic and Altaic language-families is still widely held. Yet, the Uralic-Altaic hypothesis (or the "Mongolian theory") has certainly never found such an enthusiastic acceptance by the general public of Finland as the so-called "Turanian theory" once found in Hungary. The fiery Hungarians, desiring to be thought warlike, would rather claim the brave Turks and Mongols as relatives than the poor, fishgrease-eating Siberian Voguls and Ostjaks. Even the most zealous Finn, however, is unlikely to be pleased by the thought that the mighty Mongol princes or the Turkish Great Khans are his distant relatives. Those involved in Finnish cultural endeavors, both at home and abroad, have observed with satisfaction that the embarrassing "Mongol problem" has apparently lost its former significance. Anthropologists have decisively shown that the Finns as a race have nothing in common with the Mongolians; rather the Baltic Finns belong partly to the Germanic and partly to the East-Baltic races.

Among linguists, however, the theory of a common origin for both the Uralic and Altaic language-groups still holds place. A relationship of language does not imply a relationship of race. For example, the fair-complexioned Scandinavians do not represent the same "race" as the darker Hindus, although their languages most certainly are related. The same is true of the Finns and the Samoyeds.

On the other hand, in modern Turkey the Finns are considered welcome relatives, for there the Uralic-Altaic hypothesis enjoys general acceptance. Many scholarly journals printed in different countries often mention, perhaps only from habit, that the Uralic and Altaic languages and peoples are related. One could mention many noted European scholars who have subscribed in the last decades to the theory that the Uralic and Altaic languages may have originally sprung from a single proto-language spoken some ten to fifteen thousand years ago somewhere in Western Asia.

This theory is supported first by certain common words that belong to the elemental vocabularies of those languages and that in some cases point to a common primitive culture. In the second place, the structure of the Uralic and Altaic languages, that is, their phonology, morphology, and syntax, includes many apparently clear-cut correspondencies. Dr. Marrti Räsänen, professor of Turkish philology at the University of Helsinki and an expert student of both language-groups, has defended the Uralic-Altaic hypothesis and, having critically examined the entire bibliography in this area, has presented a substantial number of lexical items in support of the theory.

All other Finnish linguistic scholars of this century have denied the relationship of the Uralic and Altaic languages. The Finns have directed their attention toward another far-reaching problem, namely, the possibility of a common origin for the Indo-European and the Uralic languages. This hypothesis had been advanced by some eighteenth-century scholars who attempted to demonstrate, for example, that Hungarian was related to the Indic and Persian languages.

It is quite natural to consider the possibility of the Finnic tongues having been originally related to the "Aryan" languages, for the races speaking these languages have lived as near neighbors from very ancient times and the languages have many similar sounding words. The newer critical philology has, however, proven that the majority of these words are loans from various Indo-European languages into Fenno-Ugric. Yet, even after all of these newer loanwords of several millennia have been carefully eliminated, there remains a group of common words and—what is most significant—various inflectional and derivational endings, which have clear correspondencies on one hand in several Indo-European languages, and on the other in the Uralic languages, including the Samoyed dialects of Siberia. Such ancient elemental features cannot be easily explained away as loans, but rather seem to indicate that the proto-Uralic and the proto-Indo-European languages may have been derived from a common original language. Among scholars supporting and developing this theory are the well-known Scandinavian linguists: Holger Pedersen, K. B. Wiklund, Hannes Sköd, and Björn Collinder.

At present, therefore, in respect to the Uralic (or Finnish-related) languages, on the one hand it is held that they contain a group of such primitive features that would seem to point to their having long since been very closely connected with the Altaic languages, and on the other hand the proto-Uralic languages seem already to have included some lexical items and some inflectional endings similar to those of the proto-Indo-European language. Some of the correspondencies appear, indeed, in all three language-groups. So one could well ask: Does this not show that these

three groups, Uralic, Altaic, and Indo-European, are related among themselves, having developed from one and the same ancient language. This is
certainly possible, even probable, but it is difficult to prove beyond all
doubt. For when the object of study is such a changeable element as a
human language, no one can predicate very definite probabilities concerning the form of any "original proto-language," spoken, let us say, twenty
thousand years ago. At present at least, very few of these "three-in-one,"
Altaic-Uralic-Indo-European, elements can be discerned. The reconstruction of Proto-Uralic and Proto-Altaic, moreover, has not advanced as far
as the reconstruction of Proto-Indo-European, and it is only by comparing
the earlier forms of several languages that conclusions about their relationship can be drawn.

      Present-day discussions about language relationships often neglect
M. A. Castren's words: "We must little by little accustom ourselves to the
thought that we are descendents of those despised Mongols, but we can at
all events put this question forward for the future to answer: Is there any
real difference between the Caucasian (or Indo-European) and the Mongolian races? I do not think there is. From a linguistic point of view such a
difference cannot hold its place." Castren's position, therefore, is essentially
the same as that held today on the basis of far more material than he
possessed. But we must, nevertheless, make the usual qualifying statement:
before we can progress beyond general conclusions, we must have completed much additional detailed study in the area of all of these language
groups.

NOTES

TRANSLATOR'S NOTE: For a recent statement by American scholars on this question, see *Anthropological Linguistics,* VII, 1 (January 1965), special supplement
"Languages of the World," "Boreo-Oriental Fascicle One," section 1, "Relationship of Uralic to Altaic and the Scope of Boreo-Oriental," pp. 2–8, co-authored
by Professor Alo Raun, Mr. David Francis, and Professors C. F. and F. M.
Voegelin. The authors include the Uralic language-family in the Altaic phylum.

EDITOR'S NOTE: Wuorinen, in *History of Finland,* reaches the following conclusion regarding linguistic and anthropological research into the problem:

      What are we to conclude, then regarding the people who inhabit
Finland today and their recognizable forebears in historic times? The
question, if freed from the romanticist notions which the past few generations have accepted as congenial articles of Finnish nationalist faith, is no

more complex than the same question applied to the other peoples in the West European culture area. The earliest "origins" of all of them are obscure and seemingly unknowable. The nations of today, however, can be observed and measured and the conclusions stated in reasonably clear and definite terms.

Finland is no exception. Research and observation have delivered a verdict free from ambiguity. The verdict is, as one would expect, that the Finns and their "racial forebears" are "purely European." More specifically, a study of the physical characteristics of the people of Finland has brought to light that the Finns are relatively tall, being slightly shorter than the Swedes or the Norwegians but somewhat taller than the Danes or the Germans; that they are overwhelmingly blond, in that light and mixed types predominate, only about 6 percent being classified as brunette and less than 2 percent having dark brown or black hair; that they are somewhat more broadheaded than their Swedish neighbors, but less so than the Danes or the majority of the Germans; that the differences between the Swedish-speaking and Finnish-speaking elements of the population are, in so far as they exist at all, small and unimportant; and that blondness, tall stature, longheadedness, and other so-called Nordic characteristics are most frequently found in the western, southwestern, and southern parts of the country, and decrease toward the north and east. At least one of the basic physical characteristics, stature, has undergone marked change since it became the object of record and study some seventy or eighty years ago. The average Finn today is appreciably taller than his grandfather. The reason is probably a greatly improved standard of living during the past half-century and more.

Finally, the Finns obviously represent, in common with all the other peoples of Europe, a mixture of various strains. The primary strains, the anthropologists claim, are two: the element popularly known as the Nordic, and another, which several anthropologists have designated of late as the East Baltic. Both of the categories are rather arbitrary approximations, needless to say, and stand for no sharp differences. The East Baltic is more prevalent and is distinguished from the former primarily on the basis of a broader head form; otherwise the physical characteristics of the two classifications do not differ conspicuously. The East Baltic element, together with some others, is also found in Sweden and Norway, and while its presence in Denmark is unimportant, Denmark discloses another broadheaded strain that is significant. Except for differences in degree, the peoples of the four Scandinavian nations seem thus to represent pretty much the same physical characteristics.

To sum up, the explanations and assumptions of philologists, or the interpretations formulated by many historians and other writers, have for the most part thrown no real light upon the origin or distant background of the Finns. Not infrequently, they have obscured the problem for the student and baffled and misled the layman. The distant origins of all European peoples, including those of the Finns, are hidden in the impenetrable mists of the faraway past. They are likely to remain forever

hidden and the puzzle insoluble. In the circumstances it is clear that the
"racial" classification of the Finns and their place among the other
peoples of northern Europe can be defined in only one way. That is to
classify according to the abundant available facts that relate to the
physical characteristics of the people of Finland. The facts, left to speak
for themselves and unmarred by fanciful interpretation, place the Finns
in the category of the other northern peoples. Political, religious, educational, and other aspects of Finland's general development in the distant or more recent past merely underscore the same conclusion. This
fundamental fact is writ large over the entire recorded history of Finland.

Eino Jutikkala

❧ TOWARD INDEPENDENCE: A SURVEY OF THE HISTORY OF FINLAND TO 1920

Establishment of Finnish Autonomy

For about six hundred years Finland was part of the Kingdom of Sweden, and its inhabitants had the same rights and obligations as those of Sweden proper. When Sweden became a modern, centrally governed state at the beginning of the seventeenth century, Finland was seen from the capital merely as a group of provinces existing alongside the provinces of Sweden. The language of administration and culture in Finland was Swedish; the educated classes, whether of Finnish, Swedish or foreign stock, all eventually adopted Swedish as their mother tongue. Church services, however, were conducted in Finnish except in the small area where the entire population spoke Swedish. Moreover, an interest in the Finnish language and national culture began to develop at the University of Turku (Åbo), the country's intellectual center. In the Diet, the Finns sometimes found themselves opposing the Swedish representatives of Sweden; a frequent complaint was that posts in Finland were given to Swedes with no knowledge of Finnish. Despite these grievances, the Finns remained loyal subjects of the Swedish crown.

By the middle of the eighteenth century, however, the balance of power in Northern Europe had changed considerably and the Finns were

9

obliged to reconsider their position. The Peace of Uusikaupunki (Nystad, 1721) had ended Sweden's status as a great power by giving the Baltic States and South-Eastern Finland (roughly up to the present frontier) to Russia; the Peace of Turku in 1743 ceded a further strip of territory in Southern Finland to Russia. During the two wars the Russians had occupied the whole of Finland. Having lost faith in Sweden's ability to defend the country, many Finns were ready to fling themselves into the arms of the Russians when war threatened. Inducements were not lacking, for at suitable intervals from 1742 onwards Russia offered Finland the status of an autonomous protectorate of the Empire. Thus the Swedish government, not only for military reasons but also in order to influence Finnish opinion, found it necessary to devote more attention to strengthening the defense of Finland. This policy achieved some degree of success, but in the 1780's an "independence movement" developed among members of the Finnish officer class. Colonel G. M. Sprengtporten, its leader, summed up the movement's aim: "We are destined sooner or later to come under Russian domination in any case, but it will be much more onerous if we do not submit voluntarily."

This line of thought, however, received comparatively little support even among the upper classes; only a few of the Finnish officers who mutinied during the war against Russia in 1788 were separatists and the great majority were disaffected because Gustav III had taken up arms against his powerful neighbor. But the attitude of the population as a whole was governed by the revulsion inspired by the many cruel wars that had been fought against the Russians. "The hatred of our people for the Russian and his protection is so deeply felt," wrote H. G. Porthan, an outstanding figure in the intellectual world, referring to Sprengtporten's program, "that I would not advise anyone to put such a programme before them." But Porthan himself died in the worried conviction that "Finland will sooner or later come under Russian Suzerainty." This vision of the future imposed itself more and more clearly on the minds of the Finns during the Napoleonic wars.

In June 1807, the two rulers of continental Europe, Napoleon and Tzar Alexander I of Russia, met at Tilsit and agreed that the stubborn Swedish king, Gustav Adolph IV, must be forced to break his connection with Napoleon's chief enemy, England. In February 1808, Alexander, who would have preferred Russian expansion in the direction of the Balkans, yielded to pressure from Napoleon and launched an attack on Sweden.

The Swedish plan of campaign completely disregarded Finnish interests: the Finns were at first to rely entirely on their own forces and, in order to conserve them, were to retire to Ostrobothnia, thus leaving practically the whole country at the mercy of the enemy. This plan, coupled with a possibly exaggerated idea of Gustav Adolph IV's political incompetence, aroused great bitterness against Sweden and made it easier for the Finns to sever their old connections. The defeatism that had already begun to affect the educated class was intensified by Napoleon's almost legendary military reputation. It is not surprising, therefore, that the fortress of Sveaborg (today Suomenlinna) outside Helsinki, which was considered one of the strongest in Europe and which—according to the plan of campaign —was to have been held, surrendered to a weak attacking force without a struggle. Although the annexation of Finland to the Empire was not one of the original Russian war aims, the ease of the Russian advance, coupled with political setbacks in the Balkans, led the Tzar to revise his plans. The annexation of Finland to Russia was proclaimed and its inhabitants were required to swear the oath of allegiance.

Many high officials readily entered the service of the occupying power, but in the field the officers and, to an even greater extent, the rank and file of the army remained unshaken; the peasant population was unwavering in its loyalty to Sweden. The Finnish forces had withdrawn to Northern Ostrobothnia. From there they launched an attack and advanced several hundred miles; after bringing up reinforcements and some hard fighting, the Russians finally gained the upper hand.

Having obtained Napoleon's consent to Russia's annexation of Finland at the Congress of Erfurt, Alexander proceeded to organize the occupied territory. Since the map of Europe could still be regarded as fluid (as indeed it remained until the fall of Napoleon), it was expedient for the Tzar to try to win the sympathy of the Finns. Speransky, Alexander's influential advisor, advocated a policy involving the formation, outside the purely Russian areas, of a zone which could be used as a testing ground for the ideas of the Enlightenment. Sprengtporten, who had for some time been living in exile in Russia, was agitating strongly for the convening of the Finnish Diet. A similar stand was taken by the Finnish delegation summoned by the Tzar to St. Petersburg to acquaint him with the wishes of the population; they stressed that they were not able to speak in the name of the Diet. Faced with the threat of a new European war, Alexander I, without waiting for the end of his own war against Sweden, summoned the Finnish Diet to assemble at Porvoo (Borgå) in March 1809. He had already ordered that questions relating to Finnish affairs be submitted directly to him and not through the Russian ministries; this instruction was one of the factors that helped to pave the way for Finnish autonomy.

It was fortunate for Finland that the Swedish constitution was strongly monarchical. The Tzar would have found the drafting of a special constitution for a conquered territory extremely difficult. By guaranteeing the Finns the continuation of the rights they had hitherto enjoyed (including that of worshipping as Lutherans), he was able to confirm the existing constitution without appreciably diminishing his own status as an absolute ruler. In the Diet, a bipartite agreement was reached: the Finnish people swore allegiance to the Russian Imperial House, and Alexander, to quote his own phrase, "promoted the Finnish people to the status of a nation among nations." The old title of "Grand Duchy of Finland," coined in the sixteenth century to add luster to the titles of the Swedish kings, now took on real meaning.

Thus the Finns agreed to their future status before the conclusion of peace. The significance of this chronological order of events can hardly be over-emphasized: Finland never became a province of Russia, as it would have if the Diet had been postponed until after the peace treaty came into force. For in the peace treaty signed at Hamina (Fredrikshamn) in September 1809, Sweden ceded the eastern half of her kingdom to Russia.

In their new position, the Finns had no share in the exercise of authority in Russia and the rulership of Finland was determined by the order of succession to the Russian throne. But within the Grand Duchy the Finns had all those powers which were not held by the Tzar in his capacity as Grand Duke of Finland. This power did not initially amount to much, but the constitutional enactments which Alexander I had promised (and bound his successors) to uphold, and which every succeeding Tzar confirmed in his turn, did guarantee a certain minimum.

According to the Swedish constitutional laws of 1772 and 1789, which remained in force in Finland until 1919, power lay exclusively in the hands of the ruler, to whom the government was responsible. The convening of the Diet was also a matter for the ruler to decide, but no legislation on the most important questions, including the imposition of new taxes, could be implemented without the Diet's assent. As the existing tax revenue was sufficient for the needs of the Finnish state, Finland was governed for over half a century without the Diet being convened, and yet without any significant breach of the constitution.

In 1809, the Tzar set up a government composed entirely of Finns, which later came to be known as the Senate to indicate that its status was comparable to that of the Russian Senate, the highest governmental body in Russia. The government made its own decisions on less important matters; it submitted its views on more important matters to the Tzar. All matters relating to Finland were placed before the Tzar by a resident Finnish minister, the Secretary of State in St. Petersburg, who added his own comments; these, though no doubt suitably worded for Russian consumption, would nevertheless stress the Finnish point of view. The Tzar was also influenced by the advice of his representative in Finland, the Russian Governor-General. The intention had been that this high official should act as Chairman of the Senate; however, the Governors-General, not knowing Swedish, usually stayed away from Senate meetings, and the Vice-Chairman, a native Finn, thereby obtained a status comparable to that of a Prime Minister. Finnish autonomy was thus manifested in the Diet, in the Senate and government offices, and in direct submissions to the Tzar; other marks of autonomy were the small enlisted army, the customs frontier with Russia, and the special rights of Finnish citizenship which were not automatically enjoyed by Russians settling in Finland.

The Finnish educated classes were gratified by the number of official posts now open to them. The peasants with their strong monarchistic instincts saw the Emperor–Grand Duke as a kind of national ruler. Although the position of the Grand Duchy was in fact determined by the relative strength of Russia and Finland, it was theoretically possible to speak of a personal union between the two countries, different though they were in size. There was even one occasion when the Tzar put the interests of his Grand Duchy before those of his Empire, or at least appeared to do so: in 1811, Alexander I decided to return to Finland the territory in the southeast which had been ceded to Russia under the treaties of 1721 and 1743. In fact, the Tzar was afraid that the miserable conditions prevailing in these areas might lead to anti-Russian prejudice, since the Finns might fear that a similar fate awaited the rest of Finland now that it had been conquered by the Russians.

The National and Political Awakening

Such misgivings proved groundless, for Finland was allowed to retain her Scandinavian social system. Although the reign of Nicholas I (1825–1855) saw the beginnings of a chauvinistic movement in Russia and demands were heard for the Russification of every part of the Empire including Finland, such a policy was out of harmony with the spirit of the Holy Alliance. The Tzar himself turned a deaf ear to such suggestions.

Nicholas I made no distinction between the various peoples of his great empire: in principle each was as good as another so long as they remained loyal to the throne. Since Finland lay on the boundary between East and West it was especially important to keep its population contented. The Finns gradually learned to trust the Tzar, and the Tzar trusted them. The outstanding virtue of the Finnish leaders was their caution, and they paid careful heed to what was expected of them by St. Petersburg. Nevertheless, under the wing of this autocratic regime, a sense of nationality developed, reinforced by Finland's autonomous status. J. L. Runeberg's poem-cycle, "The Tales of Ensign Stål" (written in Swedish in 1846–1860) which treated the Russo-Swedish war of 1808 as a purely national struggle by the Finns against Russia, inspired a sense of self-dedicated patriotism in one generation of Finns after another. Despite strict censorship, the book was published. Works printed in Finnish, however, were subjected to stringent control: it was feared that the simple common folk might be infected with democratic ideas from the West. Indeed, for some years after the February Revolution nothing was allowed to be printed in Finnish except religious and economic texts.

This ban should not be taken as proof that the regime was averse to the development of Finnish culture. Up to a point the cult of Fennicism was actually encouraged, as this trend would help to loosen the intellectual ties with Sweden. But the demand for the adoption of Finnish as an official language was dismissed by the ruling bureaucracy as a romantic daydream.

After the break with Sweden, Swedish had continued to be the language of both administration and education. As the common people understood not a word of the documents they received from official quarters, the literacy which had been virtually universal since the seventeenth century was of no advantage to them in civic life. All applications or requests to officials had to be translated into Swedish, and there was no certainty that an official dealing with the common people, such as an examining judge, knew enough Finnish to understand what they said. In the Finnish-speaking areas, by far the greater part of the country, the language frontier was also the social frontier. Thus, even from the practical point of view, there were strong arguments for improving the status of the Finnish language. In this atmosphere the ideology of romantic nationalism began to spread.

This nationalism was based on the notion that every people has a distinctive character of its own, made up of inherited characteristics and revealed in its language. Autonomous Finland, it was felt, could become a national state only if Finnish were the official language: only in and through the Finnish language could creative cultural activity be carried on in Finland. The "Fennoman" movement which now appeared demanded that Finnish be adopted by the educated classes and insisted that Finnish be allowed in government offices and schools. The reform must be put into effect while "the Finnish national spirit is repressed by a force (i.e. the Swedish language) other than that which fetters Finland's political independence (i.e. Russia)." If Russian were to become the official language of the country, these two forces would be identical and there would then be no hope of ever raising the status of the Finnish language.

The leader of the Finnish language movement was the philosopher J. V. Snellman (1806–1881), one of the most famous statesmen of the period of autonomy. During the 1840's, the entire educated class felt the impact of his ideas. Some opposed them, either because they believed a change of language presented too many difficulties or because they doubted the ability of the Finns to create and maintain a culture of their own. These doubts were largely swept away in the enthusiasm that followed the publication (in 1835 and 1849) of the folk-epic *Kalevala,* compiled by Elias Lönnrot from ancient folk poems taken down from the lips of country people. A large number of educated people did begin to speak Finnish, with varying degrees of proficiency, in their homes, and the foundation of a Finnish-speaking educated class was laid.

Under the bureaucrats who had run the country during the reign of Nicholas I, anyone who advocated ideas as revolutionary as Snellman's would have been kept severely in his place, but during the reign of Alexander II (1855–1881), Snellman became a Senator and for a time his opinions were treated with respect in St. Petersburg. The first Finnish secondary school was founded in 1858; in 1863 the Tzar decreed that in the course of the next twenty years all public departments were to initiate the issue and acceptance of documents written in Finnish. Thus, although Finnish had by no means attained full equality with Swedish, which remained the internal language of all official departments, the worst of the practical handicaps had been removed.

During the same period a Swedish nationalist movement, under A. O. Freudenthal, also arose. This movement's aims were to make the Swedish-speaking commoners conscious of their nationality and to awaken in them a love for their native tongue. The Fennoman and the Svecoman movements were inspired by the same romantic ideology; they might have been able to flourish side by side had they not disagreed over the question of the educated classes. While the Fennomans demanded that these should adopt Finnish, the Svecomans regarded the educated classes as Swedish by both nationality and language and warned them not to change their mother tongue. After the 1870's, fewer and fewer moved from one language group to the other, and the only recruiting method left open to the Finnish-speaking intelligentsia was to encourage greater social mobility through the medium of the Finnish-speaking secondary schools.

The Swedish nationalists formed themselves into a political party, as the Finnish nationalists had already done. Only about one-seventh or one-eighth of the total population was Swedish-speaking, but in the Diet, where three of the four chambers represented the upper strata of society, the two parties were roughly equal in strength. By the end of the century the two language groups were about equally strong throughout the administration, from the Senate downwards. On the language front every inch of ground was hotly contested. The bitter hostility between the two language parties, the outstanding phenomenon of the 1880's and 1890's, was the result.

The Liberal movement, which had originated in the years following the February Revolution, attempted to strike a balance between these two parties until the 1880's. The Liberals considered the language question secondary; their principal goals were an autonomous land constitutional system of government, freedom of the press, and the liberation of trade and commerce from government tutelage. Regarding Russia as backward, the Liberal movement failed to recognize the strength a great power possesses merely in being able to call upon the blind obedience of its subjects. The tendency of Liberalism was to estrange the Finns spiritually from Russia and the Tzar.

Partly as a result of the Liberals' demands and partly because of Snellman's realistic statesmanship, Finnish autonomy was substantially strengthened during the reign of Alexander II. The Diet was eventually convened in 1863; in 1869 the Tzar ratified a new Procedural Law which required that the Diet meet regularly. The Finnish monetary system was gradually dissociated from that of Russia (1860–1878) and the gold mark became the official unit of currency in Finland. In 1878, Finland obtained its own conscript army with Finnish officers; its function was the defense of the homeland and the thrones—not, that is to say, of the whole empire.

Had it not been for the general patriotic awakening that found its expression in Runeberg's poetry, the Finnish and Swedish nationalist movements, and Liberalism which forged firm links with the West and strengthened constitutional thinking, the Finnish nation would have been ill prepared for the onslaught made upon it by the Empire. A docile bureaucracy such as existed in Nicholas I's reign could never have stood up for Finnish autonomy with the toughness and confidence shown at the turn of the century by the educated classes of the country, behind whom stood a nation well on the way to political consciousness.

The Struggle for Constitutional Rights

Towards the end of the nineteenth century the ideology of Liberalism in Europe was giving way to nationalism and imperialism. In Russia where Liberalism, even in its heyday, had never been particularly strong, these two movements aimed primarily at absorbing the peoples of foreign extraction in the borderlands and making these areas into integral parts of the Empire. The Russian jurists attempted to demonstrate that the agreement at the Diet of Porvoo was in no sense bipartite: that what Alexander I, in his omnipotence, had conceded to Finland, the Tzar of Russia, exercising the same omnipotence, could take back again whenever he wished. A new term, pan-Imperial legislation, was coined to describe both those Finnish laws which affected the interests of the Russian Empire and those laws which were held to be valid throughout the Empire. Such laws were to be enacted according to Russian legislative procedure, i.e., by Russian government officials and the Tzar, for there was as yet no Diet in Russia. The strong-minded Tzar Alexander III (1881–1894), however, had a personal affection for his loyal Finnish Grand Duchy, and—with a few unimportant exceptions—turned down every proposal that would have threatened Finland's autonomy. His weak successor, Nicholas II (1894–1917), allowed himself to be guided by rabid nationalists; his reign opened a new phase of Finnish history, the struggle for constitutional rights.

Some minor reorganization in Finland may well have been desirable from the viewpoint of Russia's real interests: it may, for example, have seemed unfair that the burden of the military system should fall so much more lightly upon the Finns than upon the Russians. In questions of this kind a compromise should have been possible, but the Tzar demanded much more. Consequently, when Russian measures violated the rights of the Finns and ignored the Finnish point of view, relations deteriorated suddenly and a once loyal nation became hostile and undependable. One result of this deterioration was that Russia's real interests now called for measures which previously would have been to her disadvantage, such as the disbandment of the Finnish army. And now, too, the ambitions of a great power called for obedience from a small nation.

Russification began in earnest in 1899. Nicholas II issued a proclamation that he was entitled, without the consent of the Finnish Diet, to enact laws enforceable in Finland on matters involving Russia's interests. He then began to implement his proclamation. Finns were ordered to serve in Russian units and Finland's army was disbanded. Measures were initiated for the gradual imposition of Russian as the official language of Finland. Increasing executive power was conferred upon Governor-General Bobrikov, who was extremely hostile towards Finland. Bobrikov became, in effect, an absolute dictator.

Two opposing factions crystallized out of Finland's old political parties: the Constitutionalists and the Compliers. The gap between them was unbridgeable. The Constitutionalists adhered strictly to the law of Finland and demanded that no one observe the illegal enactments of the Tzar or carry out any order of the Governor-General that was contrary to law. Trusting idealistically in the victory of justice, the unarmed nation was to fight back with every means short of violence. A group of extremists, the Activists, went so far as to endorse acts of violence as well. The Compliers, on the other hand, took what they believed to be a more realistic view of history: they had no faith in the triumph of justice and realized that a great power motivated by ambition is inexorable. They were therefore ready to give way in everything that did not, in their opinion, affect Finland's vital interests. One of their decisions was not to refuse to obey a regulation merely because it had been issued illegally.

But the Constitutionalists, too, rested their case upon a realistic argument. They saw that Russia's demands arose from an ideological nationalism that would not be satisfied until Finland had been completely absorbed into the Empire; that compliance would merely accelerate the process of Russification.

When the Constitutionalists were dismissed from their offices and their leaders were exiled, the Compliers accepted their posts on the grounds that the posts would otherwise have been taken over by the Russians. This argument hardly mitigated the bitterness of the Constitutionalists deprived of their offices and positions. The bitterness of the conflict was intensified by the fact that the opposing sides coincided to a great extent with the two parties to the language dispute: the Fennomans led by Y. S. Yrjö-Koskinen adopted a policy of compliance; the Svecomans led by R. A. Wrede and the former Liberal leader, Leo Mechelin, clung firmly to the constitution. A considerable number of Fennomans, however, disapproved of Yrjö-Koskinen's policy, particularly of his refusal to cooperate with the Svecomans. Out of this split arose a new party, the Young Finnish or Finnish Constitutionalist Party (as opposed to the Old Finnish Party). The Labour Party, which had been founded in 1899 and a little later adopted the tenets of Marxism, was the most uncompromising of the parties. The Labour movement brought the unfranchised and now politically awakening masses into the constitutional struggle but was reluctant to cooperate with bourgeois elements. The Tzarist dictatorship, and the fact that almost the entire working population was without a vote, naturally inclined the Socialists to a policy of class warfare: in a country where even the right wing was systematically sabotaging the ordinances of the government, it is hardly surprising that the left wing should have leaned towards revolution.

Resisting Russification even at the sacrifice of immediate advantage not only had a stronger ethical appeal but also seemed to be the more effective long-run policy. When recruitment for the Russian army was begun under the illegal Military Service Act, the Constitutionalists refused to answer the call-up. After three unsuccessful notices the Tzar had to give in: the Finnish army remained disbanded, but no Finns were drafted into the Russian army, and were thus spared participation in the Russo-Japanese War and World War I. When an Activist assassinated Bobrikov, reprisals were feared; instead, a more lenient Governor-General was sent to the country. And when the Constitutionalists, availing themselves of Russia's momentary weakness, combined with the workers to organize a general strike of all citizens, including civil servants, the Tzar was forced to revoke the illegal orders. Although he soon reinstituted the policy of Russification, he went so far that even the Compliers were forced to agree that he had overstepped the extreme limit. Thus, in a way, they acknowledged the failure of their own policy. They resigned from the Senate, then unconstitutionally filled with Russians. In 1910, the responsibility for all important legislation was transferred to the Russian Parliament, to which the Finnish Diet was to send representatives. Needless to say, these representatives were never elected. Thus a conflict which had begun as a dispute between the Tzar and the Finns took on the character of a dispute between the two nations now that Russia had a Parliament of its own.

The general strike led to a reform of the Diet in 1906. At one stroke the four-chamber Diet was changed into a unicameral Parliament elected by equal and universal suffrage. Here, then, was a reform brought about by an act of violence. Again it was noted that when the supreme authority, the Tzar, had broken his oath, he was induced to honor it only by coercion. Purely external factors had combined to undermine the citizen's respect for law and order and to shake that confidence in governmental institutions and legal methods which is the foundation of democratic life. Such a psychological shock could not fail to have an effect on the political mentality of the country.

Parliamentary reform brought with it the political emergence of the Social Democrats. In the 1916 parliamentary elections, in which the electorate participated only half-heartedly because the Tzar had announced that he would not summon Parliament until World War I was over, the Social

Democrats obtained an absolute majority. In March 1917, the Tzarist regime was overthrown in Russia; the provisional government hastily summoned the Finnish Parliament and appointed a Parliamentary Senate with a majority of Socialists and the Socialist O. Tokoi as Prime Minister. At the same time the Russians restored to Finland its autonomous rights. But this concession no longer sufficed. Because of the policy pursued by Russia since 1899, what had once been the distant dream of a politically contented people—complete independence—was now a genuine political aim.

The Achievement of Independence

The Russian government, however, claimed all the legal rights that had belonged to the Tzar in Finland. There were many opinions as to the revolution's effect on Finland's status, and the controversy over the degree of independence that could be claimed was accompanied by a dispute as to the form of government.

In July 1917, the Finnish Parliament, on the initiative of the Socialists, issued a proclamation by which it arrogated to itself the powers of the Tzar in Finland. Foreign policy and military matters, however, remained the responsibility of the authorities in Russia. The proclamation did not satisfy the majority of the Finnish bourgeois members of Parliament, since it amounted to the creation of a form of government without a recognizable head of the state. Nor did it satisfy those who had made complete independence their objective. Supported by the Finnish bourgeois parties, the Russian provisional government dissolved Parliament and thus invalidated the July proclamation.

In the new Parliament the Socialists were a minority party. The latent dissension within the party, between the democratic wing and those who advocated a dictatorship of the proletariat, now became more acute. The dissolution of Parliament and the Socialists' loss of their parliamentary majority tended to strengthen the left wing of the party, which saw its opportunity when the Bolsheviks seized power in Russia.

As a result of the economic isolation brought about by the World War, Finland was at this time in the grip of famine and unemployment. In November 1917, the revolutionary wing of the Socialists called a general strike and resorted to acts of violence. The country had no army and only a weak police force, as the Tzarist gendarmerie of the Russification period had been disbanded. The democratic wing of the party, however, was still strong enough to end the general strike and effect a reconciliation with the bourgeois parties over the issues of independence and governmental form.

After the Bolshevik revolution even the most discreet bourgeois politicians declared themselves in favor of independence; the majority of these men demanded a strong central authority. The proclamation now issued differed from that of July in two essential respects: first, Parliament, while again arrogating to itself the powers of the Tzar, did not exclude foreign policy and military matters; second, the question whether there should or should not be a head of state was left open, Parliament announcing that it would assume the powers temporarily. The actual power was then vested in a government composed of all the bourgeois parties and headed by P. E. Svinhufvud, who had served for a long period as Speaker of Parliament, and who, having been exiled to Siberia for his uncompromising constitutionalist attitude, enjoyed immense popular favor. The declaration of independence drafted by this government was passed by Parliament on December 6, 1917.

But there were Russian military forces in the country, and independence implied recognition by foreign powers. Svinhufvud was reluctant to seek recognition from the Bolshevik government, which was not considered likely to remain in power for long—a view held fairly generally in Europe at that time. However, on the suggestion of Germany, Finland sought and was accorded recognition. The Russians probably had good political reasons for recognizing Finnish independence; moreover, the Bolshevik government assumed that a Communist revolution would soon take place in Finland.

Finland at this time enjoyed very close relations with Germany, the enemy of Russia. Even before the collapse of the Tzar, Germany had given military training to Finnish youths who had gone secretly to Germany intending to start a rebellion in Finland when the opportunity offered. This "Jaeger" movement was animated by the same spirit as Constitutionalism. It was a game of chance, calling for great personal sacrifices and trusting idealistically in the triumph of justice when every effort to restore the rule of law in the country had failed. Once again, the risks taken turned out to be justified.

Before the Russian revolution the Socialists had been well disposed towards the Jaegers, but relations were severed when the revolutionary wing of the party began to form its own armed force, the Red Guard. The bourgeois parties also established their own force, the Civic Guard, from which Svinhufvud formed the government army. He found a commander-in-chief for the army in C. G. Mannerheim, an able Finnish-born general who had served in the Imperial army. Mannerheim was given the task of expelling the remaining Russians from Finland. Germany promised to send

back the Jaegers and, later, to provide military aid herself. The German
military leaders favored participation in the fighting that had broken out in
Finland, as they considered that this would enable them to obtain concrete
strategic advantages, but for a long time the political leaders opposed
intervention. Mannerheim was initially opposed to accepting the expeditionary force: he argued that the Finns would lose their self-confidence if
they were treated as though they were incapable of liberating their country
by themselves.

While Mannerheim was evicting the Russian military detachments
which had remained in Finland and were supporting the extreme left, the
revolutionary wing of the Socialists seized control, first of the party and
then of southern Finland. The situation, although extremely serious, was
not as dangerous as it had been in November when the government had no
military forces at all. A virtually improvised army was now engaged in
simultaneous operations against the Russians in Finland and against the
"Reds." It was both a war of independence and a civil war. During the
fighting which lasted from January to May 1918, thousands of civilians
were killed in the Red area; many times more Red prisoners died of starva-
tion and disease in the government's prison camps. Although the decisive
victories were won before the German expeditionary force arrived, German participation shortened the war.

After the civil war the majority of the members of the Parliament,
which contained only a few Socialists, favored retaining a monarchical
system of government. The question was settled provisionally by electing a
regent, in accordance with the constitution inherited from the Swedish
period. To this office they appointed, first Svinhufvud, and then—after the
collapse of Germany—Mannerheim. In the meantime a German prince
was nominated as King of Finland, but when Germany collapsed, the
Prince refused to accept the office. Mannerheim succeeded in gaining the
favor of the Western powers for Finland, and at the Versailles Conference
Finland was not treated as an ally of Germany. But since Russia was regarded as in a state of disintegration, the question of possible Finnish
intervention in Russia became a matter of acute interest. Such intervention
was demanded by some of the parties to the Peace Conference; the counter-
revolutionary Russian generals repeatedly asked Mannerheim for support
against the Bolsheviks; but as these generals did not even recognize the
independence of Finland, Mannerheim refused. The refusal was repeated
in the autumn of 1919 by the President of the Republic, K. J. Ståhlberg.
During his regency, however, Mannerheim had permitted Finnish volunteers to join the Karelian irregulars who were resisting the Soviet govern-

ment on the other side of Finland's eastern frontier. The motive behind this policy was not mere romantic nationalism but a desire to secure a safer eastern frontier for Finland.

Peace between Finland and Russia was concluded at Tartu (Dorpat) in October 1920. In addition to the territory of the former Grand Duchy, the Soviet Union ceded to Finland a corridor to the Arctic Ocean at Petsamo and guaranteed the autonomy of Eastern Karelia.

In March 1919, less than a year after the conclusion of the civil war, free elections were held. The new Parliament did not support the idea of a monarchy, but neither did it associate itself with the radical proposals put forward during the year of the revolution for the creation of a "headless state." The opinions of the Center prevailed: Finland would have a President with fairly extensive powers. K. J. Ståhlberg, the principal author of the Constitution of 1919, became the first President of the Republic of Finland. The language question was settled by giving equal status to both Swedish and Finnish. Unlike the numerous new states that came into being after World War I, Finland did not have to build the machinery of government from the very beginning as she had inherited the necessary institutions from the days of Finnish autonomy.

Francis P. Magoun, Jr.

❈ MATERIALS FOR THE STUDY OF THE KALEVALA

Elias Lönnrot: Epitome of a Finn [1]

Elias Lönnrot was born April 9, 1802 in the parish of Sammatti (province of Uusimaa, Swedish Nyland), on Lake Haarjärvi, in a cottage which later became Paikkari Farm, state-owned for the benefit of veterans (now a little museum), and died November 19, 1884, at Lampi Farm in the same village. He was a physician and discoverer of our traditional poetry. His father, Fredrik Juhana Lönnrot, was a tailor; his mother, Ulriika Wahlberg, a peasant's daughter.

Life was hard in Lönnrot's childhood. Elias, the fourth of seven children, was first apprenticed by his father to learn tailoring, but his son's overwhelming desire to read drew him to books. In 1814, his eldest brother got the boy into an elementary school at Tammisaari (Swedish, Ekenäs), where he studied for three terms. From 1816 to 1818, Lönnrot attended the cathedral school at Turku (Swedish Abo), and after learning Swedish, which at first caused him very great difficulties, he worked his way in spite of this to the top of his class. Finally the lack of means seemed to become an insurmountable obstacle. The curate at Samatti, Juhana Lönnqvist, then began to give private instruction to the boy who was so eager for knowledge, advised him to get the necessary means by soliciting in his parish

24

scholarship-money for high school, and in the spring of 1820 took him to the high school at Porvoo (Swedish, Borga). For lack of means he moved after a few weeks to Hämeenlinna (Swedish, Tavastenhus), where L. J. Bjugg needed in his pharmacy an apprentice competent in Latin, a post to which he was bound for five years. Besides working for his living, Lönnrot, helped by both the district doctor, J. E. Sabell, and the school principal, H. Langström, continued his studies, and in October 1822 he became a student at the University of Turku.

Study at the University of Turku threatened to become an unbearable struggle against poverty. Happily, on the recommendation of Professor Johan Agapetus Törngren, M.D., Lönnrot got the position of private tutor in the parish of Eura on Lake Pyhäjärvi in Satakunta and in 1824 in Törngren's own family. Under the circumstances, Lönnrot spent his winters in Turku, later in Helsinki (Swedish, Helsindfors), his summers on the Törngren family estate "Laukko" in the parish of Vesilahti (Swedish, Vesilax), which in his adult years he visited as a family friend. This fine and hospitable home counted greatly in Lönnrot's development. Five years later, in June 1827, Lönnrot passed the examination for his Master's Degree at Turku after defending a thesis "De Vainamoine, priscorum fennorum numine" (Väinämöinen, a Divinity of the Ancient Finns), done under the guidance of Associate Professor Reinhold von Becker. This pamphlet aimed, on the basis of the then-known songs, to explore the time and place of the origin of their main hero, matters of family relationship, characteristics, and so forth. Of the actual conclusion nothing is known, for the end of the thesis was destroyed in the 1827 fire of Turku.

Using to his advantage an opportune period of free time, Lönnrot set out in April 1828 on a song-collecting trip to Häme (Swedish, Tavastland), Savo (Swedish, Savolax), and through Finland's Karelia. On the trip, Lönnrot got a clear idea of eastern Finland's wealth of song and met at least one man especially expert in the old songs, Juhana Kainulainen, in the parish of Kesälahti (province of Kuopio), and at Rautalampi (province of Kuopio) a couple of composers of newer songs, Paavo Korhonen and Pentti Lyytinen. Already while on the trip, Lönnrot had arranged his collection for the press, he published in 1829–1831 in four fascicles as *Kantele* (The Harp). There would have been material enough for two more fascicles, but in the meantime his plans had changed.

In October 1828, Lönnrot began to continue his studies at the medical school of Helsinki University. After procuring his first medical degree, he was assigned as an intern to the cholera hospital at Hietälahti near Helsinki and then as an inspector with a roving commission to the eastern part of the province of Uusimaa and the southern part of the province of Häme. On one such trip of inspection he noted down the spring-festival songs at Ritvala in the parish of Sääksmäki (the province of Häme). After defending his final thesis, "Om Finnarnes magiska Medicin" (The Magical Medicine of the Finns), later published in *Finska Läkaresällskapets Handlingar* (Transactions of the Finnish Medical Society), I (1842), 199–244, Lönnrot got his M.D. at the first graduation exercises of Helsinki University in 1832. Thus the materials of both the M.A. and M.D. theses were the old poetry and lore of the Finnish people which the Finnish Literature Society (Suomen, later, Suomalaisen Kirjallisuuden Seura), founded in 1831 and of which Lönnrot was the first secretary, aimed to bring to light. In the latter half of 1832, Lönnrot was assigned as an assistant circuit physician in the province of Oulu, which had been afflicted with epidemics, and in January 1833, first as a temporary, and then a few months later, as a permanent doctor for the Kajaani (Swedish, Kajana) area, town, and castle. In this district, about sixty miles in extent, there were hundreds of sick people who lacked food and the most rudimentary knowledge of the treatment of epidemics and of contagion. Lönnrot began at once to take energetic measures until in February 1833, he came down with typhus and for a month hovered on the brink of death, so that a report of his death spread to southern Finland. To mitigate the distress of future years of crop-failures, Lönnrot adapted and translated into Finnish, Gustafva Schartau's pamphlet *Hyväntahtoisia neuvoja katovuosina* (Well-intentioned Advice in Crop-Failure Years) (1834), and, adapting Carl Nordblad's *Sundhets-lärobok för menige Man* (Health-Manual for the Common People), drew up a set of instructions for the treatment of common diseases, *Suomalaisen talonpojan koti-lääkäri* (The Finnish Peasant's Home Doctor), (1839, 3d ed. 1867).

In the summer of 1833, Lönnrot conceived the idea of collecting and arranging in groups everything sung about Väinämöinen, Ilmarinen, and Lemminkäinen. Evidence that Lönnrot's non-professional efforts were gaining recognition among the authorities was a year's leave of absence from his medical work. The Finnish Literature Society gave him 1000 rubles (about $500) traveling money. From September 1836 to October 1837, Lönnrot traveled about, first in the Archangel district of Karelia, eventually farther on right up to the Arctic coast and back through Petsame (formerly a province of Lapland), Lake Inari (Swedish, Enare) (a province of Lapland), and Sodankylä, (a province of Lapland), and immediately after that, he wandered back and forth across Finnish Karelia. The spoils were unexpectedly rich and included all kinds of traditional poetry.

Lönnrot undertook to arrange the lyrical songs for the press, and for this purpose made a few more short "collecting" trips into Finnish Karelia. As new additions continued to increase, the manuscript had to be recopied four times. The songs finally numbered 650. On his thirty-eighth birthday, in 1840, Lönnrot signed the preface of the *Kanteletar* (The Spirit of the Harp), in which the author's aesthetic views are best reflected. At about two-year intervals, there appeared the two remaining cornerstones of our traditional poetry, *Sananlaskut* (Proverbs) and *Arvoitukset* (Riddles); the former contains 7077 proverbs, the latter 1679 Finnish and 135 Estonian riddles.

On his long trip, Lönnrot had become familiar with Lappish and Karelian, and from these languages began to collect materials for a comparative Finnish grammer and a vocabulary of the eastern dialect. In 1840, the Finnish Literature Society asked Lönnrot to complete the big Finnish-Swedish dictionary which, after Kaarle Niklas Keckman's death, had remained unfinished. For this work, the Cabinet granted him a two-year leave from his official medical duties. In January 1841, Lönnrot set out for the Olónetz area of southern Karelia, always intending to go clear to Archangel, but on account of an unsatisfactory passport, he had to return from Petrozavodsk (Finnish, Petroskoi) (Karelian, SSR) with almost nothing accomplished. In the autumn of the same year, he set out again with M. A. Castrén on a roundabout course by a northern route through Inari, Norway, and Russian Lapland and came back alone via Archangel and the Veps country in the Olónetz area. In 1844, Lönnrot made a final exploratory trip to Estonia lasting half a year. On his return journey through Ingria in the rectory of Kattila, Lönnrot noted down Vote songs from an excellent woman singer, Anna Ivanovna.

Apart from the above-mentioned publications of traditional poetry, Lönnrot's correspondence in the thirties and forties absolutely teemed with literary projects: a Finnish-language lawbook, a medical guide, geography, history, and arithmetic books sought to enlighten the peasantry in all fields of knowledge. To this end, Lönnrot in 1835 founded the first Finnish-language periodical, *Mehiläinen* (The Bee), in order to publish specimens of different kinds of traditional poetry and articles in a rustic style in the above-mentioned fields of knowledge. As an appendix there appeared in serialized form von Becker's Finnish translation of a history of antiquity, Juhana Fredrick Cajan's history of Finland, and a history of Russia adapted by the author himself and Gustav Ticklén. *The Bee* appeared in 1836–37 and 1839–40. In 1840, Lönnrot was busy establishing the scholarly and patriotic periodical *Suomi* (Finland). During the first most difficult years,

Lönnrot's share was noteworthy on the side of both quality and quantity. Among the newspapers of the capital, Lönnrot enthusiastically supported *Helsingfors Morgonblad* (*The Helsingfors Morning Journal*), during those years when Runeberg and Fabian Collan were its editors. When in 1844, Snellman began to issue in Kuopio *Maaniehen ystävä* (The Farmer's Friend) and the Swedish language *Saima,* Lönnrot was associated as a contributor to both. Of the articles sent in by Lönnrot to the former, the most significant was a serialized and popularly written account of the vicissitudes of Finland; of those sent to the latter, a presentation of the fundamentals of the metrics of Finnish traditional poetry. Here Lönnrot insisted firmly on the quantitative basis of the meter of the classical languages and of the ancient *Kalevala*-type verse. When *Saima* was suppressed in 1846, Lönnrot edited with Snellman *Littera Turblad för allmän medborgerlig Bildning* (*A Literary Journal for General Civic Culture*) from 1847 to 1849. His articles touched on popular education, temperance, native literature, and the preparation of the *New Kalevala* ("Anmärkningar til den nya *Kalevala*-upplagen," 1. Jan. 1849, pp. 15–21.)

At the beginning of 1844, Lönnrot got a five-year leave for the preparation of the big Finnish-Swedish dictionary, but his many outside activities got in the way of the main work. He was forced in 1847 to undertake the task of preparing *Ruotsin, suomen ja saksan tulkki* (A Swedish, Finnish, and German Interpreter) and the Finnish part of Chief-of-Protocol Agathon Meurman's Russian-Swedish dictionary. From the first-mentioned, there grew a work containing nearly 10,000 words and some 2000 idioms. Other tasks during the period of leave were the posthumous publication of Paavo Korhonen's collected poems and the editing of the *New Kalevala,* the preface of which he finished on April 17, 1849.

The second edition of the *Kalevala* was not received with nearly the same enthusiasm as the first—such great expectations had had time to develop. Many persons expressed the hope that Lönnrot himself or someone else would edit another new revised edition. The greater the passage of time, the less did anybody want this, apart from abridgments for school instruction like the one that Lönnrot himself got out in 1862. The *Kalevala* is the great creation of our period of national romanticism and is an integral part of it; its second (1849) edition in particular has attained an unrivaled and dominant position in our literature and spiritual life.

In 1849, when the five-year leave was coming to an end, Lönnrot petitioned for an extension of it, or for a discharge from his medical post, in order to prepare the dictionary. Revolutionary movements abroad had, however, made Governor-General Alexander Sergevitch Menshikov extremely suspicious, and both requests were denied. Accordingly, in the summer of 1849, Lönnrot again began to attend to his medical practice and married Maria Piponius, the energetic, practical, pious daughter of a dyer in Oulu (Swedish, Uleaborg). As a sideline, he edited in 1852–53 the Oulu *Wiikko-Sanomat* (The Weekly News) without complaining about the restrictions of the very worst and most rigid censorship.

When a professorship for the Finnish language and literature was established at Helsinki University, no amount of persuasion changed Lönnrot's opinion that M. A. Castren was best-qualified for it. When on Castren's death in 1852, the chair again fell vacant, Lönnrot was persuaded at the last moment to accept it. After the defense of his inaugural thesis "Om det Nord-Tschudiska spraket" (*The North Tschud Language*), Lönnrot was named professor of Finnish language and literature in October 1853. His scholarly publications of this period are, apart from one, *Ueber den Enarelappischen Dialektt* (The Inari-Lapp Dialect), fairly short articles.

Much greater then as a theoretical investigator is Lönnrot's significance as a practical linguist who, from out of the confusion of the struggle of the Finnish dialects, efficiently guided the standard literary language that was gradually being accepted—and this regardless of the fact that his own style, particularly during his early years, is characterized by long sentences, is very stiff, and would be quite tiresome to read but for a playful turn that now and then brightens it up. His chief aim was to write in language that as many people as possible might understand easily. In all main points, he kept the West Finnish morphological system, already to some extent established in earlier literature, but as the need arose, he enriched it with additions borrowed from East Finnish dialects, for example, with the reflexive verb forms and above all with a rich stock of words. As a many-sided expert in Finnish dialects, Lönnrot was an incomparable coiner of neologisms. Most of Lönnrot's word formations are in the fields of history, linguistics, medicine, arithmetic, botany, and law. Basic and exemplary in this connection are his *Flora Fennica: Suomen kasvisto* (The Flora of Finland) (1860, 2d ed. 1866), and Johan Philip Palmen's *La'in opillinen kasikirja yhteiseksi sivistykseksi* (Juridical Handbook for General Enlightenment), done into Finnish by Lönnrot in 1863.

Lönnrot was charged with reacting coolly to the political movement of pro-Finnicism, apparently because the greater part of his scholarly production was in Swedish and because as a known man of peace he presumably did not try to fight for recognition of the Finnish language. He often openly expressed his appreciation of the Swedish language and Swedish culture, but in the annual main addresses which he delivered as head of the Finnish Literature Society he pointed out again and again that in both educational institutions and government offices, Finnish must become the equal of Swedish. In the spring of 1862, Lönnrot was invited to be a member of a committee which was to deliberate the abolishment of the bad practice whereby the majority of the people got their official documents in Swedish, a language incomprehensible to them. Because of the attitude of the majority of the committee, the committee's report contained only cautious hope. In Lönnrot's opinion, newly appointed judges and officials ought to be obliged to use Finnish as well as Swedish. In order not to be left alone, Lönnrot associated himself with a rather firm demurrer in which a five-year respite was prescribed.

In the summer of 1857, when crop failures threatened northern Finland, the government sent Lönnrot there to direct the preparation of food substitutes. At that time he published in Finnish and Swedish *Neuvoja erästen jäkäläin käyttamisesta ruuaksi* (Advice on Using Certain Lichens as Food) (2d ed., 1867). To check infant mortality, Lönnrot wrote in 1859 a pamphlet *Minkätähden cuolee Suomessa niin paljon lapsia ensimmäisella ikävuodellansa?* (Why do So Many Children in Finland Die in Their First Year?). Lönnrot adapted to Finnish several books of popular instruction to promote temperance and a decent life.

In the spring of 1862, Lönnrot retired from his professorship. From a neighbor near Paikkari Farm, the home of his birth, he bought Niku Farm, put it in first-class shape, and a few years later got Lampi, a backwoods farm in the middle of the forests of northern Sammatti, situated back at the end of inconvenient roads, so as to be able in peace and quiet to devote the powers of even his old age to the Finnish language and literature.

In 1863, Lönnrot was invited to join a committee whose task was the publication of a radically modernized Finnish hymnal. He was the most active member of the committee. Leaving out of account the hundreds of hymns left more or less complete in manuscript and those published in the newspaper *Tähti* (The Star), Lönnrot has to his credit about ten hymn publications. Of these the most important is *Suomalainen virsikirja valiaikaiseksi tarpeeksi* (A Finnish Hymnal for Temporary Use) (1872), of which there appeared in 1883 an edition emended and noted for four voices. The greater part of the contents of these publications is old material linguistically revised. Lönnrot's own hymns are not especially poetical nor at all smooth as to rhythm, but they are devout, simple, and easy to understand.

Another work, which Lönnrot had started on from time to time since 1840 but did not really get going on until he retired, is the big *Suomalais-ruotsalainen sanakirja* (Finnish-Swedish Dictionary), which appeared in fourteen parts between 1866 and 1880 (2d printing, 1930; 3d printing, 1958). It aimed to include the whole Finnish vocabulary. The collecting of this was, however, carried out unevenly, casually, and with too little help; it is unreliable especially in the derivatives, material made according to a pattern which had never appeared in living Finnish. Regardless of its shortcomings, it was, while appearing, an indispensable aid, and indeed even now is incomparably the largest Finnish vocabulary, containing more than 200,000 words.[2]

During the last years of his life, Lönnrot returned to traditional poetry. In 1880, he published *Suomen kansan muinaisia loitsorunoja* (Old Metrical Charms of the Finnish People), and on J. V. Snellman's seventy-fifth birthday in 1881 a poem *Turo, kuun ja auringon pelastaja Inkerin kansarunoista kokoon sovittanut Elias Lönnrot* (Turo, Savior of the Sun and the Moon. From Ingrian Songs concatenated by Elias Lönnrot). As a very last work, Lönnrot made a new arrangement of the *Kanteletar* (The Spirit of the Harp), of which he managed to reorganize and greatly enlarge the third volume. Julius Krohn published the manuscript in 1887 in the third printing of the *Kanteletar*.

Already during his lifetime, Lönnrot received public recognition and marks of distinction in abundance, but these seem to have brought him less pleasure than distress. Lönnrot was in his proper milieu at home at a work-desk that he had ingeniously made, in well-worn peasant clothes with a pipe in his mouth, and all his manuscripts and equipment in fine order. When taking time off from work, as his relaxation, he sang traditional songs and lays, accompanying himself on a harp, and took regular walks, swam, and skied up to the last years of his life.

In his old age, Lönnrot, like a great patriarch surrounded by his family, was the all-in-all of his local chapel. There having been for years no clergyman, he conducted divine services every third Sunday in the church at Sammatti; sick people went to him for treatment without charge, often getting at the same time their medicines, which were concocted from native herbs. As a memorial to his nearest relatives, many of whom died before him, he at one time paid for an addition to the district school; at other times, he had the church repaired, presented it with an altar piece painted by Adolf von Becker, out of his own means established a lending library, and finally assigned in his will the largest part of his estate to found a school of home economics at Sammatti. Lönnrot left the Finnish Literature Society his literary residue with all rights.

Without being a writer in the proper sense of the word, as a publisher of traditional poetry, compiler of our national epic, "second founder of our written language"—the first being Michael Agricola (ca. 1510–1557)—Lönnrot created the basis on which one could and can build. As a human being, Lönnrot is the epitome of a Finn, and, even if one tries, it is hard to find in him any objectionable traits; indefatigable assiduity and power of concentration, a quiet firmness and a kindly sense of humor under all circumstances, reasonableness and tolerance, extreme unpretentiousness, and truly Christian humility were characteristic of him.

Of Lönnrot's writings preserved in the archives of the Finnish Literature Society, there have been published (in Helsinki), among others, *Kalevalen esityöt* (Work Preliminary to the *Kalevala*), 3 vols. (1891, 1895); *Elias Lönnrotin matkat* (Elias Lönnrot's Trips), 2 vols. (1902); *Elias Lönnrot's svenska Skrifter* (Elias Lönnrot's Swedish Writings), 2 vols. (1908–1911); *Alku-Kalevala* (The Proto-Kalevala) (1929); *Alku-Kanteletar* (The Proto-Spirit of the Harp) with addenda (1929); *Loihtoja* (Charms) (1930), facsimile of the first edition.

BIBLIOGRAPHY. Emil Fredrik Nervander, *Elias Lönnrotin nuoruuden ajoilta Laukon kartanossa* (From the Times of Elias Lönnrot's Youth on the Laukko Estate) (Helsinki, 1893); Aukusti Robert Niemi, "Elias Lönnrotin lapsuus" (Elias Lönnrot's Childhood) *Valvoja* (The Guardian), XV (1895), 455–471; Eemil Nestor Setälä, *Elias Lönnrot ja suomenmielisyys* (Elias Lönnrot and Pro-Finniscism) (Helsinki, 1898); Oskar Albin Kallio, *Elias Lönnrot* (Helsinki, 1902), reprinted in *Suurmiestemme elämäkertoja* (Biographies of our Great Men) (Helsinki, 1929); Aarne A. Anttila, *Elias Lönnrotin elämä ja toiminta* (Elias Lönnrot's Life and Work), 2 vols., (Helsinki, 1931–1935), abridged ed. 1945.

The Kalevala[3]

The idea of concatenating Karelo-Finnish traditional songs into an epic-like whole was first advanced by Kaarle Akseli Gottlund in 1817: ". . . if one should desire to collect the old traditional songs (*nationalsagerna*) and from these make a systematic whole, there might come from them an epic, a drama, or whatever, so that from this a new Homer, Ossian, or *Nibelungenlied* might come into being" [*Svensk Literatutidning* (Swedish Literary

News), No. 25, 21 June 1817, p. 394]. In 1820 Reinhold von Becker published in three installments in his *Turku Weekly News* an article of his own, "Concerning Väinämöinen," [4] which in its consequences was important for the birth of the epic. In this article, von Becker reports where the old songs are still being sung, and urges that they be recovered. He regards the songs that tell of Väinämöinen as the most remarkable. He presents in prose form what the songs know about Väinämöinen, and at the end gives a 265-line compilation which contains "Väinämöinen's Courtship," "The Wound in the Knee," "The Origin of the Harp (kantele)," a fragment of "The Boatbuilding," "The Visit to Antero Vipunen," and the "Contention" song. Soon afterwards, Zachris Topelius, Sr., published a notable collection of songs; his last musical notations were from the year 1803, and the resulting collection was published between 1822 and 1831 in five parts as *Suomen kansan wanhoja junoja ynnä myös nykysempiä lauluja* (Old Poems of the Finnish People together with Songs of Later Date). He was the first to deal with the rich store of songs in the Archangel government, and he showed that the heyday of the songs had not yet passed, as it had ever since Porthan's time been customary to bemoan.

Von Becker's influence on Elias Lönnrot appears *inter alia* in the fact that the latter chose a subject for his Master's thesis from the field of traditional poetry, completing in 1827 his investigation "De Vainamoine, priscorum fennorum numine" (Väinämöinen, a Divinity of the Ancient Finns). This influenced the history of the genesis of the *Kalevala* to the extent that Lönnrot there became acquainted with what had been collected and investigated up to then and learned to combine verses taken from different songs. Lönnrot regarded the songs as pieces of historical evidence which shed light on the ways of life, religion, and customs of the Finns. Like von Becker, Lönnrot did not in this investigation conceive of Väinämöinen as a divinity, but, on the contrary, as a hero who attained immortality only by singing. When because of the Turku fire of 1827 the university was closed, Lönnrot set out in the spring of 1828 to collect traditional songs. In the province of Häme (Swedish, Tavastland), his notes were not increased, and the results were likewise meager in the province of Savo (Swedish, Savolax), but in Finnish Karelia, the finds were unexpectedly abundant. The trip had not yet been extended to the Archangel government. After he returned from the trip, Lönnrot started to edit the songs for publication. In 1829–1831, four fascicles of these appeared, *Kantele taikka Suomen kansan sekä wanhoja että nykyisempiä ruonja ja lauluja* (The Harp, or Old and Later Poems and Songs of the Finnish People), in which there were in all, ninety old and twenty later songs.

Many of the songs were pieced together from five or even six different variants.

After he had visited Repola behind the Russian border in 1832 and gone all the way to Akonlahti, Lönnrot intended to publish a continuation, *Kantele* (The Harp), in fascicles. Then a new idea flashed into his mind, and he wrote about it to the secretary of the Finnish Literature Society: "How would it be if the Society were to reprint all the Finnish songs which have merited its esteem and assemble them in order, so that what is to be found in different places about Väinämöinen, Ilmarinen, Lemminkäinen, and others were joined together or combined, and variant readings put at the bottom of every passage?" At the same time, he reported that he had tried "to join the songs about Lemminkäinen together in that way" and had come to the conviction that variants of the same song should be woven into one song and not published separately. In the same way, one ought to combine all variants that were connected with the name of the same person. The first work, "Lemminkäinen," merely a trial compilation preserved in manuscript is relatively unpretentious, the outline of an epic 825 lines long and arranged in two parts. In the first part are told "The Origin of Beer," "The Invitations to the Wedding," "Lemminkäinen's Journey to the Sun's Domain (Päivölä)," "The Duel," and "The Flight to The Island"; in the second part, how Lemminkäinen went wooing at the Demon's (Hiisi) abode and how he was killed. Lönnrot intended to combine the narrative songs about Väinämöinen and Ilmarinen in the same way. But before he started on this he made a new expedition of discovery to the Archangel government, which was rich in results. In the village of Vuokkiniemi, Lönnrot met two such skilled singers that he got a totally new idea about the homogeneity of the songs. Vaasila Kieleyainen sang as a single song the heroic deeds of Väinämöinen, of Ilmarinen, and to an extent of Kuulervo. Antrei Malinen, in turn, had recalled that the Sampo cycle and the "Courtship Journey" belong together, for the maiden wooed is to be given to him who forges the Sampo as a task to earn her. It now began to become clear to Lönnrot that it would be possible to create a single epic out of the song, since the singers of these songs formerly chanted them as a long series. When he got back from the trip, he combined into a single whole of 1867 lines the variants telling of Väinämöinen and Ilmarinen, using for this the title, "Väinämöinen." Into this were woven Väinämöinen's unsuccessful attempts to woo first Velamo's maiden, then the virgin of North Farm (Pohjola), and finally Joukahainen's sister. Even after he had become interested in fitting songs together, Lönnrot at the same time arranged as a

one-part experiment the wedding lays into a song cycle 499 lines long.
Meanwhile he noticed that Ilmarinen gets a bride from North Farm and
that the wedding is then celebrated. He joined the wedding lays to "Väinämöinen," and thus came into being at the end of 1833 the "Proto-*Kalevala*,"
a manuscript containing 5052 lines comprising sixteen poems, which is
customarily entitled "The Collected Songs about Väinämöinen" (Runo-
kokous Väinämöisesta), published in 1929 under the title *Proto-Kalevala*
(Alku-Kalevala). In this, Lönnrot was thus able to include his compila-
tions made up to that time: the songs about Lemminkäinen, Väinämöinen,
and the wedding party. He sent the manuscript to Helsinki, but even while
sending it, he questioned whether the "Collected Songs" was as yet a work
which "future generations will possibly hold in as great esteem as the
Germanic nations esteem the *Poetic Edda* and the Greeks and Romans
esteem, if not precisely Homer, at least Hesiod." He proposed that the
printing not be begun until he had once more visited eastern Karelia, in
the Archangel government. During the journey of April 1834, new materials accumulated to such an extent that in the spring Lönnrot set out for
Helsinki in order to combine them with the "Collected Songs." To this,
there came such really notable additions as "The Birth of Väinämöinen,"
"The Death of Aino," and "Kullervo's Farewell"; these fitted into the
framework of the "Collected Songs," so that there was no need, as before,
to take the whole thing apart at the seams. Magical charms, too, were
represented. The manuscript was ready in the winter of 1835; the preface
bore the date of February 28, and since 1920 it has been unofficially celebrated as Kalevala Day. Volume I appeared before Christmas 1835, Volume II, in February 1836. The title of the work was *Kalevala taikka
wanhoja karjalan runoja Suomen kansan muinosista ajoista* (The Kalevala,
or Old Karelian Songs of the Finnish People from Ancient Times). The
epic, which is now usually called *Vanha Kalevala* (The Old Kalevala), is
divided into thirty-two poems, in which there are in all 12,078 lines.

Before *The Old Kalevala* appeared, Lönnrot, in the spring of 1835,
made a fruitful trip to the vicinity of Repola and Uhtua, and in September,
1836, he set out on his longest rune collecting enterprise, with the university
student Juhana Fredrik Cajan as his companion at the start. For two months
he moved about in far corners up north right to the Kola Peninsula and clear
to Lake Inari (Swedish, Enare). After he had rested in Kajaani, he again
set out by way of Vuokkiniemi, Repola, Eno, Liperi, and Kide to wander
through Sortavala and back again through southern Savo. On both trips he
gathered songs in abundance. In Finnish Karelia, there were above all

lyrical songs. Lönnrot started arranging the new materials just as soon as he returned from these trips. From the lyrical songs, he edited the collection *Kanteletar* (The Spirit of the Harp), which appeared in 1840.

David E. D. Europaeus, engaged by Lönnrot in 1845 to make a clean copy of his dictionary materials, collected folktales and songs between the White Sea and Lake Ladoga during the years 1845 and 1847, and brought songs from such altogether new areas as Salmi, the Karelian Isthmus, and Ingria. Nearly half of all the additions gathered into the 1849 *Kalevala* are from notes taken by Europaeus. Several scholars of the Finnish Literature Society also collected additional material: August Engelbrekt Ahlqvist in 1846 in the districts of Ilomantsi, Korpiselkä, and Taakkima; the university students Zacharias E. Sirelius and Rietrikki Polen in 1847 in southern Savo and Finnish Karelia; Henrik A. Reinholm in 1847 along with Europaeus in Ingria, and at the end of the same year with the university student Carl M. Forsberg in the Karelian Isthmus.

At the beginning of 1847, Lönnrot started to prepare a new edition of the *Kalevala*. Besides the collections already mentioned, he was able to make use of those of Anders Johan Sjögren and Matias Aleksanteri Castren. First, Lönnrot picked out all the variants dealing with the same matter and wrote them down in their appropriate places. A whole year elapsed before he could start combining the texts of the new edition into a unit. As editor, he used the same procedure as before. The main aim was a connected presentation in which through these songs the Finnish people themselves pictured their former way of life, their thoughts, and their customs. The narrative thread maintaining the homogeneity of the epic in the *Old Kalevala* and *New Kalevala* is the Sampo and the struggle between the Kalevala District (Kalevala) and the North Farm (Pohjola). Lönnrot viewed the *Kalevala*-type songs as having first been composed immediately after the events. As times changed, supplementary features were invented; the homogeneity of the songs and the order in which they were sung gradually got confused. In "Anmarkningar til den nya Kalevala uplagan" (Notes on the New *Kalevala* Edition), *Litteraturblad för allmän medborgerlig Bildning* (Literary Journal for General Civic Culture), No. 1 (January, 1849), pp. 15–21, Lönnrot himself explained his view about the songs: "I cannnot regard the order used by one singer as more authentic than another's; on the contrary, I explain both as born of that desire which everyone has to put his knowledge into some sort of order, which then according to the singer's individual way of presentation has created differences. Finally, since not a single one of the singers could vie with me in the wealth of songs, I thought I myself also had the same right as most singers, namely, the right to arrange the songs as they best-fitted into one another—or, to speak in the words of a song (cf. Poem 12, lines 167–168), 'I began to practice magic, started to become a sorcerer'—that is, I regarded myself as a singer of songs as good as even they."

In 1849, the new edition of the *Kalevala* appeared. It was divided into fifty poems comprising 22,795 lines. The arrangement of the poems was changed to the extent that Väinämöinen's shooting took place after the creation of the world, and the "Sowing of the World" and the "Aino Poem" were fitted between. The narrative materials grew, especially the Kullervo and Lemminkäinen poems; lyrical songs and magic charms were generously added, so that in its final form it reflects all the poetical genres composed in the old traditional meter.

There has been some debate as to whether the Finnish people or Lönnrot is to be regarded as the maker of the *Kalevala*. Although Lönnrot conscientiously preserved the manuscripts and rough drafts which he used, the issue is sometimes viewed as not a little obscure. The homogeneous epic is the work of Lönnrot. But Lönnrot put the *Kalevala* together not as a real scholar or literary artist, but as a singer of traditional songs. He departed from the singers only in that he used writing as an aid to his memory so that it was possible for him to command a great number of song variants. But he subsequently read and reread the notes until he knew a great part by heart and could, while composing from memory, let supplementary verses ring out just like a real singer of songs. Lönnrot, to be sure, normalized the language of the variants and corrected metrical defects, but the singers, too, used their own dialects. Lönnrot took from the variants the best features to be used, and connected verses, even whole descriptive passages from quite other contexts. The singers did the same; they, too, could expand their songs with magic charms, lyrical materials, proverbs, and so on. Thus the whole plot, indeed, of a song could be appreciably changed by different singers. Lönnrot did not wish to add to the *Kalevala* anything at all out of his own head. As far as possible, he used the verses of a traditional song—a few hundred linking verses are all that he really added of his own. The verses composed by Lönnrot in the "Collected Songs about Väinämöinen" are only five per cent of the whole, and they are adaptations. Lönnrot was ahead of the singers in that he had a more developed taste in selecting the materials; he also had the advantage of literacy and models, especially of the Homeric epics.

Epical songs of the *Kalevala* type are best preserved among the folk of Karelia; the *Kalevala* poems are, for the most part, based on variants from the latter. Songs of this type were still being sung in the last century

throughout all Estonia, Ingria, and the Karelian Isthmus, on the western
and northern shores of Lake Ladoga, in Finnish Karelia, northern Olonetz,
and the western part of the Archangel government.[5] But the farther south
we go from that basic singing area of narrative songs, from west of the
White Sea, the shorter the heroic songs become.

Lyrical material is most abundantly represented in Estonia, Ingria,
and southern Karelia. The reason is that in the southern districts singing
is just the occupation of women. As a result, the songs are rather short,
consisting of game, joke, and courtship songs and sentimental songs and
ballads. These areas have been a battleground for Germans, Swedes, Lith-
uanians, Poles, and Russians. Only in Finnish Karelia and in the Archangel
government have men had the peace and quiet to meditate on long hero-
songs while at their domestic occupations and when on hunting and fishing
trips. There foreign cultural trends have not done away with calm meditation, so that the rich old-time singing of songs was preserved there to
the last.

As to the age of the songs, Kaarle Krohn was at first of the opinion
that, in general, they originated in the Christian era, only a few in the
"semi-darkness" of the time of the transition from paganism to Christianity,
and were brought to the Archangel government only in later times. In his
later studies, *Kalevalastudien*, (6 pts., 1924–1929) Krohn almost completely reversed his earlier position, and held that most of the hero-songs
of the *Kalevala* were historical in their basic character, the personages,
heroes who lived in the Viking age. Furthermore, he saw in the *Kalevala*-
type songs a considerable number of elements based on Biblical themes and
saints' legends. The scenes of action and the place of origin would have
been almost exclusively in western Finland; the Island (Saari) of the songs,
the site of the theft of the Sampo, was the Swedish island of Gotland. The
Karelians he claimed to be merely preservers of the songs. The latter were
composed in western Finland and "traveled" across the country as integral
units, in later times reaching Karelia, where they were longest preserved.
The similarity of the songs of Estonia and the Archangel government is
explained by at least two facts; namely, contact between Estonia and
western Finland had not yet been interrupted in the pagan period, when
the hero-songs came into being; and also, to some extent, by the simultaneous invention in both regions of the same plots for their songs. The
oldest songs are supposed to have originated between A.D. 700 and 1000.
The composers were chiefly aristocratic persons, the disseminators toward
the east being mainly junior clergy. The names, too, of the *Kalevala*-type
heroes were derived in great measure from Germanic originals.

Eemil Neestor Setälä does not regard a Germanic origin of the *Kalevala* hero names as credible. In his work *Sammon arvoitus* (The Riddle of the Sampo) (1932), he takes a negative position also as to a late migration of the songs from western Finland to Karelia and Ingria and assumes that in the Karelian area and in Estonia the poetry was preserved as an inheritance from one generation to another. Setälä claims that in the very ancient songs, there are different strata and that even the Karelians composed additions to them; he thinks it is possible that some songs are of their own composition, even though the material might have been procured elsewhere.

If these songs have only in recent times become the subject of extensive and many-sided scholarly study and discussion, there have not been many facts from which scholars might draw positive conclusions. Unanimity has been reached on the point that the plots of the hero songs originated near the sea, namely the Baltic and its gulfs of Finland and Bothnia, and that the oldest are from before the twelfth century, possibly many centuries earlier. No movement of songs with *Kalevala*-type material from Estonia or western Finland took place before the seventeenth century, since no old hero songs have been handed down from the Savakko and Äyrämö peoples, originally of the Karelian Isthmus, who were relocated in Ingria after the 1617 Treaty of Stolbova; only Ingrians of Karelian origin preserved them.

Kalevala variants and the ancient Finnish songs have been published as follows: Aksel Borenius (later Lähteenkorva) and Julius Krohn, *Kalevalan toisinnot* (*Kalevala* Variants), 2 vols. (1888–1895), and *Kalevalan esityöt* (Preliminary Work to the *Kalevala*), 2 vols. (1891–1895); Aukusti Robert Niemi, *Vanhan Kalevalan eepilliset ainekset* (The Epical Materials in the *Old Kalevala*) (1895); and A. R. Niemi, Väinö W. Salminen, et al., eds., the series *Suomen Kansan vanhat runot* (Old Songs of the Finnish People), 13 vols. in 33 parts (Helsinki, 1908–1948).

Kalevala translations—In English, the first information about the *Kalevala* was furnished by the botanist Professor Thomas Conrad Porter of Marshall College, later of Lafayette College, who wrote on the connection between the *Kalevala* and Longfellow's *Song of Hiawatha* in "*Kalevala* and *Hiawatha*," Mercersburg Quarterly Review, VIII (1856), 255–275, and to demonstrate the relationship published in English the opening words of the *Kalevala* from Anton Schiefner's 1852 German verse translation of the 1849 *Kalevala*. The chemist Professor John Addison Porter of the Yale Sheffield Scientific School posthumously published *Selections from the Kalevala, Translated from a German Version* (New Haven, Conn., 1868,

2d printing 1873), including Poems 3–4 and parts of Poem 2 together with
an analysis, all based on the 1849 edition. In *Stray Leaves from Strange
Literatures* (Boston, 1884), pp. 137–165, Lafcadio Hearn likewise translated a few prose excerpts based on Louis A. Leouzon le Du's complete
French prose translation of the 1835 *Kalevala,* included in his *La Finlande;
son histoire primitive, sa mythologie, sa poesie epique, avec la traduction
complete de sa grande epopee le Kalevala* (Paris, 1845) Vol. I, pp. 1–130
(Poems 1–16), Vol. II, pp. 1–133 (Poems 17–32). Professor John Martin
Crawford of Pulte Medical College published the first complete *Kalevala*
translation, *The Kalevala: The Epic Poem of Finland* (New York, 1888);
based on Crawford's verse translation was a rather complete prose adaptation for young people with illustrations, mostly of Lappish scenes, by R.
Eivind, *Finnish Legends for Children,* The Children's Library (London,
1893; New York, 1894). In 1907 (with many later printings), there appeared in Everyman's Library a two-volume verse translation by the English
entomologist William Forsell Kirby, made directly from the Finnish. There
is also an abridged prose translation by Aili Kolehmainen Johnson (Hancock, Michigan, 1950), and an adapted verse translation of part of Poem
50 ("Marjatta") in *Flower of Finland from the Kalevala* (Helsinki, 1954),
by Margaret Sperry. For a survey of the American translations, see Ernest
J. Moyne (Formerly Möykkynen), *"Kalevalan* kaannokset Amerikassa"
(Translations of the *Kalevala* in America), *Kalevalanseuran vuosikirja,*
XXIX (1949), 121–140.

   Aesthetic studies. Many foreigners have studied and interpreted the
Kalevala from an aesthetic point of view as, for instance, Jakob Grimm
(1785–1863), Johann Karl J. Rosenkranz (1805–1879), Heymann
Stenthal (1823–1899), Wilhelm J. A. Von Tettau (1804–1894), Domenico
Comparetti (1835–1927), Karl B. Wiklund (1868–1934), and Ferdinand
Ohrt (1873–1938). Among Finnish students of the subject are Matias
Aleksanteri Castren (1813–1853), Johan Robert Tengstrom (1823–
1847), Fredrik Cygnaeus (1807–1888) [*Om det tragiska Elementet i
Kalevala* (The Tragic Element in the *Kalevala*), 1853], Frithjof Perander
(1838–1885), August Engelbrekt Ahlqvist (1826–1889), Julius Krohn
[*Kaunotietellinen katsaus Kalevalan* (An Aesthetic Look at the *Kalevala*),
1855], Bernhard Fredrik Godenhjelm (1840–1912), Eliel Aspelin-Haap-
kylä (1847–1917), Kaarle Krohn (1863–1933), Viljo Tarkiainen (1879–
1951), Rafael Zacharias Engelberg (1882–   ) [*Kalevalan sisällys ja
rakenne* (The Content and Structure of the *Kalevala*), 1914], Franz Akseli
Hästesko (in Finnish, Keporauta) [*Kalevalan kauneuksia* (The Beauties of
the *Kalevala*), 2 vols., 1920, 1927], and Augusti Robert Niemi (1869–

1931) ["Kalevalan esteettisesta arvioimisesta" (An Aesthetic Appraisal of the *Kalevala*), *Kalevalanseuran vuosikirja* IV, 1924, 110–134].

The aesthetic interpretation and appraisal of the *Kalevala* depends in great measure on the position taken in an investigation of the history of the origin of our old epical poetical corpus, whether mythological or historical, arriving, of course, at one aesthetic result if he interprets the basic material of the corpus as mythological. For example, in this issue, one may interpret Väinämöinen as the tutelary genius of water, Joukahainen as the genius of snow, and the "Contention" poem (poem 3), accordingly, as a contest between summer and winter, or if one interprets *Pohjola* (The North Farm) as the vicinity of the North Star in the heavens, the maiden of North farm as the glow of light in the heavens, the Sampo as the pillar of the world, and the Sampo expedition as a sailing trip through blue space taking place in an imaginary vessel, or as a horseback rider on an imaginary colt, as Setälä has interpreted it. One arrives at quite another result, if in the manner of Kaarle Krohn, one views our old poetic corpus as from the beginning fundamentally historical, its personages as heroes of the Finnish Viking Age, the Sampo directly as a costly tangible object, a decorated pillar, for example, and the Sampo expedition as a Viking expedition from the original Suomi area in southwest Finland overseas to Gotland, called "the land of Vuojo" (Vuojonmaa). Up to now, aesthetic study of the *Kalevala* has, generally speaking, set out from the historical point of view, which Lönnrot represented, and has viewed its epical events and its personal portraits as based on historical reality, even though styled by the imagination and here and there fancifully colored. Starting from this basis, the relations between two tribes and the contest over the Sampo have been viewed as the narrative framework. The *Kalevala's* narrative structure is not, to be sure, as close-knit as the Homeric poems, for instance, nor was its action ever really developed into an exciting physical conflict; witness the entire peaceful character of the Aino and Kullervo episodes, also the lyrical wedding lays and the magic charms. But coherence is given to the poetical narrative by the consistency of the personal characterizations, which remain unchanged through the whole work, the animistic-magic underlying tone of view of nature, and above all the epical verse form, with its alliterative runes and variations or parallelisms. One can say that certain typical fundamentals of the Finnish national character are outlined in the *Kalevala's* great personal characterizations. For example, in Väinämöinen, he sees meditative stability and wisdom; in Ilmarinen, workaday industry; in Lemminkäinen, sportive recklessness; in Kullervo, dark defiance; in Aino, a tender dreaminess; and in many of the mothers, loving affection. Domestic conditions and everyday tasks are pictured in the wedding lays (Poems 21–25), in the greatest detail and with the greatest clarity. Manly heroism and resourcefulness occasionally flash out for a moment on the military expeditions, while in the Finnish landscape, nature is a singularly living and richly nuanced backdrop and has a part in every description of an action, not least in the numerous lyrically sentimental bits. But fancy and feeling every now and then transform and enhance in dimension—to a remarkable degree embellish and extend—the descriptions both of nature and of persons, and often give a story a free-soaring and glowing fantasy, just as is the case in certain folk epics of India. Taken from this point of view, the *Kalevala* has sometimes been called a folktale or sorcery epic, even though some sort of historical fact might have been the starting point of its stories. In certain respects, it represents a more primitive stage of spiritual development than the old epics of the Western peoples. For this reason, an aesthetic appraisal of its poetry entails special difficulties.

The influence of the Kalevala on literature and art. The *Kalevala* has influenced Finnish literature and art in a most fructifying fashion. The Finnish-language lyric derives one of its main sources of inspiration from the traditional poetry. Already in Kallio (pen name of Samuel K. Berg, 1803–1852), Oksanen (pen name of Aukusti Engelbrekt Ahlquist, 1826–1889), and Suomio (pen name of Julius Krohn, 1835–1888) echoes of the traditional poetry can be found. Johana Heikki Erkko (1849–1906), also Kasimir Leino (originally Lönnbohm) (1866–1919) and Eino Leino (1876–1926) often took material from it; one need only mention Eino Leino's *Tarina suuresta tammesta* (Story of the Big Oak), *Tuonelan joutsen* (The Swan of Death's Domain), and *Helkavirsiä* (Spring Festival Songs). From the literature of the drama, note the play by Aleksis Kivi (originally Stenvall, 1834–1872), *Kullervo,* (1864); Erkko's play of the same title (1895), also his *Aino* (1893) and *Pohjolan häät* (The Wedding at North Farm) (1902); Eino Leino's *Sota valosta* (The War for Light) and *Karjalan kunningas* (The King of Karelia); the *Lemminkäinen* (1907) of Larin Kyösti (Kyösti Larsson, 1873–1938), and the *Lemmin poika* (Lempi's Son) (1922) of Lauri Haarala (1890–1944). Among novels in which *Kalevala* figures appear, the most noteworthy is *Panu* (1897), by Juhani Aho (1861–1921).

Among sculptors who have fashioned works of art based on *Kalevala* subjects, one should mention Erik Cainberg (originally Haino) (1771–1816), Carl Eneas Sjöstrand (1826–1906), Johannes Takanen (1849–1885), Robert Stigell (1852–1907), Emil Wikström (1864–1942), and Eemil Halonen (1875–1950). Among artists, the foremost is Akeseli Gallen-Kallela (1895–1931), who became especially absorbed in *Kalevala* and from it created many notable works, such as the National Museum frescoes "Sammon puolustajat" (The Defenders of the Sampo), "Lemminkäisan Aïti" (Lemminkäinen's Mother), "Joukahaisen Kosto" (Joukahainen's Revenge), "Kullervon kirous" (Kullervo's Curse), and "Kullervon sotaanlähtö" (Kullervo's Setting out to War). In 1922 appeared Gallen-Kallela's *Koru-Kalevala* (The Decorated *Kalevala*), in which the songs are embellished with illustrations at the beginning and the end of each. Gallen-Kallela only lived to prepare the illustrations for the first few poems of a large scale "Suur-Kalevala" (The Great *Kalevala*). Among the numerous other artists who have treated the *Kalevala,* further mention may be made of the Swedish artist Johan Zacharias Blackstadius (1816–1898), Robert Vilhelm Ekman (1808–1873), Berndt Abraham Godenhjelm (1799–1880), Sigfrid August Keinanen (1841–1914), Pekka Halonen, (1865–1933), and Joseph Alanen (1885–1920).

In our music, *Kalevala* subjects hold a distinguished place. One may cite, for example, among operas Oskar Merikanto's (1868–1924) *Pohjan neiti* (The Maiden of North Farm) (1899), Erkki Melartin's (1875–1937) *Aino* (1909), Armas Launis' (1884–   ) *Kullervo* (1917), also *Die Kalewainen in Pohjola* (The Men of the Kalevala District at North Farm) (1891) by the German composer Karl Muller-Berghaus (1829–1907), who worked in Turku in 1886–1895; among symphonies, Robert Kajanus' (1856–1933) *Aino* (first performance February 28, 1885); among symphonic poems, Johan Julius (known as Jean) Sibelius' (1865–1956) "Kullervo" (1892), "Lemminkäisen's Homecoming) (1899), and "Tuonelan joutsen" (The Swan of Death's Domain) (1895), Leevi Madetoja's (1887–1947) "Kullervo" (1913), and Johan Filip van Schantz's (1835–1865) orchestral prelude "Kullervo"; among vocal works with orchestral accompaniment Sibelius' "Tulen synty" (The Origin of Fire), Madetoja's "Väinämöisen kylvo" (Väinämöinen's Sowing), and "Sammon ryöstö" (The Theft of the Sampo); and among some choral works, Sibelius' "Venematka" (The Boat Journey) and "Terve, kuu!" (Hail, Moon!)

The *Kalevala* brought into being two other poems in which use is made of materials from this traditional poetry; in 1853 the Estonian *Kalevipoeg* (Kalev's Son), by Fredrich Reinhold Kreutzwald, and in 1855 *The Song of Hiawatha* by the American poet Henry Wadsworth Longfellow (on which see E. J. Moyne and T. F. Mustanoja, "Longfellow's *Song of Hiawatha* and *Kalevala*," *American Literature,* XXV (1953), 87–89).

BIBLIOGRAPHY. (In this selective list, the place of publication, unless otherwise noted is Helsinki.) C. J. Billson, *The Popular Poetry of the Finns,* Popular Studies in Mythology, No. 5 (London, 1900); Kaarle

Krohn, *Kalevalan runojen historiaa* (The History of the *Kalevala* songs), 7 pts. (1903–1909); Kaarle Krohn, *Kalevalastudien,* 6 pts. (1924–1928); Laina Hänninen, *Luettelo ennen vuotta 1927 painetusta Kalevalaa koske-vasta kirjallisuudesta* (A Catalogue of the Literature Touching the *Kalevala* Published Before the Year 1927) (1928); Vaino W. Salminen, *Kertovien runojen historiaa* (The History of the Narrative Songs), Vol. I: Ingria (1929); Kaarle Krohn, *Kalevalan opas* (A Guide to the *Kalevala*) (1931); Eemil Nestor Setälä, *Sammon arvoitus* (The Riddle of the Sampo) (1932); Vaino W. Salminen, *Suomen muinaisrunojen historia* (The History of the Ancient Finnish Songs) (1933); Onni Okkonen, *A Gallen-Kallelan Kale-vala-taidetta* (Kalevala Art) (1935); Väinö Kaukonen, *Vanhan Kalevalan kokoonpano* (The Compilation of the *Old Kalevala*) (1939–1946); August Annist (born Anni), *Kalevala taideteoksena* (The *Kalevala* as a Work of Art) (1944); Väinö W. Salminen, *Kalevala-kirja* (A *Kalevala* Book), 2d ed. (1947); Bjorn Collinder, *Det finska nationaleposet Kalevala* (Stockholm, 1951); Martti Haavio, *Väinämöinen, Eternal Sage,* Folklore Fellows Communications No. 144 (1952); Jalmari Jaakkola, *Suomen Varhaishistoria; Heimokausi ja "Kalevala-Kultturi"* (The Early History of Finland: The Tribal Period and *"Kalevala* Culture"), 2d ed. (1956), esp. pp. 381–430, 459–462; V. Tarkiainen and Eino Kauppinen, *Suomalaisen Kirjalli-suuden Historia* (History of Finnish Literature), 2d ed. [n.d. (1961?)], pp. 15–75 ["Kansanrunous" (The Traditional Poetry)], and pp. 385–386 (bibliography); Matti Kuusi et al., eds., *Suomen kirjallisuus* (Finnish Literature), Vol. I: *Kirjoittamaton kirjallisuus* (The Unwritten Literature) (Helsinki, 1963), esp. pp. 129–417 (on *Kalevala*-type poetry of various periods), and pp. 624–630 (bibliography).

NOTES

1. By Aarne A. Anttila, in *Iso Tietosanakirja,* 2d ed., Vol. VII (Helsinki, 1935), coll. 277–84, with a few minor omissions.

2. Now in many, though not all, respects surpassed by the monolingual *Nyky-suomen sanakirja,* 6 vols. (Porvoo–Helsinki, 1951–1961).

3. By Väino W. Salminen and Viljo Tarkiainen, in *Iso Tietosanakirja,* 2d ed., Vol. V (Helsinki, 1933), coll. 1141–55; material of secondary interest for the English-speaking reader has been omitted.

4. "Väinämöisesta," in *Turun Wiikko-Sanomat,* No. 10 (11 March), pp. 2–4, No. 11 (18 March), pp. 1–4, No. 20 (20 May) pp. 2–3.

5. Four such *Kalevala*-type songs or variants by two distinguished women singers from northern Russian Karelia, followed by five lyrical pieces, including cradle songs, are finely recorded on a 24 cm. or 9¾″ LP record,

"Runonlaulua Kalevalan Syntysijoista," *Otavan* Kirjallinen *äänilevy* 8 ("Song-singing from the Birthplaces of the *Kalevala*." Otava's Literary Record 8) (Helsinki, 1960); there are accompanying transcripts of the texts, references to corresponding portions of the *Kalevala,* and biographical data on the singers.

Lauri Honko

❀ THE KALEVALA AND FINNISH CULTURE [1]

FEW WORKS HAVE HAD so pervasive an effect upon a nation's life as the epic *Kalevala*. Its influence upon Finnish music, art, and poetry is recent enough to be remembered by everyone; its unique place in Finnish literature is recognized by all.

Two characteristics of the age, romanticism and the awakening of the Finnish national consciousness, prepared the way for an enthusiastic reception of the *Kalevala*. Admiration for the undefiled "folk," a basic trait of romanticism, led to attempts to preserve folk literature. The publication of folk poetry and literature by Thomas Percy in England and Johann Gottfried von Herder in Germany, and the songs of Ossian, composed in Scotland by James Macpherson, are representative of such attempts. In time, these products of the late eighteenth century became known in Finland among the "pre-romantics," a group which included Henrik Gabriel Porthan, a professor of rhetoric; Frans Mikael Franzen, a poet; and Kristfrid Ganander, a pastor at Rantsila. However, these foreign works did not initiate Finnish romanticism; rather they stimulated a movement which had already begun. For example, Porthan was uninfluenced by Herderian romanticism when he began his broad researches into the poetry

46

of the people with his Depoesi fennica 1766–1778. If anything, Porthan should be regarded as a predecessor rather than an imitator. When Finland was joined to Russia, the inheritors of the Porthan tradition, the so-called romanticists of Turku, strove to produce an awakening of the national consciousness and collected materials necessary to the study of the Finnish language and poetry.

The ties with the Swedish romanticists were particularly strong at this time. One of the many Finnophiles studying in Sweden was K. A. Gottlund. While a university student at Upsala in 1817, Gottlund wrote: "If we wished to gather together the ancient folksongs and compile and order them into a systematic whole; whatever may become of them, an epic drama or what have you, it may bring to life a new *Homer, Ossaid,* or *Nibelungenlied;* and in its singular creative brilliance and glory, awakened to its sense of independence, the Finnish nation would receive both the admiration of its contemporaries as well as that of the generations to come." But considerable time elapsed before his dream became a reality.

After the University of Turku was destroyed by fire, it was moved to Helsinki, where the Saturday Society was soon organized. A cultural and political discussion group, the Society had about thirty members, the majority of whom achieved a significant place in science, art, or politics. In 1831, some of the Society's members organized the Finnish Literature Society, an original and effective supporter of Elias Lönnrot's efforts to collect and publish folk poems and songs.

In 1834, Lönnrot wrote to a friend:

> As I compared these (the results of my collections on my fourth journey) to what I had seen before, I was seized by a desire to organize them into a single whole in order to make of the Finnish legends of the gods something similar to that of the *Edda,* the saga of the Icelanders. So I threw myself into the labors before me immediately and continued working for a number of weeks, actually months, at least until Christmas, when I had quite a volume of poems about Väinämöinen in exactly the order in which I desired them. I gave attention especially to the time sequences of the feats accomplished by the heroes of the poems.

Thus, the concept of a Finnish epic was born, with prototypes from the ancient Scandinavian epics uppermost in Lönnrot's mind. However, recognizing the magnitude and importance of the task, he doubted his ability to carry out such a work:

I am not certain whether the task or compilation or concatena-
tion of the sagas of the gods should be accomplished by a single
individual, or preferably by a number of persons working together,
since our posterity will probably place this compilation on a par
with the *Edda* by the Gothenborgains or at least those of Hesiod,
if not Homer, by the Greeks and Romans.

Lönnrot's fifth trip, on which he discovered the most knowledgeable of
the singers of ancient runes, Arhippa Perttunen, was so fruitful that it was
February 28, 1835, before Lönnrot was able to write the preface to his
work, *The Kalevala,* or *Old Karelian Songs from the Ancient Times of the
Finnish People* (Kalevala Taikka Wanhoja Karjalan Runoja Suomen
Kansan muinaisista Aijoista).

At the 1835 annual meeting of the Finnish Literature Society,
J. G. Linsén announced:

> In collecting a vast number of runes in the Archangel district,
> Lönnrot, in fitting them together into a whole, has made the re-
> markable discovery that there exists, in fact, a great and complete
> mythological national epic which has now been compiled by its
> collector into thirty-two runes in which the principal songs tell of
> Väinämöinen's deeds of a heroic nature and also of his destiny.
> Painstakingly and with almost superhuman application to his task,
> the discerning discoverer and compiler achieved a marvelous result
> in the success of his endeavors in that he has fitted together the
> scattered pieces of these ancient Finnish runes and thus preserved
> them from certain disappearance; or more rightfully, he has brought
> to the light of day that which already existed only as fragments and
> were indeed hidden and forgotten. The poems were published
> under the name *Kalevala*—an invaluable gift not only to Finnish
> but also to European literature, which must add these precious
> memorials to Finnish poetry and the songs of the Ionians as well
> as those of the Caledonians.

This concept of Lönnrot's contribution is in complete harmony with the
romantic view of the nature and creation of folk songs and epic poems.
The *Kalevala* was seen as a complete epic saved by Lönnrot from fragmentation. Now restored to its pristine form, it could tell the tale of the
ancient Finns, the phases of their history, and their customs and religion.
No single individual, neither Lönnrot nor the rune-singers, played a critical
part in the *Kalevala*'s creation; its creator was "the people," the collective
creative genius active in the earliest language and poetry of all cultures.

If someone questioned this collective creative process, the explanation was that folk runes and epics were born gradually: in being communicated from mouth to mouth, they occasionally received an addition here and another there until "the people's creative spirit" modified its creation into completeness. In fact, few questioned this process. The basic romantic viewpoint was so strong that the nature of Lönnrot's labors was never actually recognized, although he spoke about it quite openly. The *Kalevala* was—or so it was acknowledged—from its inception, a pristine and complete epic poem, born in antiquity. Lönnrot was simply the successful reconstructor of this ancient masterpiece.

The flaws in this hypothesis are revealed by Lönnrot's letter to Fabian Collan: "I suppose you are amazed that in all this I have nothing to do but to follow the runes. Therefore, I must explain to you that from the runes collected to date I could get at least seven volumes of *Kalevalas*, each unlike the other." This letter, dated 25–5–1848, was written a year before the manuscript for the new *Kalevala* was completed. Lönnrot had in his possession the results of four trips made by himself as well as the collections of A. J. Sjögen, M. A. Castrén, D. E. D. Europaus, H. A. Reinholm, August Ahlqvist, Fr. Polén, and Z. Sirelius. The sheer magnitude of the materials forced Lönnrot to choose among alternatives, even to the extent of modifying the theme and structure of the old *Kalevala*. He wrote of this problem: "The poems, especially those at the beginning will be in a different order from the previous ones, to bring about a more cohesive and natural entity. The many repetitions afford so vast a selection in form and verbiage that one could often wish for fewer riches from which to make a choice." However, when the researchers began to argue about the place and time of the *Kalevala*'s birth, they forgot completely that the epic as they knew it was born at the desk of Elias Lönnrot.

The publication of the old *Kalevala* awakened a powerful national consciousness. J. G. Linsén said in 1836, that if Porthan still lived, he would bless this unexpected victory for the land of his birth. Declaring that Finnish literature could now claim a significant place in European literature, Linsén added: "In making these oral runes her very own, Finland can thus, encouraged and self-informed, learn to known its antiquity and also the future potential of its intellectual development. Finland can now say to itself: 'I, too, have a history' (Suomi voi sanoa insellensa minullakin on historia!)." M. A. Castrén, a young scholar from the North, conjectured: "If I wished to prophesy a future for Finland, when its young men enlivened by true patriotism and willing to lay aside foreign cultures and confessing only that to be true, which had developed from their very own intellectual life and effort; I could well seek the foundation for these hopes in the very *Kalevala* itself."

The powerful need for a national political self-consciousness was the greatest single factor in the *Kalevala*'s success. Interest was first aroused by the fact that the Finnish "hoi polloi," of whose language little was understood, had now been proved to be the protector of a great treasure. In addition to the influence of the romantic milieu, Ruenberg threw the weight of his prestige in defense of the work. Comparing it favorably with the greatest artistic accomplishments of the Greeks, he thus helped the *Kalevala* to achieve recognition. Ironically, each of these inspired pronouncements was delivered in Swedish; the Swedish-speaking intelligentsia were especially interested in the *Kalevala* although their acquaintance with it was rather superficial because of the difficulties of language. Even such a Finnophile as Volmar Schildt-Kilpinen acknowledged ten years after its publication that "I feel like a blind man with regard to the runes, in many instances playing a guessing game at what may have been in the mind of the creator, for I cannot grasp it completely."

On the other hand, the Finnish-speaking people knew very little about the *Kalevala*. The only Finnish-language newspaper in the country, *Sanan-saattaja Viipurista,* did publish a brief but dry article in which both the name of the epic and its author were misspelled. The first edition of the *Kalevala,* consisting of five hundred volumes, was sold out twelve years after the date of publication. Nevertheless, this apparent lack of interest is in no way indicative of the *Kalevala*'s importance. It was, as Martti Haavio has since expressed it, not only "the symbol of Finnish nationalism; but it was actually its crown jewel. It formed a kind of capital, which could hardly as yet be fully drawn upon. It was a cultural goal toward which the oppressed spirit of the Finnish nationalism groped."

Before long, the discussion concerning the *Kalevala* was joined more closely to the program of awakening the national consciousness and was a factor in the struggle over the language question. In 1845, the new editor of the *Mehilainen,* J. V. Snellman, began directing his readers to become acquainted with the *Kalevala:* "Young men, each Swedish word which you utter from this moment onward shall be, relatively speaking, lost from this literature, from the name of Finland, and from your own dignity. Only your mother tongue will afford your works and name a place in the world." When the decree of censorship in 1850 threatened to put an end to the strengthening cause of Finnish patriotism, scores of university students, helped by gifts from their home districts, journeyed to the backwoods and towns with the *Kalevala* in their knapsacks to continue Lönnrot's work.

The peacefully begun national awakening was seriously impeded when the country was torn asunder by political factions and the language struggle. The Swedish movement challenged the originality and true nature of the *Kalevala;* C. G. Estlander contended that the epic was nothing more than a counterfeit based upon runes of the Ossian-type. As Lönnrot's original notations of the runes had been lost (they were later discovered by chance among some discarded papers), the task of quickly gathering "replications of the *Kalevala*" was begun. This task was doubly beneficial, for it not only refuted Estlander's contentions but also helped to renew the lagging interest in rune collection. The *Kalevala* is original in the same sense that the Homeric epics, the *Edda* legends and the *Niebelungenlied* are original. It is based upon original, although separately sung, runes and upon smaller folk epics (the Sampo-epic, the Lemminkainen-epic and the Kullervo-epic). Both Homer and Lönnrot compiled the runes of the rhapsodists and runesingers into a broader and systematic whole. On the other hand, the *Kalevala* cannot be compared either to Macpherson's *Ossiad,* which contains only a sprinkling of original folk songs, or to the two literary epics inspired by the *Kalevala,* the *Kalevipoeg* by the Estonian Kreutzwald and *Hiawatha* by the American Longfellow.

About 1860, numerous *Kalevala*-inspired works began to appear: Aleksis Kivi's Kullervo-tragedy, Sjöstrand's sculptures, Ekman's paintings, von Schantzin's *Kullervo* overture, and Topelius' *Princess of Cypress.* The 1890's were the golden age of folk romanticism. Artists journeyed to the wilds of Kauko-Karjala in search of the milieu from which the runes had come. Four names are pre-eminent among the multitude of artists in this period: Jean Sibelius, Akseli Gallen-Kallela, Juhani Aho, and Eino Leino.

About the same time that realism began to be a factor in literature, the maturation of research in folk poetry caused a re-evaluation. Julius Krohn in his lectures on the *Kalevala* in 1875 reported that he had concluded "that the published *Kalevala,* although it is so carefully compiled, or, better, especially because it is so carefully concatenated, does not lend itself at all to scientific research." In other words, it had become quite clear to the researcher that the problem of "replication of variant readings of the *Kalevala*" indicated that one could solve the problem of the variant forms and rich folk-runes only by attaching the original runes themselves as basic sources. Examination should be focused primarily upon the developmental history of the separate poems, their structure and age, and not upon the synthesis created by Lönnrot which did not contain all of the runes and therefore could not reveal the richness of the variant readings and the nature of folk poetry. The researcher must also investigate the prose forms contained in the descriptive runes, legends, proverbs, and riddles. A similar impulse to extend Finnish literary culture can be observed in the other works of Elias Lönnrot, who had published works on incantations, proverbs, and riddles (arvotuksia), and was presently at work on a monumental Finnish dictionary. At this time, *Kalevala* research became separated from research on Finnish folk runes. The latter utilized geographic-historical methodology to uncover a cultural basis for the creation of runes. The former devoted itself to delineating the problems related to the compilation of the *Kalevala* and to critically examining the epic as literature. Today, nearly one hundred years after this work was published, it is possible to mark the excellent achievements of both schools. The "Finnish method" used in the investigation of sagas achieved prominence in its day, even in foreign countries; later, when the methodology used in folk research became multifaceted, it served to illumine the history and nature of folk poems and lyrics. *Kalevala* research, in its investigation of the individual runes, has clarified the sources of the verses and has revealed the creativity of Elias Lönnrot. Contemporary scholars assign the modern *Kalevala* research to literary science; the special artistic creative process which resulted in Elias Lönnrot's *Kalevala* is best explained through the methodology of literary criticism.

The foregoing has attempted to trace the meaning of the *Kalevala* in terms of the cultural-historical situation into which it came. Neither the *Kalevala* nor the folk-songs which comprised it were understood in any profound sense for a long time. A considerable interval elapsed before it was possible to interpret the strange words and obscure language of the runes, and to recognize the poetic values in the text. In spite of these obstacles, the effect of the *Kalevala* is immeasurable. It has been said that the greater part of Finland's history during the past generation is a direct or indirect result of the publication of this folk epic. Simply in the area of political history it has been crucial. In almost all the fields of artistic endeavor the *Kalevala*'s influence has been pervasive: it gave birth to new branches of learning; it fructified the Finnish language, thus laying a cornerstone for Finnish literature; and it brought the name of Finland to the attention of the world. Only an epic and only a folk epic at that could have accomplished so much.

NOTE

1. *Suuri tietokirja* (The Large Encyclopedia), 1960.

FINNISH EMIGRATION
TO AMERICA

Reino Kero

❈ THE BACKGROUND OF
FINNISH EMIGRATION

THE MAJORITY OF Finns who emigrated to America in the mid-nineteenth century came from the central Bothnias. A considerable number also emigrated from northern Satakunta, northern Tavastland, and the regions of Rauma and Aland. On the other hand, relatively few left the provinces of southern Tavastland, Savo, Uudenmaa, and Karjala. Therefore, any examination of the factors influencing Finnish emigration to America must determine what motivated so many citizens of certain areas to seek a new homeland in America. One such factor was the increase in population. Although the population grew appreciably in the eighteenth century, crop failures and communicable diseases kept it within reasonable limits. In 1800, Finland had a population of about nine hundred thousand; a century later, the figure stood at three million. The country as a whole experienced a rapid increase in population, but the average growth was far surpassed by that of the newly pioneered areas such as Bothnia and northern Satakunta. In Satakunta, for instance, it is possible to trace the influence of population growth upon emigration: in the late nineteenth century, emigration from the northern part of Satakunta where the population had grown rapidly was significantly larger than emigration from the central and southern parts of the province where the population growth

55

had been average or minimal. However, the mere increase in population was not the sole factor producing emigration since the Finnish cities and the general economic life of the country offered the excess rural population other ways of earning a living. It is clear that in certain areas, Bothnia for example, migration to America became the fashion whereas the inhabitants of other places such as Savo were more likely to move to the Finnish cities.

It is evident that as the nineteenth century wore on, it became an economic necessity for ever increasing numbers of rural folk to seek a living either in America or in the cities of the homeland. In the beginning of the century, the vast majority of Finns were farmers. Consequently, when the population increased in the nineteenth century, the arable land per capita decreased. Farmlands were divided; a nation in which a small farm economy was already the norm was divided into still smaller working units. The small farms were unable to produce a livelihood for all their inhabitants. Yet the rural population without property or farms increased. The areas boarding on the towns were dotted with small huts whose inhabitants had no land and no employment, but often did have eight to twelve children to feed. At the same time, significant changes were taking place in agriculture. As hay became the principal crop, a farm economy developed which was based on dairy cattle, but even this was not sufficient. This accelerated growth required more and more employment and greater income. In the forest-covered areas of the country, the solution was relatively simple for the value of timberlands increased appreciably in the nineteenth century. The sale of forests and lumber gave the peasants a sizable income, and the lumbering industry offered them new possiblities for a livelihood.

However, not all of Finland benefited from the forests and lumbering. Many of the best forests, especially in Bothnia, had been spoiled by the practice of tar-burning. The distillation of tar (tervanpoltto) had for several centuries been one of the country's secondary producers of employment for the rural population, and the tar economy had in the best of recent centuries, especially in Bothnia, been a significant competitor with the economy based upon agriculture. As late as the 1860's, tar-burning constituted an important source of livelihood for the residents of Bothnia. However, after the Civil War in the United States, the price of tar dropped drastically, and a major Finnish industry built around the distillation of tar came to an end. As has been pointed out, tar-burning had destroyed the forests to such an extent that the healthy lumbering industry was unable to gain a place in Bothnia. The era based on lumbering brought about an economic crisis in that province. Similar economic crises were set off in northern Satakunta and northern Tavastland when a lack of workable forests put an end to the work of hand-sawing lumber and carting the planks by horse to Pori. Thousands of farmers, small tenant farmers and cottagers thrived on the forest economy during the 1860's, but by the end of the nineteenth century, the whole industry was a thing of the past. Furthermore, the advent of steam-powered ships brought an end to the building of sailing vessels by the close of the nineteenth century. The Gulf of Bothnia had a number of ports where shipbuilding was a key industry, for example at Luvia, Merkarvia, Kokkola, and Pietarsaari. As steamships gradually took the place of sailing vessels, the workers in the shipbuilding industry lost their jobs.

Thus, when the burning of tar, shipbuilding, and the transportation of lumber each saw its conclusion, Bothnia and its environs were left on the periphery, economically speaking. The heart of the Finnish economy of Finland shifted to the southern coastal cities. The rural population was forced to seek its existence outside the home provinces. The Bothnians were the first to leave their homes; as early as the 1850's, they were seeking employment in the great construction areas of southern Finland. The construction of the Saima Canal, especially, gave employment to many, but a few northern woodsmen went as far as Russia where they were employed in the shipyards at Petrograd and Kronstadt. However, the crop failures of the 1860's also increased the movement to the south. This created a problem for the southerners who during the years of dearth sought ways in which to deal with "those beggars," from Bothnia and Satakunta, "who go from house to house to seek their livelihood." In the next decade, ever-increasing numbers of people left their home provinces. Although railroad building provided employment for many, it could not supply nearly enough jobs to fill the demand. A newspaper account of the construction of the line from Tampere and Pori reported that hundreds of men presented themselves each day at the Kokemaki employment office, in spite of the fact that comparatively few were successful in obtaining work. Thus, the end of the nineteenth century saw a decided movement into the urban areas. Helsinki, in particular, was inundated by men from the provinces of Uusmaa, Hame, Savo, and Bothnia seeking employment.

It was fairly obvious that the existing urban centers were unable to keep pace with the rapid rise in the ranks of the unemployed. Gradually word about the opportunities in America spread from parish (pitäjä) to parish. Thereafter, the number of emigrants increased each decade. By the close of the nineteenth century, thousands of Finns had left for America; in the early twentieth century the number of emigrants rose to tens of thousands.

The political situation was also a factor in increasing emigration. Under the decree of 1878 regarding compulsory military service, every Finnish male was subject to a three-year term of service with the regular army. The average citizen regarded a three-year term during peace-time as unreasonable. By 1880, the newspapers contained statements that the new conscription law had only served to increase emigration to heretofore unpredictable proportions. Then in the 1890's, when Russia's political machinations threatened Finland's existence, increasing numbers of Finns decided to seek better conditions across the ocean. The new military service law of 1901 was yet another source of discontent; this law stipulated that all Finnish conscripts were, when called upon, to fight anywhere in Russia or possibly outside its borders as the situation at a given time demanded. An attempt was made to discourage the number of emigrants seeking to avoid military service by refusing passports to them, but many still succeeded in leaving the country. It is estimated that from Ostro-Bothnia alone, thousands managed to leave either without a visa or with a false passport.

The oppressive measures taken by the Russians created a grim atmosphere which heightened the appeal of emigration. Furthermore, the growth of the workers' movement at the turn of the century made emigration acceptable. Leaders of the workers' movement, such as Matti Kurikka, Taavi Tainio, and Oskari Tokoi, had made trips to America and generally affirmed the cause of the emigrants. In *Työmies* (*The Worker*), Matti Kurikka presented powerful propaganda favoring emigration. He wrote, for example, "We shall discover the historical salvation of our people through emigration. In Finland the working class may eat only raw herring and drink skimmed milk. Everything is much better in America. It is not worthwhile for the working people to remain in Finland." The workers' newspapers produced an attitude severely critical of the social conditions in Finland. Knowledge of the contrasting socio-economic conditions in America and Finland became one of the primary factors affecting emigration. The Finns did not become really interested in emigration until they learned that America offered better possibilities for economic advancement. In fact, it was only after the comparison with the American situation was firmly established, that they became severely critical of their own social conditions.

Finnish interest in America began to develop in the mid-nineteenth century when the news of the discovery of gold in California trickled to Finland. Finnish seamen began to escape from their ships when they docked in American harbors. In the 1860's emigrant recruiters began to travel in Finland; in the following decade, steamship companies propagandized to stimulate out-migration. For example, in 1874, one steamship company spread literature from Sweden depicting Canada as an earthly paradise. It argued that the world's best potatoes, turnips, and cabbages grew in Canada. During the next decade, Canada sent emigrant agents on recruitment trips to Finland. It is reported from Kiikoinen that an "emigrant-runner" at the turn of the century, probably in 1902, took the region's first emigrant to Canada to work on a railroad. The newspapers of the day contained advertising which depicted Canada as an agricultural nation, where good arable land was offered at a supposedly cheap price. The majority of the Canadian emigrant-runners probably recruited Finns for Canadian farms and its labor force. The U.S. agents sent by the railroad companies were especially active during the 1880's. It was impossible, they said, to convey the beauties of the United States. America contained multitudes of good fields and pastures; there were many silver, gold, and coal mines. Nature was beautiful beyond comparison.

The newspapers warned the people not to believe the promises of the emigrant-runners. For example, one of the leading papers described the activities of the recruiters: "Their promises are pure lies and a fraud. The recruiters are seeking simple-minded folk to fall into their trap. Men of Finland, keep your eyes open." It is impossible to know what the farmers, peasants, and poor cottagers thought about the promises made by the recruiters or how they reacted to the warnings in the newspapers. But America was able to entice over three hundred and eighty thousand Finns, one-third of which later returned to Finland. It is possible that many of the first emigrants left because of the lures of the emigrant-runners.

Once the first Finns reached America, they wrote letters to their friends and relatives in Finland describing the wonders of their new country. These descriptions were trusted even by those who refused to heed the promises of the recruitment people. The letters assured them that no one need fear starting off as an emigrant; if some hesitated because of the difficulties of travel, he need not, for the emigrants were shepherded so carefully from Hanko onward that they could never get lost. When they had crossed the ocean and reached land, interpreters would be there to receive them. Once in America, it was quite simple to find one's way to his destination. Those who came were promised much good fortune. The residents of the Ii-parish in 1866 learned from one such letter that "in America even the grain grows up in a week, that peas there rotted in a pile at the base of trees, and that the supply of red wine flowing from between cracks in the cliffs never became exhausted, not even by drinking it." At Pudasjarvi,

it was common knowledge that "in America every common 'Maija' walked
the streets in silk, and with a hat on her head to boot." The residents of
Puolanka heard that "in America there were vast piles of all good things
gathered together: gold, silver, wheat, punch, and whiskey." Visible proof
of these wonders was provided by photographs showing ordinary Finnish
workers transformed into ladies and gentlemen of wealth. The simple,
rural hometowns of the Finns paled in comparison to the stories of America's bounty. No wonder that the recipient of such letters and photographs
was prepared to cross the Atlantic on the very next ship.

The Finns found the wages in America practically beyond belief.
A good worker there could save three hundred dollars a year—or about
fifteen hundred marks according to the rate of exchange prevailing at the
turn of the century. In Finland, a good worker could save at the most two
to three hundred marks a year. And women were paid a far better wage
in America than in the old country. For example, a servant girl in Bothnia
at the beginning of the century would earn about one hundred and twenty
marks per year in addition to her keep. In America, the going rate was
from ten to forty dollars per month, or the equivalent of from six to
twenty-five hundred Finn-marks annually.

Yet another enticement was knowledge of the social conditions
prevalent in America, which was regarded as the freest country in the
world. In 1866, a well-known newspaper man wrote the following about
America: "Why does the mention of the name of the U.S. cause our hearts
to pound so strongly? Why has the U.S. grown from a miserable land of
immigrants to become the number one country in the world? Because in
America, the individual may sacrifice himself on the altar of liberty." Letters from the new country spread the news of the ideal conditions in
America among the rural population. It was said that the new world was
the loving mother of mankind which had given birth to a new concept of
freedom. The upper classes hated this freedom, but the people loved it.
The United States was, among the nations of the world, a child of good
fortune for there it was possible for the people to rule themselves. Quite
the reverse was true in Europe and in Finland, where the nobility had
made slaves of the people. In America even the poor man was noble. The
American was always prepared to help his poor neighbor. In Finland, the
people were forbidden to speak their own language by the aristocracy;
the schools trod upon the values making for human dignity and brought
the citizen to a state of hopelessness. In America, all was different. There
a woman received the dignity she deserved. It was rumored that in America

even the most corrupt person received a new mind and spirit; as no one inquired into the sins of his past, he was free to seek something higher and better.

These letters extolling the economic, social, political, and spiritual opportunities in America are typified by one written by a Finnish immigrant living in Kaleva, Michigan:

The area is exceedingly fertile. The fruit trees, which are everywhere, are adequate proof of the matter. The branches of the fruit trees again this year bend under the burden of the lush fruit they bear. I have never seen such large apples as I have seen here. They also grow numerous kinds of fruit, which I have never seen in Finland. Of these I recognize only the plum. Grapes grow here wild in the woods. The farms grow corn and potatoes, which have a different taste from those in Finland. The Finns here have begun to take up chicken farming. It is possible to purchase ready-built homes here from the older members of the community because when the Finns came and moved in among them, they sold their farms for fear of the Finnish sorcerers. Last year it was possible to buy these farms cheaply, but now when we have asked about the prices, they have risen by about twenty percent. But, in any case, you can still purchase an exceedingly good farm of 80–100 acres for from $2000–3000. Those who have no money buy uncleared land for $6–10 an acre, and do the clearing themselves. The soil is good sandy loam and absolutely free of stones. The area is surrounded by fresh water lakes, rivers, and creeks, and the shores are filled with hundreds of types of deciduous trees. If you intend to come here as a farmer, do it immediately because the prices of land keep rising as more and more immigrants swarm here from Finland. It is not worth your while to stay in Finland. If the gentlemen (herrat) leave something for you, the Russians (ryssät) will come and take it from you slowly but surely. Therefore, with all the persuasion at my command, I would persuade all those who have even only 3000 marks to come here as farmers, for with such a capital one can eat his bread here as though it were nothing but play. The farming region is replete with schools. You know here we govern ourselves. The Finnish language is heard wherever one goes, and all of us have our roots deep in Kaleva. The government, you know, favors Finnish immigration. The climate is favorable. Kaleva needs a lot of active people like yourself.

The reports from America forced the Finns to take a critical look at their own surroundings and awakened secret prospects for a better life. The first emigrants had proved that in America the poor Finnish cottager could prosper and live a life of dignity. America thus became the goal for thousands of Finns.

Tauri Aaltio

❖ A SURVEY OF EMIGRATION FROM FINLAND TO THE UNITED STATES AND CANADA

EMIGRATION FROM Finland to the United States and Canada started as late as the latter half of the nineteenth century. Because of her remote location, Finland had been sheltered from the earlier migratory movements which transferred millions of people from other western European countries to the new continent during the centuries following the discovery of America. The flow of Finns to America soon became a real exodus: more than three hundred and fifty thousand citizens—out of a total population of about three million (1900)—left their country in search of better conditions on the other side of the Atlantic Ocean.

There had been, however, a much earlier attempt at Finnish settlement in northern America, although not actually initiated by the Finns themselves. During the sixteenth and seventeenth centuries people in certain parts of Finland, then part of the Swedish kingdom, moved to Sweden, either to work temporarily in the mines or to settle there permanently for farming, hunting, and fishing. This emigration increased notably after King Charles IX. To promote the settlement of the uninhabited areas in Vermland, western central Sweden, Finnish settlers were even promised taxfree years for clearing the forests for cultivation. It is estimated that some forty

63

thousand Finns moved across the ice of the Gulf of Bothnia or drove their cattle before them hundreds of miles around it.

Accustomed to hard work and experienced in clearing forests, the Finns seemed to have made a good start in Vermland. Fairly soon, however, conflicts developed both with envious Swedish neighbors and with the authorities. A new law which made burning woodlands for cultivation illegal created further problems. Sweden, then one of the great powers in Europe, was planning to establish a colony on the new American continent. The first shipment of settlers consisted of a few volunteers from Sweden and Finland, but the majority were Vermland Finns, put forcefully aboard as punishment for violating the new forest laws. The first ship landed at the mouth of the Delaware in 1638. During the short history of "New Sweden," conquered by the Dutch in 1655, an estimated five hundred Finns arrived in Delaware. They were soon assimilated by their neighbors. When the famous Finnish scientist, Peter Kalm, visited the area a hundred years later, he could not find a single Finnish-speaking family, but certain typically Finnish traditions still prevailed. Some geographical names of Finnish origin were retained much longer.

In 1938, three hundred years after the arrival of the first ship from Sweden, a monument by the Finnish sculptor, Wäinö Aaltonen, was erected in Chester, Pennsylvania, an area earlier called Finland, to commemorate the earliest Finnish pioneers in America.

During the first half of the nineteenth century, well before the days of the great migration to the United States, when Alaska still belonged to Russia and Finland was a Grand Duchy under the Russian Czar, a number of Finns moved to what is now the state of Alaska. Most of them were either fishermen or whale and fur hunters, but two Finns served as governors of Alaska. After the United States bought Alaska in 1867, some of the Finns returned to Finland, others moved to the United States proper or to Canada. In the 1880's, however, when gold was found in Alaska, the Finns started moving there again. During the first decades of the present century, the Finns, together with the Norwegians, were the largest foreign-born national group in Alaska. It was not by chance that the last acting governor of Alaska before it became a state, Waino Hendrickson, was born of Finnish parents. The Finns' most notable strongholds in Alaska have been Sitka, Juneau-Douglas, Fairbanks, and Anchorage. As early as the first years of the 1840's, a Finnish church was built in Sitka—the first Protestant church on the west coast of North and South America.

The great emigration from Finland to America can be said to have begun during the 1860's. A copper mining company in Hancock, Michigan, had sent recruiters to northern Norway, and Finns working there were the first to bring reports of the wonderful country in the West to their country-men back home. As the conditions in Finland at the time forced part of the population to seek their livelihood elsewhere, the tidings of available cheap farming land, plentiful employment, and good wages—in a word, of better prospects for energetic young people and their offspring—found more and more eager listeners particularly in the western and northern parts of Finland, and especially in Ostrobothnia. The example of those who had met the challenge of unfamiliar conditions successfully encouraged others to follow. Thus began the so-called "American fever," which raged from 1870 until 1920.

The earliest official statistics cover only the principal emigration provinces of Vaasa and Oulu; figures on the entire country are not available before 1893. The following figures demonstrate the intensity of the emigration from Finland to America at its peak:

Year	Number of emigrants
1883–1892	36,401
1893–1900	47,557
1901–1910	158,832
1911–1920	67,346

In 1920, there were 149,824 persons in the United States born in Finland. That year, a new immigration law introduced the so-called quota system, which limited the number of immigrants from Finland to approximately five hundred and sixty per annum. The main flow, although greatly reduced, was now directed to Canada. The older immigrant generation gradually died, however, and many—according to most estimates up to a third of the total number of emigrants—returned to Finland. By 1950, the number of Finland-born persons in the United States was only 95,506; the number has continued to decrease.

When the American fever was at its peak in 1902, twenty-three thousand emigrants left Finland: that is, 83.8 persons per ten thousand inhabitants for the whole country; 237.6 per ten thousand in the province of Vaasa. Nevertheless, the population of Finland, with the sole exception of the province of Vaasa, continued to increase. In Ostrobothnia and adjacent areas, however, the loss of young people from twenty to thirty was considerable. More than sixty percent of the young emigrants were men; from sixty to seventy percent came from farming areas.

The Finns, like other immigrants, had to face many hardships in

America. New conditions, unfamiliar customs, a strange language, and homesickness were among the many factors causing them to seek the company of other Finnish immigrants, which in turn led to the formation of several "Finnish" communities in the United States. The first of these was in the Hancock area in northern Michigan. Finns originally went to Hancock to work in the numerous mines, but later, more and more turned to farming. The strength of the Finnish element in those parts is still reflected in the many Finnish place-names such as Toivola, Tapiola, Nisula, etc.

As a rule, Finnish immigrants tended to settle in the northern states, where the climate and scenery were similar to those of the home country. Speaking little if any English, yet accustomed to hard manual labor, they usually had to earn their living in the heaviest kind of work: mining, lumbering, loading and clearing uninhabited forests for cultivation. There were Finnish miners all over the country, even as far west as Colorado and California. Partly due to mining, partly to lumbering and farming, large Finnish areas developed in northern Minnesota, with Duluth and Virginia as the most important centers. The harbors of the Great Lakes offered plenty of loading work and gave rise to the concentration of Finns in Ashtabula and Fairport Harbor. In the industrialized East, Finns worked as factory hands in cities like Worcester and Fitchburg, Massachusetts. The latter was gradually to become, next to Hancock, an important center of the cultural activities of the Finns in America, and the Finnish element in Fitchburg has remained strong and active. By the time the Finns had arrived, much of the best farm land had been seized by others, but there were still homesteads in the north available on favorable terms. Finnish farmers opened up extensive areas in the states of Minnesota, Michigan— the two states with the largest Finnish population—and the Dakotas. Other Finns took up farming in the eastern and western coastal states. In addition to the more traditional forms of farming, the Finns began specializing: some grew cranberries, blueberries or other fruits; others raised cattle or poultry. The large cities like New York, Chicago, Los Angeles, San Francisco, or Seattle exerted their drawing power on the Finns as well as on other nationalities. Finnish fishermen were not uncommon in the big western rivers and on the northern coast of the Pacific. Finnish maids and housekeepers were much sought after on account of their great skill and dependability. Many immigrant girls also worked in textile mills and other factories, but the great majority of the Finnish women in America did their long day's work at home, often toiling hard on the farm and raising a large family.

The greatest obstacle to adaptation and assimilation was the immigrants' poor command of English. Those who had left Finland as adults encountered almost insurmountable difficulties in mastering a new and totally different language. On the other hand, Finns were uncommonly eager to provide their children with as good an education as possible, thus making it possible for the second generation to obtain a better position in American society.

As the number of Finns in America increased, the immigrants soon discovered a need for common activities. This need was the more urgent as the first generation of immigrants, having lost their old roots and environment, easily fell prey to dangers like alcoholism in the cultural vacuum of their new non-Finnish surroundings. It was no surprise, therefore, that temperance societies were among the earliest Finnish community activities to flourish in America. Dozens were established in different parts of the country. Besides maintaining halls and arranging social evenings, many temperance societies included activities such as gymnastics, music, choral singing, and drama clubs; many implemented Finnish libraries.

The need for an organized religious life also became apparent soon after the Finns started forming groups and communities in America. They had brought their psalm books and Bibles with them from the old country, but lacked established congregations and ordained Finnish-speaking pastors. Gradually, however, more and more congregations were established until every major Finnish community had at least one Finnish church, in many cases even more, as the different denominations established congregations and built churches of their own. Churches have had an important role in maintaining the Finnish language and Finnish traditions among immigrants and their children. It was common in earlier times that children were taught to read and write Finnish in Sunday schools. The most important cultural contribution of the Finnish church in America has probably been the establishment of Suomi College by the Suomi Synod seventy years ago.

Other interests favored by fairly large numbers of Finnish immigrants have been the labor movement, strongest before the First World War, and the cooperative movement, a field in which the American Finns have pioneered. The Finnish-language press, both political and non-political, has had an important function, particularly during the most intensive immigration from Finland, as most of the newcomers could not read English and postal connections with Europe were uncertain and slow. Finns are avid readers; in addition to the literature shipped from Finland, there has been a considerable amount of American-Finnish publishing activity.

The history of Finnish emigration to Canada greatly resembles that to the United States. There are, however, two notable differences: emigration from Finland to Canada started later but has maintained a greater numerical strength, as Canada has not permanently limited the number of immigrants allowed to enter the country.

Approximately ten percent of the Finns who emigrated during the first two decades of this century went directly to Canada. After 1920, when the quota system was introduced in the United States, Canada received the great majority of Finnish emigrants. From 1921 to 1931 the number of Finnish-born people in Canada rose from 12,156 to 30,354. Canada was soon forced by the great depression, however, to limit the entrance of new immigrants. As there was also a considerable tendency during the late thirties to move to the United States or return to Finland, the number of Finnish Canadians was reduced to 24,387 by 1941. In the early 1950's, the time of the most recent "Canadian fever," emigration from Finland to Canada again grew to noteworthy proportions. In 1951 alone, more than five thousand Finns crossed the Atlantic to Canada; a couple of years later, the figure reached eight thousand. Towards the end of the decade, however, the number of Finns leaving for Canada fell under one thousand per year. Acute unemployment in Canada and a rising standard of living and full employment in Finland caused many Finns to return home, especially during the sixties.

In Canada, there are also a few distinctly Finnish areas. In terms of the Finnish proportion of the total population, the most important of these is Port Arthur, Ontario, and the surrounding vicinity. The city has a number of Finnish stores and several Finnish halls. It is surrounded by extensive farm lands cleared by the Finns and large forests giving work to many Finnish lumbermen. Other Finnish centers are Sudbury, Ontario, where Finns mine for nickel and run neighborhood farms; Toronto, with Finns employed mainly as artisans and in various service occupations; Sault Ste Marie (metal foundry); Timmins (mining and lumbering); Montreal; and certain areas on the West Coast, especially Vancouver. Unique among the Finnish settlements in Canada was Sointula ("Harmony"), a utopian community established in 1901 on Malcolm Island by a group of Finnish socialists. Although the experiment failed after only a few years, most of the Finns stayed on, and the island population still contains a strong Finnish element.

The community activities of Finnish Canadians have retained an intensity and variety no longer seen in the Finnish areas of the United States. Both cultural and athletic interests flourish; the impressive annual Finnish-Canadian festivals are attended by thousands of Finns from all parts of that large country. There is also some Finnish publishing in Canada, including three newspapers in the Finnish language.

BEGINNINGS OF A FINNISH COMMUNITY IN AMERICA

David T. Halkola

※ FINNISH-LANGUAGE NEWSPAPERS IN THE UNITED STATES

REMINISCING IN THE twentieth-anniversary publication of the *Amerikan Suometar* (The American Finn) in 1919, a veteran worker in Finnish-American endeavors, J. H. Jasberg, noted as a major reason for the founding of that newspaper the great need for a "voice" by the Finnish Evangelical Lutheran Church, Suomi-Synod. Jasberg suggested that the founders had reached the stage where they could be compared to individuals who played on someone else's horn. Those who owned the instrument (i.e., the newspaper) were willing to hear only tunes that they favored. If the causes of the church body and of Suomi College were to be heard correctly by the immigrant Finnish people, it was imperative that the interested leaders secure their own trumpets regardless of cost.[1]

This problem faced all of the religious groups among the Finnish Lutherans in their formative years. Ultimately, it led each one to undertake the publishing of a newspaper or some other form of periodical that could disseminate information in a favorable light to the sponsoring church body. Therefore, in addition to the *Amerikan Suometar* of the Suomi-Synod (1899), there appeared the *Auttaja* (Helper) of the National Evangelical Lutheran Church (1906), and the *Walwoja* (the Guardian, 1915) and the *Opas* (Guide, 1930) as organs of the Apostolic Lutheran Church.[2]

73

Sundry other religious periodicals, more strictly devotional in nature, added to the impact the respective church bodies sought to make among the immigrant Finnish people and their descendants.

There was no paucity of newspapers in the Finnish language to justify the launching of such a venture by the church body involved. According to J. I. Kolehmainen's bibliographical guide, over three hundred and fifty newspapers and periodicals have been published in the Finnish language in the United States. The first was the *Amerikan Suomalainen Lehti* (The American-Finnish Journal), a weekly launched by A. J. Muikku in Hancock, Michigan, shortly after his arrival in 1876. Muikku published only eleven issues; similarly short-lived was a successor, the *Lehtinen* (Leaflet), which Muikku published briefly the same year. However, it was the beginning that led to the proliferation of Finnish-language papers. In 1899, the year that the *Amerikan Suometar* first appeared, there were no less than ten weekly, four monthly, one semi-monthly, one quarterly, and one annual publication that catered to the needs of the growing Finnish population in the United States.[3]

None of the earlier ventures in the publishing of a Finnish-language newspaper was formally incorporated into the program of an organized church body. However, a second *Amerikan Suomalainen Lehti,* started in 1879, was printed by a firm in which the controlling interest was held by the Apostolic Lutherans, and the editor, Alex Leinonen, fostered that particular denomination's point of view. Since sharp divisions existed among the Apostolic Lutherans of that day, Leinonen's position was made very difficult, and eventually the paper ceased to take a strong editorial stand on any religious issue. Years later, when the Suomi-Synod was established in 1890, the editor did lean more in the direction of the Evangelical Lutherans, but for the fourteen years or so of its existence, the *Amerikan Suomalainen Lehti* was basically an independent newspaper.[4]

In the latter part of the nineteenth century, the church leaders tended to rely upon the more strictly devotional type of periodical in order to reach their scattered congregations. Thus, the leaders of the future Suomi-Synod, such as J. K. Nikander, J. J. Hoikka, and K. L. Tolonen, established the *Paimen-Sanomia* (Shepherd's Tidings) in 1889, and through this monthly publication, advanced the cause of an Evangelical Lutheran Synod. As a result, when the Suomi-Synod was founded in 1890, the *Paimen-Sanomia* became the official organ of that church body although it remained for some years in the hands of its founders rather than become the property of the church. In 1892, Pastors Nikander and Tolonen began to edit a publication designed primarily for children, the *Lehti*

Lapsille ja Kuviakin (Journal for Children and Pictures Too). In 1894, Nikander personally started the *Joululehti* (Christmas Journal). With the founding of Suomi College in 1896, this journal became the first of a series of quarterly festival publications that were issued by the institution at Easter, Mid-summer, Reformation, and Christmas.

As worthy as the purposes of these publications were, they did not satisfy the Synod's need for an actual news media. Difficulties with the existing independent papers increased the pressure for such a publication. From its beginning, the Synod had run into considerable hostility from certain quarters of the press. Ino Ekman's *Kansan Lehti* (The People's Journal), published in Calumet, Michigan, and Fred Karinen's *Työmies* (Worker) from Ishpeming, Michigan, led the assault against the formation of the Synod. It was claimed that a Synod would bring about a forcible collection of dues, that it would be dominated by the clergy, and that the very word "Synod" suggested something sinister. Other newspapers, such as V. Burman's *Amerikan Suomalainen* (American-Finn) and A. Nylund's *Uusi Kotimaa* (New Homeland), were more friendly to the strivings of the Suomi-Synod. However, the railings in the *Amerikan Uutiset* (American News), edited by Kalle Haapakoski, were more typical of the press. He bitterly attacked the Suomi Synod and its institutions, notably the recently established Suomi College.[5]

This hostility was a leading factor in the start of the *Amerikan Suometar*. Writing some years later, F. V. Kava stated that it was undeniably due to the conditions of the Finnish-American press then extant that the newspaper was begun. The existing publications did not further the causes of the church. Instead, Kava claimed, they were coldly critical of the Synod, and their policies and editorial stands did not satisfy the needs of the more serious-minded people. To the people to whom the heritage of the church from the old homeland was precious, a more positive promotion of Synodical causes seemed desirable.[6] About a year after it had been started, the *Suometar* [7] editorialized strongly on this point:

When the Suometar was established, . . . there was not a single newspaper in the United States upon which the Synod could rely in the slightest. All had to a greater or lesser extent taken a stand that was contrary to the best interests of the church, despite the fact that the church could do so much good for the immigrants. Neither had Suomi College received the support from the newspapers that it deserved. Thus long before the *Amerikan Suometar* appeared, a hope for just such a newspaper to support the congregational and educational aspirations of the people existed. From these people, letters flowed to the leaders pleading that a proper newspaper be started.[8]

Again, in 1912, the *Amerikan Suometar* stated flatly: "This paper was not established to provide a means of livelihood for some private individuals, but a general agreement concerning the more valuable endeavors and common causes of our people has created the *Amerikan Suometar*." [9]

Yielding to the increasing demand for a newspaper that would truly represent the growing Suomi Synod, the leaders finally took action in 1899. On February 28, an *Amerikan Suometar* publishing firm was organized and a constitution for the group was approved. In addition to Pastors K. L. Tolonen, J. K. Nikander, J. Back, and R. Ylonen, J. Holmlund was present at the meeting. Not present, but also founding members of the firm were A. Leinonen and I. Silberg. A capital of seven hundred dollars was subscribed by the founders; Pastor Ylonen became the first chairman of the firm, with Nikander as secretary and Back as treasurer. From the many applicants for the editorship, N. J. Ahlman of Finland was selected at a monthly salary of sixty dollars. A decision was made to print a "presentation number" of five thousand with the subscription rate for the weekly paper to be two dollars per year.[10]

In the very first issue of the *Suometar,* the basic purpose was clearly stated. Deeming most important the preservation and dissemination of the faith of the fathers, the paper would seek to nurture the precious seed that the fathers had planted and left as a great heritage. More specifically the *Suometar* stated that its editorial stand would be based on the following points: (1) the furthering of Finnish nationalism and culture, (2) support of the temperance movement, (3) preservation of Finnish culture and education, (4) information about the United States, (5) worthy fiction or literature, (6) thorough coverage of news from Finland, (7) reliable reporting from Finnish-American communities, (8) as much world news as space permitted, and (9) underlying all, a Christian outlook and strong support of the institutions and activities of the Suomi Synod and its pastors.[11]

It soon seemed inconsistent for a newspaper so thoroughly dedicated to the causes of the Synod to remain in private hands. The *Amerikan Suometar* had joined the *Paimen-Sanomia* as products of the same press and essentially the property of the same small group of individuals. It was only natural that serious thought be given to the possibility that they would become the direct concern of the entire church body. In return for the reimbursement of their investment, the various owners were willing to sell their shares to the Synod. When the annual convention of the Synod met in 1900, a committee was assigned to look into the feasibility of purchasing the entire operation—papers, presses, and building. The committee report recommended a purchase price; it was accepted by the convention and what became known as the Finnish Lutheran Book Concern was established under Synod auspices. In regard to the *Suometar* specifically, the value of the property was deemed to be the same as the indebtedness, a figure recorded at the time at $1,186.19. Thus, for slightly over a thousand dollars, the Synod gained the desired "horn" with which to trumpet to an audience of some two thousand. The Consistory of the Synod was assigned the task of directing the operation during the first year; in 1901, the board of Suomi College assumed responsibility for the enterprise. This arrangement continued until 1908, when the church created a separate board for the Book Concern.[12]

The early years were ones of growth. Immigration from Finland increased precipitously, reaching a high for a single year with twenty-three thousand in 1902. While only a minority of these immigrants became actively associated with organized religious bodies in the United States, the sheer size of the immigrant wave was sufficient to bring about notable increases in such churches as the Suomi Synod. Membership in the Synod rose from 12,000 to 22,964 in 1905 and to 27,252 in 1910. This growth was reflected in the circulation of the *Suometar*: 4,000 subscriptions were reported in 1903; in 1913, when the *Amerikan Suometar* became a triweekly, circulation reached 5,300 and a high of 7,000 was recorded in 1917.[13]

The *Suometar* had fifteen editors before 1913, when Emil Saastamoinen became editor-in-chief. Usually it was a part-time position combined with the role of a parish pastor or a teacher at Suomi College. From the spring of 1905 to the summer of 1906, the first seminarians of Suomi College were an editorial group under the direction of faculty members and interested local clergy. Only John Parkkila, editor from 1908 to 1911, served any appreciable length of time. Undoubtedly low remuneration was a factor that caused editorial tenure to be so unstable.

As befitted a church newspaper, the *Amerikan Suometar* sought to spread its service in behalf of the church. Separate sections were devoted to reporting the events for various localities. Special "Gogebic County (Michigan)" and "Iron County (Michigan)" sections appeared in 1902. Gradually the *Suometar* took on a national character. "Eastern" news, an "Ohio-Pennsylvania" section, and the "Minnesota" columns may be noted in early issues. Meanwhile, the publishers of the *Suometar* sought to remain faithful to the concepts of its founders. No theater, dance, or tobacco advertisements were accepted. In the first issue of the new tri-weekly in 1913, the editors stated emphatically:

> The *Amerikan Suometar* is the only Finnish language newspaper in the United States that does not print advertisements for miracle drugs and doctors, mining company stock, or any other means by which money is bilked through fraudulent claims. Granting the columns to such sales, a newspaper lowers itself to betray the reader in return for advertising revenue.[14]

On leading issues of the day, issues that affected many of its readers, the *Suometar* tended to be conservative. When the coal strike of 1902 had finally been settled, an editorial questioned the wisdom of strikes noting that the workers would have to spend years in making up the losses while the operators could recover quickly. During a particularly bitter strike involving many Finnish workers at the Rockland mine in Michigan, the *Suometar* did publish pleas for assistance to the miners, but in the same issue, an editorial stated strongly that the Social Democrats could not be Christians. Politically, however, as a strong supporter of Theodore Roosevelt, the paper expressed the hope that legislation could be secured to control the railroads, and it was harshly critical of the Payne-Aldrich tariff.[15]

No issue challenged so strongly the *Suometar's* attempts to maintain a balanced, if somewhat conservative, viewpoint on social and economic problems as the Copper Country strike of 1913–14. The striking miners, a large portion of whom were Finnish immigrants, were unable to find any local voice to express their viewpoints, other than the Socialist newspaper in Hancock, the *Työmies*.[16] In a way, the *Suometar* became the protagonist to answer the Socialists in the Finnish language. Seeking to report as objectively as possible the critical local conditions, the *Suometar* was increasingly attacked in the *Työmies* as the tool of the corporations and was forced to defend its editorial position. In counter-attacks, the *Suometar* emphasized the charge that the Socialists were seeking to divert the cause of the strikers to their own ends and warned that only defeat would come of such maneuvers. The *Suometar* pointedly called attention to the "pay" that Finnish Socialist agitators drew from strike funds and bemoaned the loss of reputation that Finnish-Americans suffered in the eyes of other Americans. During the heat of the strike, the *Suometar* was compelled to defend Suomi College as well. The paper hotly denied that Suomi College was unneutral, nor was it an "agitator's school." Probably the most serious attack on the *Suometar* was the charge that it had been paid by mining corporations to provide articles in the Finnish language favorable to the side of management. The Board of the Book Concern thought it better to ignore the charges of the Socialist *Työmies* because as "Esa" (a pseudonym) noted, "If they are sued because of these libelous charges, then it would prove a good excuse to collect money from people on the grounds that the capitalists and bourgeois have again begun to persecute 'the word of truth.' " [17] The *Suometar* emerged as victor; the *Työmies* was relocated in Superior, Wisconsin, and the failure of the strike cut deeply into the ranks of the Socialists. But it was a costly victory. The strike and its aftermath contributed heavily to a deficit in the operations of the Book Concern in 1914, and undoubtedly many readers of the *Amerikan Suometar* were not happy with the position that their newspaper had taken on some of the controversial issues that had arisen.

Surely some people associated with the *Suometar* had rejoiced in the battle against Socialism and had been pleased at the sharp rebuttals to the charges of the *Työmies*. But many others felt the purpose of the newspaper could be better served by less conflict and by more emphasis upon the work of the church. Running controversy with other newspapers might build up circulation; whether it always redounded to the credit of the Synod was questionable. The establishment of a clear political policy reveals the nature of the paper's difficulty. In earlier years, the *Suometar* had tried to promote Finnish candidates, other than those on the Socialist ticket, for various local offices. Usually these candidates did rather poorly in the elections, or, as frequently happened, their claims for recognition by the Republican party, then dominant in the area, were ignored. When Parkkila was editor of the *Suometar,* he recommended drastic retaliation for such slights. Withdrawal of support from Republican candidates was considered proper. In the fall of 1908, the paper printed instructions on how a voter could split his ticket. Not all of the Synodical leaders appreciated the *Suometar's* heavy involvement in local politics; their criticism of such action along with Parkkila's spirited defense of his stand appeared periodically during his editorship. This difference of opinion was an important factor in his eventual dismissal from the newspaper.[18]

The *Suometar* was more nearly in its element, however, when it was advancing the causes of the Suomi Synod. The fluctuations in the fortunes of the Synod and its major commitment, Suomi College, were kept almost constantly before the people. Stories about the leaders of the church were prominently featured. When Pastor Tolonen, then president of the Synod, died in 1902, the weekly paper devoted more than ten columns of a single issue to the report of the funeral. Another instance of church leaders making news occurred when Dr. J. K. Nikander, then president of both the Synod and the College, questioned whether the clergy should belong to temperance societies. His long article on the subject was an outgrowth of a heated exchange between two other Synodical leaders, Pastors Hoikka and Back. Emphasizing that soul care was a pastor's main concern, Nikander wondered how effective the clergy could be in temperance societies, particularly if many of the members were unchurched.[19]

The special purpose of Suomi College and its Theological Seminary received much attention, and apparent slights to the institution were quickly noted. When a congregation in Hibbing, Minnesota, restricted its search for a new pastor to men trained in Finland, the *Suometar* expressed great regret that no consideration had been given to a clergyman trained at Suomi College.[20] The College could rely upon the *Suometar* for generous promotional publicity on financial drives that were launched periodically in behalf of the school. Thus, in 1909 and 1910, the newspaper strongly encouraged participation in efforts to liquidate Suomi's debts through ten-dollar contributions. When the debt still lingered in 1914, the *Suometar* sought to spearhead a campaign for one-hundred-dollar contributions with the challenging editorial question, "Are We Finns Inferior to Others in America?" [21]

Among other areas of particular interest, upon which the *Suometar* dwelt at length in the early years, was the matter of intersynodical relations. At that time, relations with non-Finnish church groups, even Lutheran synods, were minimal, but there was a brisk exchange of viewpoints with other Finnish churches. This was especially true of the contacts with the National Evangelical Lutheran Church, a group organized in 1898. A continuing point of controversy was whether the church needed trained clergy as the Suomi Synod maintained, or could ordain, as the National Lutherans did, relatively uneducated men who were "called" to the ministry. As early as 1902, the *Suometar* tried to correct misconceptions that had appeared in a devotional publication of the National Lutheran Church, *Todistusten Joukko* (A Cloud of Witnesses). When the mouthpiece of the National Lutherans, the *Auttaja,* claimed to be the only Christian paper in Finnish-American circles, a Synodical leader, Pastor Hoikka, sarcastically took issue with such pretensions.[22]

More protracted were the lengthy articles and reports that covered merger negotiations between the Suomi Synod and the National Lutherans. When these had reached a significant stage in 1913, the *Suometar* stated, "We are of the opinion, that all Finnish-American Lutheran Christians should be gathered at the same 'front lines' regardless of small doctrinal differences." [23] Later, the *Suometar* gave favorable publicity to meetings between leaders of the two churches and gave detailed accounts of discussions at the Synodical conventions of 1914 and 1915. However, special columnist "Esa" criticized the *Auttaja* for what he considered prejudiced reporting of negative aspects in the merger. "Esa" used a quotation from the *Auttaja*, "It may be, that this merger is a Synodical bait, by which an attempt will be made to destroy the National Lutheran Church." [24] Such negative feeling was to be found in certain Synodical quarters as well, and the merger talks collapsed in 1915. President Nikander, summarizing the situation in 1915, assured readers of the *Suometar* that he favored a merger when the time was ripe, particularly when the National Lutheran Church was ready. For the present, he stated, "a good brakeman helps to keep the car from going over the embankment." [25]

One of the persistent problems troubling the management of the *Suometar* was the difficulty of serving a widely scattered constituency with fresh news. An "Eastern section" had been started in the paper in 1911, but as of 1915, reports indicated that the circulation on the East Coast was low. Competing against several Finnish newspapers published in the eastern states, the *Suometar* was unable to deliver the news on time. Despite discussion at Synodical Conventions and in other quarters, this disadvantage affecting circulation on the East Coast was apparently never fully solved. In regard to the West Coast, however, a much more ambitious project was undertaken. Shortly after World War I, the Suomi Synod established a western branch operation of the Book Concern in Astoria, Oregon. A separate newspaper, the *Lännen Suometar* (The Western Finn) was launched in 1922, and optimism prevailed in the Synod that through this means, ties with a peripheral area might be strengthened. [26]

Astoria was a logical site for such an operation. A focal point of the Finnish people in the Pacific Northwest, it had been the base for several earlier Finnish-language newspapers and a center for the activities of the Suomi Synod in that area of the country. [27] However, the *Lännen Suometar* was called into action too late to be successful. The Finnish-Americans of the western United States were widely scattered and proportionately more unchurched perhaps than the Finns elsewhere in this country. Nor did the start of a newspaper in 1922 seem prescient in relation to the recently enacted legislation that so severely restricted immigration to the United States. [28]

The operation had scarcely started, when a disastrous fire swept Astoria in December, 1922; the plant of the Book Concern was among the buildings destroyed. Insurance on the venture had been inadequate, and a debt of more than twenty thousand dollars had been accumulated by 1923.[29] Still, a cautious optimism remained among the leaders of the Suomi Synod. When it was decided to continue the operation, F. Tolonen, an experienced newspaper man and business manager, was contracted to assume responsibility for the western plant. There followed a period of almost constant tribulations to plague the newspaper that had seemed to justify itself in the eyes of synodical leaders. The *Lännen Suometar* was published regularly throughout the 1920's, but a constantly increasing deficit aggravated a financial problem that defied solution. When the depression made it impossible for the Book Concern in Hancock to shoulder further the deficit of the western operation, the Suomi Synod made arrangements to lease the plant to private parties. Efforts to exercise some control over the *Lännen Suometar's* editorial policy after it had passed into private management proved ineffectual. The entire operation was sold in 1946 to Oke Zatterlow, the current lessee. In twenty-five years, most of them under private management, the west coast venture had cost the Synod close to fifty thousand dollars, a rather heavy burden upon the Book Concern for a synodical voice in the Far West.[30]

As in the case of the Suomi Synod, the first publishing efforts of the National Lutheran Church were private ventures. In 1901, Pastor W. A. Mandellöf, president of the church body, began publishing a semi-monthly devotional, *Todistusten Joukko,* in Ironwood, Michigan. It became part of the same operation as a weekly newspaper, *Kansan Lehti* (People's Journal). Despite a promising beginning, the devotional periodical was lost when the *Kansan Lehti* declared bankruptcy in 1904. Summarizing the adverse impact of the loss, Aho and Nopola stated:

> Saddest of all, was that in the crash, the *Todistusten Joukko* was also lost and that many lost the money invested. This awakened uncertainty and fear toward any new attempt, so that the securing of another voice even as a private enterprise became much more difficult.[31]

Pastor P. Wuori of the National Lutheran Church had sufficient optimism to make another attempt. Convinced of the great need for another voice to represent the church, he arranged to purchase the *Vapaa Sana* (Free Speech), a newspaper published by O. Massinen in Ironwood from 1904 to 1906. To the new venture, Pastor Wuori gave a name recommended by a fellow pastor, J. H. Varmanen, and the *Auttaja* appeared for the first time on January 18, 1906. In the initial issue, Wuori stated: "This paper wishes to take into its program primarily the causes of the Finnish National Evangelical Lutheran Church and become its representative and organ of expression." [32] The lead editorial went on to state: "We shall print those articles that do not seek to hide God's great love."

Pastor Wuori continued to publish the *Auttaja* until 1907, when the church accepted it as a gift from him.[33] Meanwhile, two other pastors of the National Lutheran Church, K. G. Rissanen and D. Ruotsalainen, had purchased Massinen's printing plant in 1908. The following year, this plant was acquired by the church from them for twenty-five hundred dollars. The legal transaction was completed on July 13, 1909. Pastor M. N. Westerback had become the editor of the newspaper [34] in 1908. Like the *Amerikan Suometar,* the *Auttaja* became early in its history a formal organ of the church. In that capacity, the weekly voice of the National Lutheran Church provided a similar service for the parent church body. General world news was provided, but there was also a strong emphasis upon reports from the localities where the National Lutherans had congregations, and editorial space was generously granted to matters of direct interest to the welfare of the sponsoring group.

In 1909, the National Lutheran Church had a membership of approximately nine thousand; an additional five thousand or more belonged to independent congregations served by pastors of the church. To this constituency, the *Auttaja* reported a circulation of twenty-nine hundred in the fall of that year.[35] Circulation remained as high as twenty-four hundred in the early 1920's, when a membership of under eight thousand was reported. As a promoter of the National Lutheran Church, the *Auttaja* was bound to clash with the Suomi Synod's *Suometar*. This was especially true during merger discussions, for when the relations between the two church bodies were strained, the newspapers simply reflected the respective viewpoints of the groups involved. Years later, a long-time editor of the *Auttaja,* Pastor J. E. Nopola, summarized the problem:

> In all its history the *Auttaja* has had almost nothing to say about any other Finnish-language church newspaper than the *Amerikan Suometar.* The *Auttaja* has not attacked the *Suometar* per se, only as a channel of Suomi Synod opinions rejected by the publishers of *Auttaja.* The criticism became more prominent after the National Church became oriented to the Missouri Synod.[36]

Unlike the Suomi Synod and the National Lutherans, the Apostolic Lutheran groups, also known as the Laestadians, in the United States did not have an officially controlled newspaper of their own. In general, this

was typical of the Laestadians who were reluctant to adopt any formal
organization into a recognized church body. Of the five different sects identified among the Apostolic Lutherans in the United States, only the American-Finnish Apostolic Lutheran Church, organized in 1928, had drawn up
a constitution and functioned, even in a modified way, like the Evangelical
Lutheran, Suomi Synod and National Lutheran groups. Nor can reliable
statistics on the relative strength of the Apostolic Lutherans during the
early years be readily procured.[37]

However, one of the earliest newspapers, the *Amerikan Suomalainen Lehti* begun by Leinonen in 1879, was published by a firm in which
a group of Laestadians held the controlling interest. From that time on,
more than one newspaper sought a wide circulation among the Apostolic
Lutherans by catering to and promoting their special needs. An interesting
example was the rather vitriolic *Amerikan Uutiset,* noted earlier for its
bitter attacks upon the Suomi Synod, Suomi College, and the temperance
movement. While hardly a great booster of any church endeavor, the paper
did not attack the Apostolic Lutherans who consequently adopted it as a
sort of spokesman for their causes.[38]

Like other Finnish-Lutheran groups in the new homeland, Apostolic Lutherans soon felt the need for a more strictly devotional publication.
The first such successful effort was the *Siionin Sanomat* (Tidings of Zion),
which lasted from 1891 to 1896. Not until 1916 when the *Kristillinen
Kuukausilehti* (Christian Monthly) was started, were the Apostolic Lutherans able to establish a more permanent publication. At first, this periodical was widely accepted by almost all Laestadians, but sharp doctrinal
differences between the *suurseuralaiset* (Big-Meeting Apostolic Lutherans)
and the Heideman branch of the Laestadians caused the latter group to
establish another devotional publication, the *Rauhan Tervehdys* (Greetings
of Peace), in 1922.[39]

In the aftermath and largely due to the adversities caused by the
Copper Country strike of 1913–1914, the *Työmies* had been shifted from
Hancock to Superior, Wisconsin, and the *Päivälehti* from Calumet to
Duluth, Minnesota. While the *Suometar* would surely have been willing to
fill this vacuum, the numerous Apostolic Lutherans of the area desired
another newspaper. At the "big meeting" of 1915, plans were made to
establish both the devotional *Kristillinen Kuuskausilehti* and a newspaper.
The result was the *Walwoja,* which had been launched earlier that year as
an independent, Republican newspaper. The controlling interest in the
publication was held by individual Apostolic Lutherans; however, it became a sort of "trumpet" for the various Apostolic Lutheran groups in the

country. Internal differences among the Laestadians made it impossible for the *Walwoja* to serve in that capacity indefinitely. By 1928, the Heidemanians were accusing the *Walwoja* of unduly favoring other groups, and in 1930, they were the most instrumental group in the start of still another newspaper, the *Opas*.[40] Like the *Walwoja,* the *Opas* claimed to be an independent, Republican newspaper. Both newspapers reached rather impressive circulation figures, at least by the standards of the Finnish-American press. In 1921, the *Walwoja* claimed a total of nine thousand, and even after division in the ranks, reported over eight thousand in 1935. That same year, the *Opas* reported a circulation of 6,540. Both figures were appreciably higher than those of either the *Amerikan Suometar* (forty-eight hundred) or the *Auttaja* (eighteen hundred). While these figures might suggest some idea of the relative strength and size of the various Finnish Lutheran church bodies, other factors must also be considered. Neither Apostolic Lutheran paper was an official spokesman for any church. Rather, as self-styled independent newspapers which were generally well edited, they also appealed to non-Laestadian readers, including a number of Suomi Synod and National Lutheran members.[41]

The declining years of these newspapers can be summarized briefly. They tended to become ever more concerned with the internal functions and problems of the churches that they represented, as well as with the dwindling subscription lists, a grim reminder of rapidly changing conditions. They were no longer so concerned with synodical differences, nor were they as strident in their statements about doctrinal interpretations. Nopola could not recall any particular interchange after 1955 between the *Auttaja* and the *Suometar*. As one explanation, he suggested, "This may be due to the fact that the two Synods were drifting farther apart through closer relations with other Lutheran churches." [42]

Nopola's comment epitomizes the last years. Merger talks between the Suomi Synod and the National Lutherans had recurred in the mid-1930's and some discussion extended to 1950, but the more fruitful dialogue for each group became an association with a non-Finnish Lutheran church. The Suomi Synod became party to the merger that created the new Lutheran Church in America in 1962, while the National Lutheran Church drew ever closer to the Lutheran Church-Missouri Synod. Meanwhile the number of the older Finnish-speaking members who had provided the reading public of the newspapers was diminishing rapidly. Circulation figures told the story; deficit financing became commonplace. Lacking formal church support or subsidy to meet these problems, the *Walwoja* and the *Opas* were the first voices to be stilled. A temporary merger of the two into the *Pohjolan Sanomat* (Northland News) in 1957 proved very temporary; shortly thereafter the remaining circulation lists were purchased by Russell Parta of New York Mills, Minnesota, publisher of the *Minnesotan Uutiset* (Minnesota News).[43]

The *Amerikan Suometar,* the only extant Finnish-language newspaper that had been founded before the turn of the century, was rapidly weakening. As the income no longer matched the expenses, it was necessary for the Book Concern to subsidize the *Suometar,* a painful process for a firm that was itself beset by financial problems. The Suomi Synod wrestled periodically, particularly in the yearly Church Conventions, with the affairs of the Book Concern and the *Amerikan Suometar,* but met with no real success. When no direct subsidy could be expected for the newspaper, after the merger of the Suomi Synod into the Lutheran Church of America had been consummated, the operation was abruptly terminated with the end of the Suomi Synod in December, 1962. Surprisingly, the smallest of the four, the *Auttaja* is the only Finnish-language newspaper still being published. There is a simple explanation. For years, the National Lutheran Church assumed responsibility through a direct subsidy to its publishing house for the maintenance of the newspaper; this arrangement has been continued by the Lutheran Church-Missouri Synod's Concordia Publishing House in St. Louis, Missouri, from where the *Auttaja* now appears as a monthly devotional publication.[44]

A relative newcomer has emerged as a voice for the Finnish-language press of the church bodies. In 1932, two men who had a long association with the Finnish-language press in the United States, Carl Parta and Adolph Lundquist, launched a newspaper in New York Mills, Minnesota, the *Minnesotan Uutiset.* Despite the rather unlikely timing in the depth of the depression, the paper met a need for an independent newspaper in the upper Midwest, and it gradually developed into one of the higher ranking Finnish language publications in the country. Through purchase of circulation lists, arrangements to fill unexpired subscriptions, and other such means, the *Minnesotan Uutiset* filled the void left by the termination of such papers as the *Walwoja, Opas,* and *Suometar.* During the 1960's, and with the name changed to the *Amerikan Uutiset* (American News), this same paper could still report a circulation of over six thousand. More important to the remaining church work in the Finnish language among congregations of the former Suomi Synod and the National Lutheran church bodies, as well as the still independent Apostolic Lutheran groups, was the service that the *Amerikan Uutiset* could render. Announcements, reports, and articles pertaining to Finnish-language church activities were published regularly in each issue. Even the name seemed appropriate for the *Amerikan Uutiset* had become a voice that covered the church news from Ohio to the Pacific.[45] If the fact that an independent voice replaced the newspapers founded with such sectarian fervor seems ironic, may it not also suggest the ecumenical trend of the Finnish-American Lutheran church bodies in recent years.

NOTES

1. J. H. Jasberg, "Toimihenkilöitten Muistelmia," *Amerikan Suometar,* 1899–1919 (Hancock, Michigan, 1919), p. 52.
2. Strictly speaking, the *Walwoja* and the *Opas* were not controlled in the same manner as the *Amerikan Suometar* and the *Auttaja*. The publishing houses of the Apostolic Lutheran "press" were not under direct supervision of the church itself. However, both have been traditionally associated with groups of Apostolic Lutherans and thus may be classified generally as organs of Finnish Lutheran churches.
3. John I. Kolehmainen, *The Finns in America* (Hancock, Michigan, 1947), p. 73 *passim*. Chapter VIII includes a nearly complete listing of American Finnish-language newspapers and periodicals, including the church press. As few publications have been started in the past twenty years, the Kolehmainen volume needs but minimal additions to serve most adequately.
4. See S. Ilmonen, *Amerikan Suomalaisten Sivistyhistoria,* I (Hancock, Michigan, 1930), pp. 23–24. Note also F. Tolonen, "Muutamia Historiatietoja Amerikan Suomalaisista Sanomalehdistä" in *Amerikan Suometar 1899–1919,* p. 83 and U. Saarnivaara, *Apostolis-Luterilaisuuden Historia* (Ironwood, Michigan, 1947), pp. 40–41.
5. For summaries of the attacks upon the Suomi-Synod, see S. Ilmonen, *Amerikan Suomalaisten Sivistyhistoria,* I, 62–63 and F. Tolonen, "Muutamia Historiatietoja . . . ," p. 84.
6. F. V. Kava, "Amerikan Suomettaren Historia," *Amerikan Suometar,* 1899–1919, p. 11. This article, pp. 11–44, is probably the most thorough summary of the *Suometar's* early years that has been published.
7. Thousands of readers knew the *Amerikan Suometar,* the legal name, by the more familiar *Suometar*. This article uses the two terms interchangeably.
8. Quoted from the *Amerikan Suometar,* n.d., No. 26, 1900, pp. 11–12.
9. Quoted in *ibid.,* p. 12.
10. *Ibid.,* p. 12 *passim*.
11. *Amerikan Suometar,* July 8, 1899, the same or presentation issue.
12. See *Paimen-Sanomia,* June 7, 1901; also Kava, "Amerikan Suomettaren Historia," p. 21, for actual transfer of the operation to the Suomi Synod. The most detailed analysis of the Book Concern, particularly financial matters and policies of control, is Taisto John Niemi, "The Finnish Lutheran Book Concern, 1900–1950: A Historical and Developmental Study" (unpublished doctoral dissertation, University of Michigan, 1960).

13. Statistical information may be found in the *Annuals* of the Suomi Synod. Niemi's study has compiled a number of tables and statistics about the Synod and the *Amerikan Suometar*.
14. *Amerikan Suometar*, January 4, 1913.
15. References in the paragraph are from the *Amerikan Suometar*, October 22, 1902; September 5, 1906; February 8, 1905; and February 16, 1910.
16. This particular *Työmies* is not to be confused with Fred Karinen's newspaper of the same name mentioned earlier. The *Työmies*, with which the *Amerikan Suometar* clashed, was the leading organ of the Finnish-Socialist societies of the Midwest, having moved from Worcester, Massachusetts, to Hancock, in 1904. It reported a circulation of over twelve thousand in April 1911, for the daily publication that had just been started. *Tyomies Kymmenvuotias*, 1902–1913 (Hancock, Michigan, 1913), p. 28. During the strike, the firm published an English-language "Miner's Bulletin" for some time as a means of making known the striker's side of the controversy. Another Finnish newspaper, the *Päivälehti* (The Daily Journal), published in Calumet, Michigan, also frequently took issue with the *Suometar*.
17. *Amerikan Suometar*, January 22, 1914. See also, issues for August 9, September 9, and September 27, 1913. Since the strike was the major news story, each issue during that period had a number of articles—lengthy news stories from Calumet and other strike-bound communities, columns by "Esa" and other such correspondents, as well as less frequent formal editorials.
18. *Amerikan Suometar*, October 28, 1908, contains the instructions on ticket-splitting. The Parkkila affair may be noted in the *Suometar*, November 11, 1908, and again May 7, 1911, and July 12, 1911.
19. *Amerikan Suometar*, April 16, 1902, May 9, 1905. Temperance societies were very influential among the immigrant Finns; a pastor was well-advised to be aware of local conditions. For this aspect of the Finnish immigrant "associative spirit," see A. W. Hoglund, *Finnish Immigrants in America, 1880–1920* (Madison, Wisconsin, 1960), pp. 55–56 *passim*.
20. *Amerikan Suometar*, January 30, 1907. The first graduates from Suomi College Theological Seminary had been ordained in 1906.
21. *Amerikan Suometar*, July 7, 1909, August 5, 1909, February 16, 1910. The editorial was in the issue of July 9, 1914. Special comparison was made of the greater support given by other ethnic groups to their church colleges.
22. *Amerikan Suometar*, March 10, 1909. As might be expected, the National Lutherans did not appreciate the low regard with which they were held in certain circles of the Suomi Synod. They accused the latter of excessive pride in their relationship with the state church of Finland as well as in the heavily indebted Suomi College. See *Auttaja*, September 2, 1909, as quoted in Aho and Nopola, *Evankelis-Luterilainen Kansalliskirkko* (Ironwood, Michigan, 1949), p. 290. This fiftieth-anniversary publication of the National Lutheran Church contains a valuable summary of the merger negotiations (pp. 288–293).
23. *Amerikan Suometar*, October 21, 1913.
24. Quoted from the *Auttaja*, in the *Amerikan Suometar*, July 21, 1914. See

also, earlier issues of the *Suometar* for discussions and reports, such as February 17, 1914, February 26, 1914, and June 18, 1914. "Esa's" negative attitude can be seen in his column in the *Amerikan Suometar*, June 27, 1914.

25. *Amerikan Suometar*, June 22, 1915. See also Aho and Nopola, *Evankelis-Luterilainen Kansalliskirkko*, p. 292 *passim*.
26. See *Amerikan Suometar*, June 12, 1915, for a report from the annual convention of the Suomi Synod. The first issue of the *Lännen Suometar* was published April 21, 1922.
27. See Kolehmainen, *The Finns in America*, for a listing of the newspaper ventures in Astoria, Oregon. Most prominent in 1922 was the *Socialist Toveri* (Comrade), still another reason the Suomi Synod hoped that a more conservative church newspaper would find a market among non-Socialist Finns in the Northwest.
28. While 1920 census statistics indicated over thirty-three thousand foreign-born Finns in the Mountain and Pacific census regions, and S. Ilmonen (*Amerikan Suomalaisten Sivistyshistoria*, I, p. 11) gives totals for the states of Washington, Oregon, California, and Montana of better than sixty-six thousand Finnish-Americans, the *Kirkollinen Kalenteri* (Church Calendar) of the Suomi Synod for 1923 lists only sixteen hundred and fifty members in the western states. See statistics in *ibid.*, pp. 28–33. Only the congregations in Astoria, Oregon, and Butte, Montana, reported as many as three hundred members.
29. *Minutes of the Consistory*, Suomi Synod, March 6, 1923.
30. According to the *Minutes* of the Book Concern Board for June 11, 1946, the firm had paid $47,973.28 on indebtedness accumulated in Astoria. Relatively little has been published about this western venture, but material can be pieced together from the *Kirkollinen Kalenteri*, the *Vuosikirja* (Annual) and other occasional publications of the Suomi Synod. The archival collection at Suomi College has a considerable, even if incomplete, collection of the *Lännen Suometar* as well as relevant material in the *Minutes* for the Consistory of the Suomi Synod, the *Minutes* for both the Hancock Book Concern and the Board of the Astoria firm, and some correspondence between leading individuals involved in the operation.
31. Aho and Nopola, *Evankelis-Luterilainen Kansalliskirkko*, p. 66.
32. Quoted in the *Auttaja*, June 26, 1947. See also Aho and Nopola, *Evankelis-Luterilainen Kansalliskirkko*, pp. 87–88, for a longer description of Wuori's efforts and the initial issue of the *Auttaja*. Whether the *Vapaa Sana* was a National Lutheran paper, as Kolehmainen, *The Finns in America*, p. 86, classifies it, seems problematical. Massinen, the publisher, was a brother of Mrs. Eloheimo, the wife of Pastor J. W. Eloheimo, recognized as a founder of the National Lutheran Church. Aho and Nopola did not recognize the paper as such. Instead they commented wryly that the contents of the *Vapaa Sana* were in keeping with the name.
33. *Auttaja*, June 26, 1947.
34. See both *Auttaja*, June 26, 1947, and Aho and Nopola, *Evankelis-Luterilainen Kansalliskirkko*, p. 99.

35. *Ibid.*, p. 99 *passim*, which also admits that a generous credit policy could well have helped the circulation.

36. A letter from Dr. J. E. Nopola to D. T. Halkola, August 21, 1965, gives the circulation for the early 1920's as twenty-four hundred. The reference to the Missouri Synod is to the period beginning in the 1920's, during which the National Lutheran Church gradually sought closer contacts with the much larger Lutheran church body of today.

37. The term "Laestadian" is derived from the Reverend Lars Levi Laestadius, a pastor in northern Sweden and Finland, who is considered the founder of the sect. In his generally accepted definitive history of the movement, U. Saarnivaara, *Apostolis-Luterilaisuuden historia*, pp. 324–333, notes five groups: (1) the Apostolic Lutheran Church, (2) the Heidemanians, (3) the First-Born, (4) the Evangelicals, and (5) the Newly-Awakened. Saarnivaara (p. 333) does have statistics about the size of the groups for 1946, but these are further complicated since Apostolic Lutherans differentiate between ordinary church members and professing Christians or "believers." In that year, he calculated a probable total of some twenty-seven thousand members, with the total of "believers" not even half that figure. It is worth noting that Saarnivaara does not even attempt to cite numbers in support of any over-all statistics for earlier periods. For the organization of the one group in 1928 from the Apostolic Lutherans most closely associated with the *suurseurat* (Big meeting or Big convention), see *ibid.*, p. 221 *passim*.

38. S. Ilmonen, *Amerikan Suomalaisten Sivistyhistoria*, I, 191–192.

39. U. Saarnivaara, *Apostolis-luterilaisuuden historia*, pp. 183, 210–211.

40. *Ibid.*, p. 189. See also section entitled *Sanomalehtisotaa* (Newspaper War) in *ibid.*, pp. 199–203.

41. Circulation figures are quoted in John I. Kolehmainen, "Finnish newspapers and Periodicals in Michigan," *Michigan History Magazine*, XXIV (1940), 119–127.

42. Letter from Dr. J. E. Nopola to D. T. Halkola, August 21, 1965.

43. Personal interview with Russell Parta, September 1965.

44. The problems of the Book Concern can perhaps be followed most easily in the reports submitted in the *Annual Yearbook* of the Synod beginning with the late 1940's. One should also note that the *Auttaja* in its present form can no longer be considered a newspaper.

45. Interview with Russell Parta, September 1965. Also perusal of recent issues of the *Amerikan Uutiset*. The territorial division arises from the fact that the East Coast still has such papers as the *Raivaaja* (Pioneer) and the *New Yorkin Uutiset* (New York News), but Parta's publication is the only one sufficiently independent to serve the needs of the church for the rest of the United States.

Arnold Stadius

❋ SUOMI COLLEGE AND SEMINARY

SUOMI COLLEGE IS the servant of the church, having been founded for that purpose in 1896. Although she served as an important educational institution for many young people who might otherwise have remained without schooling, the key to her origin and existence has always been her connection with the Finnish Lutheran Church. However, in the beginning, Suomi College was set apart more by language than by religion. As the only school in the United States founded by American Finns, Suomi College's defense and cultivation of the Finnish language is both understandable and praiseworthy.

This brief history of Suomi College is divided into the three periods of her development. The first phase, 1896–1919, was dominated by Juho Kustaa Nikander, one of the school's founders and the first president. During these years, the primary influence was the education system of Finland. The second phase, 1919–1958, was marked by increasing Americanization. The final period, which began in 1958, is one of expansion.

The Beginnings of Suomi College

The Finnish immigrants to the United States and Canada were part of the great Atlantic migration that continued into the first years of the twentieth

91

century. They followed the other Northern Europeans after an interval of
two or more full generations; their absorption and Americanization has
been correspondingly later.

The reasons for emigration from Finland were in the main economic
and only to a lesser degree political or social. Most of the immigrants
settled in the northern half of the United States, with denser centers of
population in Massachusetts, New York, Ohio, Michigan, Minnesota, and
Oregon. The Copper Country of the western Upper Peninsula of Michigan
has perhaps the largest single Finnish settlement in North America.

Over ninety percent of the Finns adhered to the Evangelical Lutheran Church of Finland, a state church,[1] but many had only a nominal
loyalty that could be easily surrendered in the New World. Others were
more zealous Christians, having been influenced by the various nineteenth-
century revival movements,[2] within the Church of Finland. In the freer
religious atmosphere of the New World, these groups could stand independently. In the end three Finnish Lutheran church bodies developed in
the United States.

Adherents of the Laestadian revival movement, which stood fur-
thest from the mother church and the other revival movements, were
the first to form a congregation in the United States;[3] later these loosely
organized Laestadian churches adopted the name "Apostolic Lutheran
Church" and went through their own process of grouping and splintering.
The Laestadian church bodies have established no schools or seminaries.[4]

From 1876, when the first Church of Finland pastor came to Upper
Michigan,[5] until 1890, when the first church body was formed, there were
only a few pastors to organize the congregations spread across the United
States. Needless to say, thousands of Finnish immigrants were lost to the
Church, and many from all contact with any Finnish group. Four pastors
and representatives of only nine congregations established the Finnish
Evangelical Lutheran Church or Suomi Synod on March 25, 1890. The
Synod comprised one hundred and fifty-three congregations and one hundred and five pastors in 1962, when it united with three other church
bodies to form the new Lutheran Church in America. In 1896 the Synod
established Suomi College and Theological Seminary. The Synod has always considered herself the daughter-church of the Church of Finland,
with which she has maintained cordial relations; she has had no special
revival direction, but has welcomed adherents of all the movements into
membership.

Fearing clerical domination, certain pastors and congregations opposed the formation of Suomi Synod and formed the Finnish Evangelical

National Lutheran Church in 1898. Because many former layworkers of the Finnish Gospel Society (a revival movement in Finland) were ordained as pastors in the National Church, it represented that movement among the Finnish-American Lutherans for some time. In 1903 the National Church founded an academy, *Kansanopisto,* in Minnesota, but lost it in 1906 to radical labor groups, who changed it into The Workers' School which was maintained by the I.W.W. until 1941. Later the National Church maintained a small theological seminary for a few years. Four unsuccessful attempts were made to unite the National Church with Suomi Synod. In 1965 the National Church merged with the Lutheran Church–Missouri Synod.

Three primary motives—religious, nationalistic, and cultural—led to the founding of Suomi College. Although many laymen actively supported the projected school years before it opened its doors, the major task of arousing support fell upon the pastors who founded the Suomi Synod and served its congregations between 1890 and 1896. Pastors J. K. Nikander, J. W. Eloheimo, K. Huotari, H. Tanner, J. Bäck, and E. W. Hynninen were graduates of the University of Helsinki; Pastor K. L. Tolonen of the Foreign Mission Institute in Helsinki, and Pastor J. J. Hoikka of Augustana College and Seminary. All were indefatigable writers to the Finnish-language newspapers; in 1889 three of them established a religious periodical, *Paimen Sanomia,* which soon became the Synod's official organ.[6] Numberless articles, sermons, and talks underscored the need for a training institution for the new church body.

The clergymen noted first how many immigrants, baptized and confirmed in the church, either discontinued all religious life or came under the influence of other denominations and sects. As the public schools could offer no instruction in religion, a private school seemed essential to provide Christian instruction for children and to train teachers and workers for the congregations. As there was little hope of getting pastors from Finland, the school must provide sufficient academic and theological instruction to produce an educated clergy for the Finnish Lutherans. The school was to become the model for other schools, the summer schools of religion, in which Suomi College graduates would teach.

Pastor Nikander and his colleagues also felt it important to retain the Finnish language and traditions; in this, they were following the example of the earlier Scandinavian Lutheran immigrants who had established a school for this purpose. Suomi College would serve the great numbers of Finnish immigrants and provide them with a bridge to the homeland.

The summer schools would carry on this work of preservation under the auspices of Suomi College. This avowed objective undoubtedly aided in soliciting gifts for the new school.

The founders of the projected academy had still other motives in seeking support for their plan among the immigrant families. These people were laboring in unskilled capacities, but with training they could hope for advancement. Suomi College would help them and their children to adjust to the conditions of the New World and would train them for greater opportunities. The curriculum had a practical base from the beginning: accounting and American history were taught in the English language the first year.[7]

Public opinion had been so much influenced by the pastors' newspaper articles that the Constituting Convention of Suomi Synod found time in the midst of its busy deliberations to give its approval for the necessity of such a school as Suomi College. Successive church conventions were equally warm in support; in fact, the committees appointed to study and advance the question were the units that could not obey the explicit mandates of the church assemblies, but proceeded with caution.[8] Later it was understood that this caution was quite in place, for the financial campaigns of the college always proved disappointing in the first half century.

The first important question was to decide upon a site for the projected school. Communities in several parts of the Midwest invited the new school to locate in their midst.[9] In 1890, the Constituting Convention named a committee to investigate sites in the Minneapolis-St. Paul, Minnesota area; the Convention of 1891 authorized a loan to purchase a North St. Paul site "if needed." Sites in Ohio, Wisconsin, Minnesota, and Michigan's Upper Peninsula were also under consideration. Impatience was expressed by the Convention of 1892, which authorized the opening of the college that same fall on a temporary basis in Hancock, Michigan.

Pastor J. K. Nikander traveled for several weeks through the eastern states to awaken interest in the college, to form support associations, and to assess feeling among the immigrants. Adolf Riipa, the Synod's first itinerant missionary in the Mid- and Far West, served as the college representative there.

Although preliminary architect's plans for an ambitious school building in Superior, Wisconsin were drawn up after that city promised a block of land, lack of local financial support prevented a final decision; this occurred in respect to all other suggested sites. The Synod's need for its own theological school was felt the more keenly as only a few pastors came from Finland to serve the increasing number of congregations and none from American schools. The Convention of 1896 ordered the college committee to open for the first semester in rented quarters in Hancock, on September 8 of that year. The newly elected Board of Trustees of Suomi College obeyed.

J. K. Nikander, pastor of the large Hancock Finnish Lutheran Church and president of Suomi Synod, was called by the Board to be the first rector of the institution; [10] Joseph Riippa and V. M. Burman were called to be instructors. The former, however, was fatally struck by lightning a few days before the beginning of the semester. The first full-time teachers were Pastor Nikander, Mr. Burman, and Mr. J. Holmlund; Mr. C. J. Barr taught English and American history on a part-time basis. The college continued in rented quarters for three and one-half years, until the three-story stone structure, now known as Old Main, was dedicated on January 21, 1900.

The Old-Country Impress Upon Suomi College, 1896–1919

The founders of Suomi College, none of whom had passed through the public school system in America, planned the new college to preserve the Finnish religion, heritage and culture, in the academic framework they knew from Finland. Nikander and his fellow pastors envisioned a faculty of dedicated Christian men and women who would pass on to the Finnish youth of the New World the values of the Old. That they did not lay equivalent stress upon preparing their students to become good citizens of their new country was undoubtedly the result of their realization that his surroundings would naturally affect the young educated American Finn. Therefore, the primary goal was to add what no other source could supply. From the beginning, the task of the college was to be one of preservation, a task which was ultimately in some ways fruitless.

One of the founders' aims was that the Suomi College student would become a teacher himself, wherever he went.[11] This goal was often realized. The influence of the relatively small school was broadcast by its former students through Sunday school and summer school instruction, through programs, lectures, and concerts, through activity in the temperance movement, through service as correspondents, editors, and authors, and through leadership in musical and literary organizations.

Suomi College, therefore, by the decision of her founders, approved in church conventions of the Synod, and delineated in the rules and regulations of the institution, would assume the structure of a Finnish private boarding school to prepare students for colleges and universities, for the future theological seminary, and for careers. There would be seven classes; students would pass from one to the next by successfully completing a spring examination. As in Finland, the final graduation of the first class was signalized by the donning of the university student's "white cap." All students in the first year were enrolled in the first class; in succeeding years, the higher classes were added one by one. Even in later years, there were not always students in every class. By 1906, the program was for all practical purposes limited to a six-year format, with classes three through six being the equivalent of the high-school grades nine through twelve, and the first two classes being the elastic, catch-all classes of the Preparatory Department. This was done to take into consideration requirements for entrance to the University of Michigan.[12]

The organization of the college was very simple at the beginning. The Convention of 1896 had chosen the first Board of Trustees of Suomi College. Thereafter, conventions continued to approve the actions of the administration and faculty and to implement the financial support needed by the new school. The curricula, textbooks, and schedule of "Suomi-Opisto" were left in the hands of the president, faculty and Board. Each church convention, after receiving the annual reports of the president and business manager, discussed and acted upon the affairs of the college only in a general way and made decisions only upon the most important matters.

Prior to 1896, the church convention had annually selected a college committee which was in charge of the preliminary plans, especially that of choosing the best possible site. Pastor Nikander and J. H. Jasberg drew up a projected set of rules for the operation of the school, which was approved with slight changes by the Church Convention at Calumet. Under these rules, the entire Consistory of Suomi Synod were ex officio members of the Board. The Board later chose the school's first three instructors from its own membership, which shows how few supporters of the college at that time were both dedicated and qualified. The Board consisted of eleven members, at least four of whom, the Consistory members, were clergymen; all were active and conscientious delegates of the church convention, who served the church body and the congregation in many other responsible offices. The first woman trustee, Lydia Kangas, a 1904 graduate of the college and later an instructor there, was elected in 1912.

Although the administration's relations with the faculty, the Board, and the Synod were always excellent, many Finnish immigrants in the

United States and Canada remained ignorant of or lukewarm to Suomi College, partly because of the scattered nature of the diaspora, partly because some were adherents of church bodies or congregations that were estranged from Suomi Synod, and partly because some were influenced by radical movements. This divisiveness did not help to ease the burden of debt and ongoing expenses that loaded Suomi College heavily for so many years.

Suomi College received its Old-Country impress above all through its principal founder, Pastor J. K. Nikander. Juho Kustaa Nikander was born in Lammi, Finland in 1855, the son of a craftsman. Handicapped by poverty in his struggles to attain an education, he attended preparatory schools in Heinola and Juyväskylä and received the university student's cap in 1874. Later, Nikander studied in the theological faculty of the University of Helsinki while working as a private tutor. Ordained in Porvoo in 1879, he served as assistant pastor for five and one-half years before he responded to a call from the Copper Country Finnish Lutheran churches and came to Calumet-Quincy in 1884. Nikander was the Henry Melchior Muhlenberg of the Suomi Synod and its first elected president. As head of the college and instructor for many years—indeed during one time the *only* instructor—he was in close contact with every student and impressed his personality and his thinking upon them all.

Other founders of the college included Pastors K. L. Tolonen and J. J. Hoikka, the latter a graduate of Augustana College and Seminary. These three also founded and edited the *Paimen Sanomia,* which later became the Synod's official newspaper. This periodical constantly spoke out for the college and was without doubt one of the greatest factors in presenting the plan of the college and then the infant school itself to the readers.

Eleven youths appeared on September 8, 1896 to register at "Suomi Opisto." As others enrolled later, the number for the first semester was twenty-two, fifteen boys and seven girls. During the first year, twenty-five students in all pursued their studies; seventeen of these were advanced to the second class at the end of the year following the final examinations. At one time, the ratio of students to teachers was five to one.

The variance in the students' ages was considerable. From the beginning, it was known that the Suomi Synod would establish a theological seminary in connection with Suomi College, so some young men enrolled after having worked in factories, mines, and farms, and progressed through all the seven classes. In addition, there were children of elementary and high-school age.

Because of the presence of very young students, a Preparatory Department was formed in 1901 for nine-year-old children and for those older students with little or no previous formal education and those handicapped by lack of either English or Finnish. Advanced students were placed in appropriate higher classes. The student with seven or eight years of training in an elementary public school entered the third class. Thus, classes three through six were equivalent to high school. These classes later became the academy.

Drawing up a schedule of studies for many classes with many subjects at different levels and with few teachers was difficult. It is probable that certain subjects were taught for only part of a year, that members of several classes united in the study of a certain subject, and that at times the advanced students helped teach the youngest students. Emphasis was laid on completing the final spring examinations with good marks, and an exceptional student could advance rapidly through the classes.

The only requirement for entrance into the Preparatory Department was the ability to read a little Finnish. Admission into the regular classes required some knowledge of English and a reading knowledge of Finnish.[13] Deficiencies had to be removed for advancement, so that the Suomi College student of the early days (with rare exceptions) soon became fluent in speaking, reading, and writing the Finnish language; several poets and hymn-writers developed among them.

All the classes were held in Old Main; business offices were located there; the house mother and boarding students occupied the two upper floors; and the kitchens, dining-room, and laundry were in the basement. A faculty lounge was set aside near the classrooms for the teachers. Half of the first floor was the chapel, where services were held twice daily; this room was also utilized for other meetings and programs. Sliding doors divided this into two separate classrooms.

By 1901, a second building was necessary. A modest one-story frame structure was built behind Old Main and was used for a gymnasium, music studio, and auditorium for smaller gatherings. This building underwent the same kind of remodeling as Old Main itself, receiving two-story additions at either end. It eventually housed the Commercial Department, the main library, and the seminary library before being demolished in 1940.

The Board of Trustees determined the courses to be offered in the first year of the school: religion, Finnish, English, arithmetic, geography, American history, general science, penmanship, drawing, bookkeeping, music, and physical education.[14] To these were added a course in the history of Finland. In succeeding years other courses were added, such as Latin, Greek, physiology, geometry. For practical reasons, English as well as Finnish was used in teaching bookkeeping and music.

From 1906 on, there are records of the courses and textbooks used at the college.[15] The offerings were heavy in languages: Finnish, English, Latin, Greek, and at one time, Swedish. Also included were world and American history, biology, botany, physiology, physics, chemistry, arithmetic, geometry, algebra, geography, religion, penmanship, voice, piano, and physical education. Although bookkeeping was not offered in 1906, the Commercial Department was formed that year and has continued to be a strong division of the school.[16]

The tuition and fees of Suomi College in this early phase now seem pitifully inadequate. The announcement in the *Paimen Sanomia* of August 1896, inviting interested persons to enroll for courses, states that the official fees were ten dollars and fifteen dollars for the fall and spring terms respectively; board and room for dormitory students was two dollars per week. In 1906 the following schedule was in effect: tuition in the college, ten dollars for the fall term and fifteen dollars for the spring term; in the Preparatory Department, seven dollars for the fall and eight dollars for the spring term. The boarding student paid two and a half dollars per week for room, heat, lights, board, and laundry. Books and other fees were approximately eight dollars for the whole year.[17] Dormitory students cleaned their own rooms and helped to clean the halls and classrooms. At that time, there were no scholarships or stipends available though this matter was discussed as early as the 1904 Church Convention.

The teachers that served at Suomi College during the early years were, on the whole, dedicated persons alive to the responsibilities of their calling. They fulfilled the qualifications of the ideal private-school teacher that the founders had in mind.

The majority of the full-time teachers of Finnish background were, of course, trained in Finland, either in a university, a normal school, or a technical school, and most of them had teaching experience there. John Bäck, K. V. Arminen, J. Holmlund, E. Aaltio, Toivo Wallenius, Lauri Lund, Alma Granqvist, Isaac Katajamaa, K. V. Kilkka, Rafael Hartman, Elma Aronen, Ilmari Krank, K. H. Mannerkorpi, John Kärkkäinen, Robert Ylönen are included in this group. It is unlikely that these teachers foresaw any rapid Americanization of the school.

Other members of the full-time faculty were of Scandinavian background: J. F. Lindblom, D. W. Brandelle, Oscar Nordstrom. The part-time teachers, some of them local high-school instructors, had little to do with the school outside of their own classes, so that they had less influence upon the students.

Money has always been an important and even anxious element of Suomi's life. Much later a harassed president of the school spoke of a "perpetual crisis" at Suomi College.[18] Everything that issued in print from the college office contained an appeal, direct or indirect, for love, prayers, and financial support. In the first album (1906), President Nikander wrote on the "Support of Suomi College"; the second album (1921) included Fabian Tolonen's "A Brief Glance at the Finances of Suomi College" and Pastor S. Ilmonen's "The Influence of Good and Poor Times on the Support of Suomi College."

President Nikander pointed out in 1906 that only one-tenth of the annual amount needed for the college expenses was derived from tuition fees,[19] which had to be kept low to encourage students to register. The other nine-tenths had to come from voluntary gifts of congregations and individuals. The college labored to organize supporting groups in every community, recommending regular donations by the members and also college programs and festivals to keep interest high. After 1917, "Suomi College Week" was used for fund-raising in all communities at about the same time in October under the direction of a local committee with help from the college. These coordinated efforts proved successful in developing a steady income for the school.[20]

Even before the college was established, the College Committee utilized traveling propagandizers: Pastors Nikander and Adolf Riippa in 1895. When the school doors were finally opened, almost two thousand dollars was in the treasury; this was expended on supplies.[21] The school's business managers supplied information about the college and suggested money-raising methods to the local supporting units.[22] In this first period there were efforts to secure interest-free loans, but it was noticed that the regular offerings fell off and the debts remained. A "ten-dollar drive" in 1910 for three thousand persons willing to contribute that much produced twenty thousand dollars for the reduction of debts, but the debts increased again in the recession during World War I.[23]

Early in its history the college began publishing a devotional magazine at Christmas and Easter. The series was later expanded to include a Midsummer and a Reformation issue. The quarterly publication was sold on an annual subscription basis. Several thousand dollars a year accrued from the periodicals at their peak.

Those concerned with the school's welfare lamented above all the shortsightedness of the Finnish immigrants. A large number were seemingly not interested in the fate of the Finnish college; several groups and newspapers were highly critical of the college; other groups gathered funds for the Workers' College at Smithville, Minnesota. Suomi College never had the united support of any major segment of the scattered Finns; they were not used to maintaining institutions by voluntary contributions and some could see no farther than the needs of their local congregation.

At the time of the great wave of emigration from Finland to the New World, there was a severe shortage of clergymen in the Old Country. Ministers were only very reluctantly released to accompany the stream of emigration; there was a question as to whether they could count the years of service in America toward their seniority.

Later, several American-Finnish pastors attributed the disappearance of the Delaware Finnish and Swedish settlements to the fact that these earlier immigrants did not preserve their religious and cultural heritage: clergymen and teachers were trained only in the Old Country, and no school was established in the colony.[24] The later immigrants, therefore, had to profit by that example. Almost from the beginning of organized congregational work, it was agreed that Suomi College should also have its own theological department to train pastors for the growing number of Finnish-American congregations. Pastor K. L. Tolonen officially laid the cornerstone of both Suomi College and the Seminary on May 30, 1899, when Old Main was begun, even though it would be five years more before the Seminary Department was initiated.

Seven young men who had completed the college's full seven-year course enrolled in the fall of 1904 in the theological seminary, which functioned from that time until 1958 as a separate department of the college. The curriculum was originally set up for two years of studies covering the five main fields of Christian theology, including both Greek and Hebrew. Textbooks were chiefly in Finnish, with some in English and German.

Three clergymen formed the seminary's first faculty: Pastor Nikander, John Bäck of the Hancock parish, and Alfred Gröning of the Atlantic parish.[25] Bäck had a Master's degree from Helsinki University and had been ordained by the Suomi Synod. Called from Finland to teach in the college, Pastor Isaac Katajamaa later became an instructor in the seminary. Other seminary instructors in this early phase were Pastors

Rafael Hartman, William Rautanen, Mauno I. Kuusi, Jacob Mäntta, and Kalle H. Mannerkorpi. During this period, Suomi Seminary prepared twenty-eight pastors for the Synod.

During its fifty-four-year connection with Suomi College, Suomi Seminary never had a building of its own, utilizing at the most a single classroom for lectures and another room for the library that was separate from the main college library. The seminary library eventually included all the Finnish volumes of the college. In almost every way, the seminarians were members of the student body, taking part in all college activities, and being especially active in the regular and free devotional life of the campus.

The Commercial Department had been planned for several years before it was organized in the fall of 1906. American Finns had already established businesses and needed bookkeepers and sales personnel with a knowledge of the Finnish language. That the area as a whole needed a business school was reflected in the relatively strong enrollment in this department from the beginning, with an upsurge following World War I. In several periods of the college's history, the Business Department was the largest division (1924–1931, 1937–1942, 1945–1948); in 1965–1966, one-third of the college students took business courses. By 1945, this department numbered one thousand and three graduates out of the total number of fifteen hundred graduates.[26]

This department was housed for a long time in the remodeled gymnasium building. Later it was quartered in Old Main and Nikander Hall. The fundamental courses were accounting, business methods, typing, and shorthand, and graduates received a certificate of proficiency. O. L. Nordstrom, a graduate of Augustana College, served as principal of the department from 1906 until 1918.

The Old-Country impress upon Suomi College continued in a diminished degree far into the school's second phase. First and foremost, the official language of the school, the principal language of instruction and devotion, was Finnish. The regulations governing the college were in that language as were the reports submitted to the Suomi Synod church conventions, whose discussion of school affairs was always in Finnish. The first brochures, the first periodicals, and the first historical album (1906) of the college were all in Finnish. Accordingly, an important entrance requirement was the ability to use Finnish, and all students were normally expected to study it.

It was natural under these circumstances that the full-time instructors were men and women of Finnish descent able to use that language fluently. Several of them in the earliest period had Master-of-Arts degrees obtained in Finland. In general, the part-time teachers, except those who taught English and American history, were also of Finnish extraction and familiar with that language. In 1906, two of the college's new graduates entered the ranks of the faculty,[27] something that has continued almost without interruption into the third phase of the school (in 1965–66, at least a third of the faculty were former students). As a result, continuity of outlook and tradition was ensured. Even the non-instructional staff was Finnish to a man—and woman—for at least the first forty years.

The *Tenth Anniversary Album* gives a snapshot view of the courses and textbooks used at Suomi College in 1906.[28] Though English and American history were originally the only courses taught in English, by 1906, several other courses also utilized textbooks in English (notably the sciences). It can be assumed, however, that instruction was in both languages, depending upon the instructor's own fluency in English.

In 1900, the first student organization, the *Konventti,* was formed for the cultivation of studies, esp., literary and forensic, for the strengthening of religion and morality, and for the advancement of Finnish culture.[29] Other Finnish-speaking societies were also organized in this period. In 1913, an English-language group, the *Philomathic* society, was founded for the cultivation of the English language, especially in public speaking.[30]

Finally, the actions of the church conventions constantly strengthened the position of the Finnish language and the Finnish orientation of the school.[31]

The New-Country Impress Upon Suomi College, 1919–1958

The beginning of the second phase of Suomi College's history dates from the death of Dr. J. K. Nikander. His co-founders, Tolonen and Hoikka, had died in 1902 and 1917, respectively. Other important laymen who shared in the founding of the congregations, the formation of the Suomi Synod, and the creation of Suomi College, had one by one disappeared from the scene.[32] A generation of American-born Finns had sprung up since the nine congregations had merged into an American-Finnish Lutheran church body and that infant church had produced an infant school.

Another year or event might have been chosen to mark the periods; for example, 1923 saw the end of the Preparatory Department and the formation of the Junior College program. The high tide of immigration had been abruptly checked by World War I and later by new laws limiting the admission of foreigners to the United States. Few students needed the Preparatory Department, and the stress on the preservation and use of the Finnish language was slackening.

The turning point might be considered 1920, when the Synod learned that the debt of Suomi College had been wiped out after twenty years of paying for the building of Old Main. Yet, the institution was still forced to live on daily sustenance with no opportunity to lay up anything for expansion. That same year, the University of Michigan's Department of Education informed the Suomi College authorities that thereafter the academy's graduates could enter the University of Michigan without entrance examinations, i.e., the Suomi College private high school was on a par with other approved public high schools.

Nevertheless, if Old-Country influences are considered the dominant force during the first phase of the college's history and increasing Americanization the major trend during the second phase, then the year of Dr. Nikander's death is the logical dividing point.

Although the "Suomi-Opisto" of the founders had become Suomi College, which included a professional school (the Seminary), and its first graduates were later granted the Bachelor's degree, the Hancock institution did not offer credits on the tertiary level of education until 1923. By this time, the older Lutheran synods had developed their academies into four-year, degree-granting institutions, and many Lutheran seminaries required an arts or science degree for admittance. Some young American-Finnish students had gained their degrees from such schools.

More of the Suomi seminarians were now young men who had received a full high-school education in the public schools. Some in Synod circles felt that the requirements for entrance to Suomi Seminary should be raised to include two years of college work, which, once a Junior College Department was also established, could be completed at the Synod's own school. The result would be to strengthen the school's influence upon the young men who would go out to serve the churches of the immigrant Finns.[33] The establishment of the Junior College at Suomi was, therefore, partly due to the desire to buttress the theological seminary and to implement the continued production of well-trained clergymen for Suomi Synod. In this sense, the change was consonant with the deepest desires of Nikander, Tolonen, and Hoikka, and was not a sign of a desire for experimentation or Americanization.

There was another important reason for the change: the Board and administration realized that the academy, the secondary level of education, would soon lose enrollment as good public high schools were now found in every town and even in the rural areas, and few parents wanted to send their youths away from home for this level of studies. Therefore, when Pastor Alfred Haapanen, the newly elected president of Suomi Synod and a long-time Board member, proposed at the Church Convention of 1922 in Negaunee that the Junior College be established, the Board of Trustees was prepared to act. A committee was chosen to determine the curriculum of the new department, and the Church Convention of 1923 in Conneaut approved the decisions to close the Preparatory Department and to open the Junior College Department in the fall of that year.

Only five students were registered in the new department in the first year for courses in English, chemistry, American history, Christianity, psychology, and philosophy. Courses in biology, botany, Greek, and German were added the following year. No special effort was made to obtain additional teachers, as the same instructors functioned in both the academy and the college. The University of Michigan examiners, however, soon pointed out that, in general, instructors with graduate school degrees should teach on the tertiary level. This gradually became the practice at Suomi, although the president's report for 1926 assured the church that qualified teachers of Finnish background were sought first.

The Junior College grew slowly; since the commercial and music departments continued their separate existence, the Junior College students were those in the "liberal arts" program. The Consistory of the Suomi Synod, rather inconsistently, also decided that, because of the immediate need for pastors, young men (many of them actually older men) would be permitted to enroll in the seminary without the hoped-for two years of college work. Other reasons for the Junior College's slow growth were: (1) a lack of confidence in the school because of its new debts, its smallness, and the talk of relocating the campus; (2) the school's failure to appeal to students over the appeal of larger colleges with better equipment; (3) the misconception that the institution was so thoroughly Finnish that fluent knowledge of that language was necessary; and (4) a belief that the atmosphere was too religious.[34] Apparently, the earnest effort to retain the Old-Country background had an adverse effect in this second phase, resulting in tension between the inevitable Americanization and a spirit of criticism in the Finnish-dominated church conventions. During the early part of this phase, the presidents were under pressure from two directions.

During the second phase of her history, there were an unusual number of board and convention elections or confirmations of new presidents for Suomi College. The administrative changes combined with a fluctuation in both enrollment and financial support suggest uncertainty about the role of the college in the Synod, its role on the educational scene, and even about its ability to continue. During this period, only one new structure was built on campus, and one older one was torn down.[35]

All of the presidents and acting presidents during this phase were trained at Suomi College, almost all had studied at large American universities, yet all were also fluent in the Finnish language, and by birth, tradition, and inclination, were acquainted with the Old Country and its culture. Four of them served on the powerful four-man Consistory of Suomi Synod, several were active in Luther League work, several in the pietistic movements, several were afterwards prominent in the merger negotiations of the Suomi Synod, and two later served other Lutheran colleges, one as dean and the other as department head and professor.[36] This brief summary of their characteristics indicates that the mother-church understood the uncertain conditions of the period and threw her best forces into the responsible task. Nevertheless, this was not—save for the organization of the Junior College and the building of a desperately needed structure— a period of advancement.

The Reverend John Wargelin, registered as a student at Suomi College on its opening day in 1896, was a student for ten years. With other members of the seventh class, he served as an assistant instructor in the lower classes for a year. He was one of the first graduates in 1904, one of the first seminarians that same year, one of the first graduates of the Theological Seminary in 1906, and one of the first Suomi Synod-trained men to be ordained. In 1912, he was elected to the Consistory of the Suomi Synod, the first American-born Finn to serve on that body. That same year, he was placed on the Suomi College Board. Having attended public schools in America, he used the English language as a native speaker.[37] After Nikander's death, the Board of Trustees made Wargelin first acting and then regular president of Suomi College. As vice-president of the Suomi Synod, John Wargelin also assumed executive direction of the church body until the Church Convention of 1919, thus succeeding for a time to the twin burdens of Dr. Nikander.

Pastor Wargelin had just been called to become the school's business manager when he became president. Early in his first term of office, the debts of the institution, totaling at that time twenty-two thousand dollars, were paid off. Many improvements became possible over the years: a new building, an endowment fund, scholarships and stipends, organized alumni work, and a field-secretary to help in recruiting students.

In 1922, President Wargelin was given a year's leave of absence to earn the Master's degree at the University of Michigan. Miss Wilhelmina Perttula, head of the Commercial Department, served as acting president for the year. At this time, the question of moving the college was a topic of agitation. Wargelin advised that the Board must be sure of adequate support, if the school was relocated. The Board did proceed with caution then and again in 1931, when a vacated school building in St. Paul, Minnesota, became available, and nothing resulted from the discussions.[38]

President Wargelin was, of course, instrumental in the metamorphosis of the college from academy program to junior college program. The 1920's and 1930's were also marked by subsidiary instructional programs. Special lectures were held for the students who would teach summer schools in the congregations. A projected organists' school in 1920 failed for lack of students, but evening classes for the community in English, political science, shorthand, and Swedish were moderately successful. In 1924, regular summer courses in music were arranged; these continued for over twenty years. Saturday courses also attracted some students unable to attend school on weekdays; these classes in music, public speaking, and recitation were continued from 1925 until 1932 and from 1934 until 1938.

The music courses developed into a Music Department in 1923 under the aggressive leadership of the composer, Martti Nisonen,[39] who laid a firm foundation for the school's musical reputation and lent an impetus to close school-community relationships. Under his tutelage, the Suomi College Choir began out-of-state concert tours. Since 1927, the department has granted a special certificate in music after two years of study (and later when incorporated into the Junior College, the Associate's degree).

In the 1920's, critical articles about the college began to appear in the Finnish-language newspapers, and questions were raised in the church conventions. Some of the criticism centered upon the increasing use of the English language at the college, and some upon the growing number of instructors not of Finnish descent.[40] In 1924, complaints were registered about the English appearance of the student yearbook. Delegates to church conventions also criticized the use of English in the college catalogs, although a Finnish supplement was also printed, as the administration realized that this was a sensitive area.

At this time, the Board and president hoped to have the church body approve a fund-raising campaign for an endowment fund; President Wargelin assured the friends of the college that, whenever possible, instructors of Finnish background would be hired, but he stressed the fact that the University of Michigan professors who examined the Junior College required that faculty members have the Master's degree, and qualified teachers from Finland or America were not always available. From 1931 on, this requirement was strictly enforced.

There was a possibility that the language problem, which was also apparent in other fields of church work, might lead to a split in the Suomi Synod itself, as had occurred in some other church bodies. Fortunately this did not happen, although the debate was keen, and there were probably some ill effects upon college support.[41] The Church Convention of 1926 in Maynard, Massachusetts, passed three resolutions concerning Suomi College: (1) that the instruction in Christianity—as far as possible —should be only in Finnish; (2) that instructors hired should—as far as possible—be able to speak Finnish; (3) that the seminary should secure as theologian a teacher fluent in Finnish.[42] Suomi College acted according to these resolutions—insofar as possible. The training, background, and culture of the Old Country was still evident, especially in several of the older instructors, and the seminary, from 1930 until its own departure in 1958, had a series of Finnish theologians as basic instructors.[43] But the New-Country impress was equally evident in the many young Masters-of-Arts who followed each other in rapid succession as language and science instructors.

In the spring of 1927, Pastor John Wargelin resigned. He stated that the difficult circumstances and the severe criticisms which he considered unjust made the position of president distasteful to him. The Board reluctantly accepted his resignation and called Pastor Antti Lepisto to succeed him in August of that year, first as acting president and the following year as regular president.

Pastor Antti Lepisto, a graduate of Suomi College, had received the Bachelor of Philosophy degree from the University of Chicago and had studied at Chicago Lutheran Seminary of Maywood, Illinois. He had served the college as fund-raiser and business manager from 1917 until 1919.

In response to the great demand for Bible courses for laymen, the Board authorized the formation of a new department, the Bible School, which was organized by President Lepisto in the fall of 1927. The Bible School was maintained for three years with a student enrollment of eleven, six and four students, respectively, graduating three students from a two-year course. President Lepisto felt that the Bible School was beneficial, but the Board considered it impractical to continue for so few students. Later, a curriculum for parish workers was organized from the regular course offerings.

In 1930, the Board decided that the academy had outlived its usefulness and would be discontinued after two years. Although President Lepisto opposed this decision, the Board had several reasons for this action: public high schools had been founded in almost all communities and in many cases had greater appeal; and the financial burden was too great. An observer suggested that the Finnish cultural appeal had greatly weakened and that there was also a disinterest in religion that worked against church-related schools.[44] The elimination of the academy would relieve the need for a double faculty and allow for additional courses on the college level. In all, one hundred and eighty-two students had received their diplomas from the academy.

Contacts with Finland were strengthened at this time. President J. K. Nikander had made periodical visits to Finland. In 1928, the former president, Dr. John Wargelin, traveled widely in Finland; speaking on many occasions about both Suomi Synod and Suomi College, he was able to correct some misconceptions. The college administration had been seeking a seminary instructor from Finland for several years, and in February, 1930, Pastor Ilmari Tammisto arrived in Hancock. As the government of Finland had provided funds for his transportation, there seemed some hope of getting support from that source for a professorship of the Finnish language and culture at Suomi College. This hope remained unfulfilled, but in 1931 the government sent Dr. Rafael Engelberg to Suomi College to lecture on the *Kalevala* and on Finnish history.

When Pastor Lepisto resigned in 1930, the Board called Dr. John Wargelin to be president again.

The effects of the long recession were felt at the college in the double form of a decreased student body and lessened income. The latest money-raising effort, begun at this inauspicious time, was also adversely affected. In 1927, the Church Convention at Fairport Harbor, Ohio, had given permission to the Board to use a professional money-raising firm to conduct a "great campaign" in the Synod to raise two hundred thousand dollars for endowment and equipment. The Board delayed implementing the plan and then submitted a new resolution that was approved by the Church Convention of 1929 at Ishpeming, Michigan; the campaign would seek to raise three hundred thousand dollars, half for the endowment fund and half for a new classroom building and equipment. Begun in 1930, the campaign raised only eighty-two thousand dollars in pledges and finally forty-seven thousand dollars in cash.[45]

As the college's financial support had decreased so drastically, a large part of the "great campaign" funds was used to meet current expenses; some was used to purchase a new science laboratory and to add volumes to the library. An earlier historian of the college believes that these funds preserved the life of the institution at a critical time.[46] The Junior College with its new equipment was approved by the University of Michigan's examiners in 1932, so that students transferring from Suomi to other schools within the state would suffer no loss of credits. The colleges of the United Lutheran Church in America agreed, in general, to accept Suomi transfer credits in full. At this time, the Board also discussed the possibility of full accreditation by the North Central Association.

Enrollment in the Junior College increased noticeably even during the depression. The Board had set up a program of twelve stipends a year that canceled tuition in the freshman year; this program continued for many years.

To reduce the financial pressures on the school, the teachers consented to a five to ten percent reduction in their salaries in 1932 and another ten percent reduction in 1933; these remained in force for about five years.

In 1932, Suomi College, especially the Seminary, arranged a week-long pastors' institute at a summer camp. The institutes were continued for fifteen years on campus during the spring semester. Some well-known theologian was the principal lecturer, assisted by the seminary instructors or synod pastors.[47] In the same year, the college established the Finnish-American museum, but a lack of funds and trained personnel hindered any progress, until 1945–46 when Dr. John Kolehmainen, on leave of absence from Heidelberg College, conducted research at the college, and began to collate the material on hand and to collect more. Dr. Armas Holmio now serves as curator of the expanding Archives, which comprise twenty thousand documents and other books and articles on the American Finns, some of them quite rare. An exchange system is maintained with the Helsinki University Library and other libraries in Finland.

Dr. Wargelin asked to be relieved of his responsibilities as president of Suomi College in 1937, although he continued as an instructor in the seminary. Dr. Viljo K. Nikander, son of the first president, became the next head of Suomi College, an office he held for ten years.

Dr. Nikander, a graduate of both Suomi Academy and Suomi Theological Seminary, had earned the B.A. degree from Carthage College, the M.A. degree from the University of Chicago, and the Ph.D. degree from Harvard University. He had taught at Carthage and Waterloo Colleges.

Dr. Wargelin had underscored the need for a new classroom building and for a new large-scale fund-raising campaign for this purpose. The task of directing the campaign and erecting the edifice fell to Dr. Nikander. He considered a new building essential to the survival of the institution, and presented the challenge to the church and the community in that light. The Board and convention approved all the plans. An experienced fundraiser, Dr. O. H. Pannkoke, directed the campaign which raised pledges totaling almost one hundred thousand dollars; by March 31, 1940, over seventy-two thousand dollars had been received in cash.

The college had already acquired at small cost sixty acres behind Old Main. Professor Eliel Saarinen and his son-in-law and architect-associate, J. R. F. Swanson, drew the plans for the new building, which is on four levels and includes a gymnasium-auditorium with stage, a laboratory, a library, several classrooms and offices, and the heating plant. First used in December, 1939, the building was formally dedicated in June, 1940, in connection with the fiftieth-anniversary celebrations of the Suomi Synod. The cost of the building, later named J. K. Nikander Hall, without equipment was ninety thousand dollars, and the total project, one hundred and twenty-five thousand dollars. A victory drive in 1942 raised an additional fifteen thousand dollars, but a considerable indebtedness remained for many years.

President Nikander believed in actively recruiting new students and in publicizing Suomi College in its own area. He employed college personnel regularly in summer tours of the Upper Peninsula and himself traveled in the congregations of Minnesota. Faculty members visited the Copper Country high schools during the school year. The enrollment, however, continued to fluctuate until 1941, when it began a steady decline which continued during the war years.

During the war years, it was necessary to borrow endowment fund monies for current expenses. Although in this period of high employment, the congregations' giving began to approach one hundred percent of the apportionments, loss of tuition income forced the college to borrow money. In 1942, the course offerings were drastically curtailed in the Junior College. In 1943, all the faculty except the seminary instructors were on a part-time basis. By this extreme economy, the building debt was slowly reduced to three thousand dollars.

President Nikander visited Finland in the summer of 1938, in search of faculty members. Urho Valjakka, M.A., came to teach Finnish, and Pastor Uuras Saarnivaara, M.A., S.T.M., became a seminary teacher. As Pastor Saarnivaara inclined toward the theological position of the Laestadian movement, it was hoped that his presence would bring more students and financial support from the many adherents of that movement in America. In 1939, the Synod invited two representatives of the Laestadian movement to serve as members of the Suomi College Board, but this action was never fully consummated.

The fiftieth anniversary of Suomi College was celebrated in June, 1946, in connection with the Church Convention held at the college. The institution received many gifts, among them an anniversary offering of forty-five thousand dollars raised by the churches.[48] The college published a *Fiftieth Anniversary Publication* as a gift to the anniversary fund donors; it was under the editorship of Dr. John Wargelin, with approximately half of the articles in English and half in Finnish. This album, like its two predecessors, contains valuable resumes of the school history.

In the fall of 1946, Dr. Nikander announced that he would resign the following year. The 1946–47 enrollment of one hundred and seventy-four students, eighty-nine of whom were studying under the GI Bill, was almost double that of 1945–46. In March, 1947, the Board called Pastor Carl J. Tamminen, secretary of the Board, to serve as acting president; he accepted with the understanding that the Board would continue seeking for a regular president.

Pastor Tamminen, a graduate of Suomi Seminary, had served in several Synod conferences and had been president of both the Michigan Conference and the Conference Luther League. He was later a member of the Consistory and was a commissioner of the Synod on the Joint Commission on Lutheran Unity during the merger negotiations.[49]

President Tamminen, like his predecessor, urged the church to consider seriously the possibility of making Suomi College a four-year institution. He also stressed the importance of obtaining complete accreditation.

Pastor Bernhard Hillila, a doctoral candidate at Union Theological Seminary in the field of school administration, received the call to become president of Suomi College and succeeded Tamminen in 1949.

A graduate of Suomi Seminary and ordained in 1941, Hillila received a Bachelor's degree from Boston University and a Master's from Western Reserve University. He had served in several pastorates of the Synod. As his special field of study was in school administration, it was felt that he was the leader needed by the school for vigorous advancement in the post-war years. Later, Dr. Hillila served as vice-president of the Suomi Synod,[50] commissioner of the JCLU and dean of Hamma Theological Seminary.

A reorganization of the school took place at this time. When it was formed, the Junior College had taken its place beside the older departments and included the students enrolled in the liberal arts program. Now all the students except the seminarians were enrolled in the Junior College, which was divided into three departments: liberal arts, music, and commercial. All courses in these departments earned full collegiate credit.

The enrollment increased sharply in 1949 and then decreased again during the Korean War. Another residence near the college was bought to serve as a boys' dormitory. In the fall of 1950, a vocational course in printing was added to the curriculum, but attracted only a few students and was discontinued after a few years.

At this time, the small remaining debt was paid off and considerable improvements were made on the buildings and property. Books and equipment were secured for the library, and the endowment fund was also increased. President Hillila reported that the contributions of the congregations to the college had become consistent. The college administration had planned a drive to raise money for needed improvements, but deferred this plan, because the Suomi Synod had begun its own Church Advancement Program (CAP), in which the college participated and from which it benefited.

Pastor Hillila resigned in 1952 to complete his studies for the doctorate in education. In his final report to the church convention, he pointed out that the assets of Suomi College had risen by thirty-three percent in the last three years, and the buildings, equipment, and library were in better condition than before. The reasons for this strengthened status were: more consistent support from the congregations, funds received from the CAP drive, and special bequests.[51] The president felt that a considerable amount should be spent to repair Old Main building.

The Board extended a call to Pastor Edward J. Isaac of Minneapolis, Minnesota, who became the eighth president of the school. Pastor Isaac received a B.A. degree from Tufts College and a B.D. degree from

Mount Airy Lutheran Seminary of Philadelphia, having spent one year of study at Suomi Seminary. He served pastorates in the Midwest. At the time he was called to the college, he was vice-president of the Synod.

The enrollment dropped from one hundred and twenty-four students in 1951–52 to ninety-four in 1952–53 (twenty-four of whom were in attendance for only one semester). Because the receipts from tuition were less than anticipated, CAP funds were diverted for current expenses, and the projected repairs of Old Main were postponed (and never completed).

Consultation with educators from the Department of Education of the Evangelical Lutheran Church led to some organizational changes. Mr. Waino Lehto, principal of the Commercial Department, was named dean of the Junior College; and Dr. Armas Holmio, dean of the seminary. Mr. Soine Torma was released from teaching duties to serve full time in public relations and student solicitation. The Michigan Commission on Accreditation approved Suomi College for accreditation.[52] The Board retained Mr. Peter Anderson, dean emeritus of Concordia College of Moorhead, Minnesota, as educational consultant.[53]

From 1949 to 1953, the seminary had its largest enrollment, with from seventeen to twenty students. The faculty included Dr. Holmio, Dr. Kukkonen, and Dr. Saarnivaara. The last resigned in 1954, after fifteen years of service, to return to Finland. A "Special Aid Fund" had been established in 1949 to channel gifts from the congregations and individuals to seminarians in need of aid. Some criticism was directed at the college at this time since so few of the seminarians were fluent in Finnish. President Isaac defended the school against charges that it did not attempt to teach Finnish: if students had not used Finnish at home, it was unrealistic to expect them to attain fluency during their busy seminary years.[54]

The salary scale for instructors was improved in 1954; in that year the endowment fund totaled $55,213.40 and the college's only debt was owing to that fund. Sizable gifts were received from area business concerns; much of this money was used for scholarships.

President Isaac died suddenly in the summer of 1954. The Board asked Mr. David Halkola to serve as interim-president as well as registrar, and later during the school year named him acting president for two years. As the regulations governing Suomi College required that the president be an ordained clergyman, Mr. Halkola was not qualified to become regular president.

Mr. Halkola, a graduate of Suomi College, had earned his B.A. degree at Wittenberg University and his M.A. at Western Reserve University. In 1948, he became an instructor at the college in history and political science.

At this point, Suomi College and Theological Seminary became a factor in the movement for a merger between the various Lutheran churches of America. Among the church bodies of the National Lutheran Council, there were two movements: a proposed four-way merger of the American Lutheran Church, the Evangelical Lutheran Church, the Lutheran Free Church, and the United Evangelical Lutheran Church working as the Joint Union Committee (JUC); [55] and a movement spearheaded by the United Lutheran Church in America and the Augustana Lutheran Church, working as the Joint Commission on Lutheran Unity (JCLU).[56] The Suomi Synod at the Church Convention of 1955 at Ely, Minnesota, appointed a Commission on Intersynodical Relations to enter merger negotiations. This commission proposed to the Church Convention of 1956 at Ashtabula Harbor, Ohio, that the Synod enter into discussions with the other church bodies of the JCLU. The final decision, after an intervening year, during which merger with the JUC was also discussed,[57] was made at the Church Convention of 1957 at Hancock, Michigan, in favor of the JCLU movement by a vote of two hundred and eighteen to ninety-nine.[58]

Those who wished to enter into the JCLU discussions also desired to relocate the Theological Seminary and affiliate it with some larger seminary of the United Lutheran Church in America, preferably Chicago Lutheran Seminary of Maywood, Illinois. Some who favored changing the constitution of Suomi College so that a layman could be president, felt that a layman should not be president of the seminary. These persons obviously advocated separating Suomi Seminary from the college and its relocation. There was, of course, sentiment against this action.

Mr. Halkola found himself in the middle of this tug-of-war. He served as interim head of the school and as acting president for two years before he was installed as regular president. During this time and into the first years of his tenure, the status of the seminary was uncertain while attempts were made to work out the practical details of the "moderate type" of separation that the administration and Board desired. There was certainly little opportunity to initiate any striking new plans. The situation was further complicated when the dean of the seminary applied for a longer leave of absence, another seminary instructor resigned, and a third died unexpectedly before he had delivered a single lecture.

The separation of Suomi College and the Theological Seminary on July 1, 1958 marks the end of the second phase of the college's history. On the same day, the seminary affiliated with Maywood. Although there was still a Suomi Theological Seminary, its history would henceforth be distinct from that of Suomi College.

The ability to use Finnish was necessary for the teacher and the student during the first phase of the college's history. The shift to English was the distinguishing feature of the second phase. As time went on, there was greater variance between the use of Finnish by those who spoke and wrote on behalf of the college and by the students, especially the younger ones who had attended public schools before coming to Suomi.

The use of English in the college catalogs, in the yearbooks of the church conventions, and in brochures by both indicates the everyday use of English many years earlier. Instructors from Finland made greater strides in learning and using English than the typical seminarian did in becoming fluent in Finnish. This was entirely natural, in fact inevitable, but nonetheless disturbing to the Old-Country parent who had supported his child's or grandchild's education.

Suomi College went with the stream. American-born presidents and instructors wanted an American school for American students. They did not, however, during this period, run roughshod over the sensitive feelings of the Finnish-born, but rather tried to maintain the Finnish language as well as the Finnish background of the college. It proved impossible.

The number of teachers who did not know Finnish gradually rose. Even the seminary felt this change. Even in the earlier phase, Pastor Jacob Mantta, an American-trained instructor in the seminary, had used English to some extent. In 1923, the Reverend Dr. H. D. Whittaker joined the seminary faculty, and in the same decade other non-Finnish clergymen were part-time teachers. This created a stir in the Synod, culminating in the mandate to obtain a seminary instructor from Finland or one who knew the Finnish language thoroughly. In fact, only in a few cases did the non-Finnish teacher stay any length of time at the college. Nevertheless, almost before this second phase of the history was well begun, English was in regular use in everyday student life.

The Old-Country lycée system was modified early. The rather elastic Preparatory Department vanished in 1923. With the establishment of the Junior College, also in 1923, Suomi College chose to keep in step with other schools on the American educational scene.[59] Yet, in a way, this step was also a return to the Old-Country model, for the student who secured the "white cap" after graduation from a secondary school in Finland had had the equivalent of a junior college education. Thus, the new

Junior College program was an expansion of the old seventh class of the lycée program.

The various subsidiary instructional programs initiated in this period—evening classes, Saturday classes, summer sessions, and the like—were all attempts to develop the college as an American school in an American setting.

The Commercial Department, although originally intended to help the Finnish young people in finding employment in business, served the entire area as an important vocational school.[60] This department brought in the greater number of non-Finnish students throughout the second phase of the school's history.

Change of language, change of faculty, change of program. Was there in addition a change of purpose, of tradition, of spirit? The question cannot be answered with a simple "yes" or "no." Those who prefer the school of the earlier phase would answer quickly in the affirmative, but those who feel that the transition to the second phase was not only inevitable but also necessary would be just as swift to deny any loss of tradition or turning aside from the original goals.

Although there were many teachers who remained only a short time, several instructors of Finnish background remained at Suomi throughout their careers. These were the teachers who maintained tradition, especially during the tenures of those presidents who were at Suomi only a few years. Their influence through many years strengthened and upheld the fabric of the school.

There were seven of these teachers, four from Finland and three trained at Suomi. Two taught in the seminary, two in the commercial department, two in the music department, and one in the area of Finnish. Each spoke Finnish fluently; each was considered an institution even before retirement, and each was long remembered.

Wilhelmina Perttula, a graduate of the first "white cap" class in 1904, became Dean of Women and instructor in 1911. A long-time teacher in the Commercial Department and principal in 1918, she served as acting president during President Wargelin's absence in 1922–23. After being away for some years, she returned to the Commercial Department from 1931 to 1936 and was housemother at Old Main for some years.

Waino Lehto ("Pop") was also a student at Suomi College, an instructor from 1920 to 1923, and again from 1926 to 1962 after receiving the M.A. degree from the University of Pennsylvania. For twenty years

Dean of the College, he was the first faculty advisor of the Sampo Honor Society and also served on many synodical boards.

Kosti Arho, who received a M.A. from Helsinki University, arrived in the fall of 1922 and became the Finnish instructor for both the college and seminary. He also edited the college publications for many years and served as librarian. He was secretary for many church conventions and was a long-time treasurer of the Suomi Synod and editor of the *Amerikan Suometar*. During World War II, Mr. Arho helped Indiana University organize courses in Finnish. In 1949, he retired and returned to Finland after twenty-seven years in America.

Composer Martti Nisonen organized the Music Department. Under his guidance, the Suomi College Choir gained a fine reputation in the area and a number of community musical organizations flourished under his tutelage. Several of his compositions, in particular hymn melodies, have become well known among the Finns. Nisonen died suddenly in 1946, after teaching at Suomi for almost a quarter of a century.

Nisonen's successor as head of the Music Department was his former student, Arthur J. Hill, who earned the B. Mus. and M. Mus. degrees at the University of Michigan. Under him the Choir tours were extended, not only into Michigan and Minnesota, but also to other states, and in 1957 to Europe, culminating with an appearance at the Lutheran World Federation Helsinki Assembly.

Pastor Uuras Saarnivaara, called to become seminary instructor in 1939, remained until 1954. He taught in the systematic and exegetical fields during the period of the greatest enrollment. Saarnivaara received the Ph.D. degree from the University of Chicago and later the Th.D. degree from Helsinki University. He is known also as a writer of theological works. Saarnivaara returned to Finland in 1954 and served there as a religious editor and speaker. He has since returned to the United States to serve in certain Lutheran seminaries.

The last dean of Suomi Theological Seminary was Dr. Armas Holmio, who served as a teacher from 1946 to 1958 and then for eight more years as an instructor in the Junior College. Educated at the University of Helsinki, he occupied pulpits in Finland and the United States and was a chaplain in the American army during World War II. Holmio earned the Th.D. degree from Boston University in the field of church history and has written several works. He was a member of the Suomi Synod in the JCLU negotiations. After retiring from full-time teaching in 1966 to write historical works about the American Finns, he continued serving as curator of the Finnish-American Archives at Suomi College.

During the second phase of her history, Suomi College was not completely sure of herself. Each new problem demanded so much attention that at no time could any one administration or president strike out in a bold, new fashion. Uncertainty about the fluctuating enrollment, the retention of instructors, the solution of the language question, the fluctuating support from the church, and the repeated fund-raising campaigns—in short, uncertainty about the very survival of the college—was the dominant mood of the time. While seeking to adapt something of the new yet retain much of the old and faced by the necessity of interpreting new features to a conservative supporting body, the successive administrations were handicapped by a narrowness of outlook that confined them to narrower purposes and plans than the real advancement of the school would have warranted.

The Period of Expansion, 1958–

The third phase in the history of Suomi College began in 1958. It is a time of expansion. Ironically, this period began with the desire for retrenchment or at least the maintenance of things as they were. The excision of the seminary seemed to have drained the spirit of the institution and there were still financial difficulties facing the school.

President Halkola reported in 1955 that the enrollment at Suomi was dropping while that of other schools was on the rise. The decrease in anticipated receipts from tuition plus the increased costs of maintaining the school forced the use of reserves. Although the Church Convention of 1955 had ordered the college to replace money borrowed from the endowment funds, the Board did not wish to incur outside debts for this purpose.[61] Deficit financing continued. The pressure occasioned by a fluctuating enrollment with consequent reduced income on the one hand and constant administrative expenses coupled with rising costs on the other led to a deficit in the General Fund of about sixty thousand dollars and a dangerous increase in debts.[62]

President Halkola resigned on December 10, 1959. The affairs of the college were administered for six months by a committee of the Board, consisting of the Synod's president, Dr. Raymond W. Wargelin, as executive officer; Onni A. Malila as chairman; E. E. Erickson as treasurer; and Leonard Johnson as secretary. An administrative council of the faculty met with Dr. Wargelin to oversee academic functions. A strict system of economy was initiated that succeeded in reducing the indebtedness of the college and restoring its credit status.

During Mr. Halkola's tenure the first Associate degrees were granted in Arts, Commerce, and Music (the last was terminated in 1967). Two ASLA (Fulbright) lecturers from Finland presented two series of lectures in the summer of 1955, but these were not sufficiently attended to warrant continuation.[63] The Suomi College Copper Country Art Exhibition, which was held for three summers and attracted much attention, was also discontinued in the interests of economy. The school's sixtieth anniversary in 1956 was marked by many celebrations, including the appearance on campus of the Duluth Symphony Orchestra accompanied by a massed choir in a Sibelius concert. During the year the president of the college and the dean of the seminary were formally installed.

There were some administrative advancements at this time. Suomi College called its first campus pastor, Martin Saarinen, who organized a student organization.[64] An active public relations officer and field representative, Pastor Giles Ekola, was named vice-president in charge of development; he was followed by Pastor William Avery. The college also began to publish a quarterly magazine of information, *The Bridge,* and a Finnish counterpart, the *Viesti.*

The enlarged Board of Directors functioned with five separate committees. To alleviate the college's precarious financial position, the Board planned a fund-raising drive under the direction of the temporary administering committee. This task was later given to the new president, the Reverend Ralph J. Jalkanen, pastor of Bethany Lutheran Church of Ashtabula Harbor, Ohio, who was called to the presidency by the Board and approved by the standing vote of the Church Convention of 1960 at Virginia, Minnesota. At that time Pastor Jalkanen promised a "new plan of action to create a new image of the college." [65]

Pastor Jalkanen grew up in the Suomi College community. A student at Suomi for five years, he graduated from the Junior College in 1940 and from the Seminary in 1943. He received the B.A. degree from Elmhurst and the M.A. degree from Roosevelt University, Chicago, and has continued studies toward the doctorate. He has held pastorates in Minnesota, Illinois, and Ohio, and has served in offices of the church conferences and Synod, as secretary of the Consistory and member of the SSCIR and the JCLU.

To understand the dramatic change in the fortunes of Suomi College one must appreciate the change of purpose and philosophy. Merely to conclude that a fortuitous combination of increased enrollment and increased giving were the causes of this change would be a mistake.

The Board was increased and now includes representatives of three groups, viz., educators, professional men and businessmen, and some (who may also belong to one of the other groups) who represent the background of the founders and earlier supporters of the school. Some of the members are chosen by supporting synods and boards; some are called by the Board. During the 1965 Capital Fund Campaign for the Library-Science Building, the Board contributed about forty thousand dollars.

President Jalkanen cited the school's financial condition as the first major problem to be solved. For the last half-decade (1960–1965) the budget has been balanced and the amounts borrowed from endowment funds have been replaced. This has been due to a number of factors, not least being the substantial amounts received from the supporting synods— the Suomi Synod until 1962 and the Wisconsin–Upper Michigan and Michigan Synods of the Lutheran Church in America since 1962. In 1965, however, important changes in the alignment of synodical support for various educational institutions of LCA were made, so that the support of Suomi College, both as to operating budget and capital improvements, is now a responsibility of the church body itself through the Board of College Education.

The rise in enrollment has been in line with that experienced by most schools throughout the country, but to ensure continued growth the administration has strengthened the office of Registrar and Director of Admissions. Two active recruiters visit scores of high schools in many states, and the school prints and mails out thousands of brochures describing the school and larger editions of the catalog for use by high-school counsellors. The Board now sponsors scholarships for students in the upper brackets of their classes.[66] The proportion of out-of-state students is also rising sharply. As steady growth is anticipated, several more dormitories will be built in the near future.[67]

A sharp increase in tuition costs and fees has been a significant factor in the buildup. The student paid only ten percent of his educational costs in the early days of Suomi College; he now contributes about sixty percent of his educational costs. It is anticipated that tuition costs will be increased approximately ten percent each year for some time, and that finally the student will contribute ninety percent of his educational costs.[68]

There has also been a remarkable increase in the sums the college has received from individuals, groups, and business concerns. The school's recent drives, well-planned and vigorously conducted, have been successful. Directed to a new constituency, they present the new image of the school as a private, church-related educational institution providing a valuable service to a large area and, therefore, naturally expecting to be supported by the responsible elements of that area.

The growth of Suomi College in the last half-decade is apparent in recent construction. A dormitory for one hundred and fifteen students with a student center and dining facilities was erected in 1965; in 1966, a Library-Science building became a matching edifice to Nikander Hall. An older building on campus, occupied for over fifty years by the Suomi Synod publishing house, became available to the college in 1965 and was converted for use by the business office, the office of development, the book store, and the music, commercial, and art departments. This is a temporary arrangement until a further stage of the construction phase is reached.

There is a master plan for campus development and a calendar has been set for construction. Three more dormitories, a physical education building, a chapel, a field house, a student center and administration building, and a music and arts building will be constructed during the next decade.

New courses have been added to the curriculum and others have been dropped or replaced; a few minor changes have been made in the requirements for the associate degree. As the Associate in Music degree has been terminated, music majors now receive the arts degree.

The great forward step has been the decision to seek regional accreditation. The school is now in the process of being reviewed by the North Central Association. It is expected that Suomi College will soon receive full accreditation.

NOTES

1. Although now a "national" church, for there is complete liberty to leave the church, the great majority choose to remain in it.
2. The chief movements were: (1) the "awakened" (herannaiset) led by N. G. Malmberg and Paavo Ruotsalainen; (2) the evangelicals (evankeliset) led by F. G. Hedberg; (3) the "praying folk" (rukoilevaiset) led by Henrik Renquist; and (4) the Laestadians led by L. L. Laestadius.
3. In 1873 in Calumet, Michigan, the *Salomon Kortetniemi Lutheran Society* (Rautanen, ASK, p. 20); the name of one of the Laestadian preachers was tacked on by the registering clerk who did not know Finnish and thought the man was a saint.
4. At one time many of the adherents scorned an educated clergy, but this attitude has been modified.
5. Pastor Alfred Elieser Backman, later Rector of Hauho, (1844–1909); in America 1876–1883 (see KT, p. 9015).
6. The *Paimen Sanomia* (Shepherd's Sayings) was established by Nikander,

Tolonen and Hoikka in 1889 and was published in the Hancock Parsonage; it was taken over by the Suomi Synod in 1890 and continued until 1960.

7. S–OA, p. 26.

8. S–OA, p. 19.

9. Minneapolis, St. Paul, Duluth, Little Falls, Nurmijarvi, Minnesota; Hancock, Houghton, Marquette, Michigan; Superior, Wisconsin; Painesville, Ohio, and others.

10. Nikander was freed from the presidency of the Synod in 1898 by Tolonen, but on the death of the latter in 1902 he again became president.

11. Nikander spoke about this on the opening day of the school, S–OA, p. 31.

12. S–OA, p. 196.

13. S–OA, pp. 201f.

14. S–OA, p. 26.

15. S–OA, pp. 206–209.

16. SC25, p. 9.

17. S–OA, p. 203.

18. SSY 1958, p. 103.

19. S–OA, p. 190.

20. SC25, p. 61.

21. SC25, p. 55.

22. J. H. Jasberg served as the first business manager (1896–1908), and was followed by Fabian Tolonen (1908–1913), Pastor S. Ilmonen (1913–1916), and Antti Lepisto (1917–1919). The position was then incorporated for a time with the president's office.

23. SC25, pp. 58f.

24. Pastor K. L. Tolonen at the cornerstone laying of Old Main, see S–OA, p. 136.

25. S–OA, pp. 93f.

26. SC50, p. 22.

27. Miss Lydia Kangas and Victor Koivumaki; the latter had completed the seminary course but was underage to be ordained.

28. See note 15.

29. S–OA, p. 68.

30. See SC25 for a lengthy discussion of the early societies of the college, pp. 82–97. Apropos, the Finnish *Konventti* outlined the English *Philomathic* society (although, of course, little Finnish is heard anymore in the *Konventti* meetings).

31. See the article "kielikysymyksemme" (Our Language Problem) by Pastor V. Rautanen in KT, pp. 220–226. He writes about the situation in the church: "There seems to be two opinions concerning the use of Finnish in the congregations. The one group would want to retain it as long as possible and tries to have the young people taught Finnish, wanting to get more teachers and support from Finland itself. The other group, knowing that there is no future for Finnish here, would want to change as rapidly as possible to the use of English; to this group belong above all the clergymen born in America and other young people, whose sense of nationality is weak and who have no ties with Finland. . . . In the church conventions these groups have already collided" (pp. 223f).

32. See the article "Pioneer Laymen of the Suomi Synod," pp. 64–67 in SC50.
33. A committee appointed to study the possibility of a four-year college suggested the establishment of the two-year college, SC50, p. 18.
34. Pastor Edward J. Isaac lists these reasons, SC50, pp. 18f.
35. The first was the present Nikander Hall, the second the small frame structure built in 1901.
36. The former was Dr. Hillila, the latter Dr. Viljo Nikander.
37. Pastor John Wargelin served as principal of the Mountain Iron, Minnesota high school 1927–1930 and for a time as County Commissioner of Schools in Houghton County, Michigan.
38. See SSH, pp. 222f.
39. See SC50, pp. 23f.
40. See Rautanen's article on the language problem, KT, pp. 220–226.
41. See SSH, pp. 212f.
42. These resolutions were proposed by the Ohio–Pennsylvania Conference (later considered more "progressive" than the conservative Michigan and Minnesota Conferences) and approved by the Church Convention.
43. Pastor (later licentiate of theology) Ilmari Tammisto (1930–1936), Pastor (later Ph.D. and Th.D.) Uuras Saanivaara (1939–1954), Dr. Armas Holmio (1947–1958), Pastor (later Th.D.) Olaus Brannstrom of Sweden (1956–1957).
44. Pastor Isaac in SC50, p. 18.
45. A description of the "great campaign" is found in SSH, pp. 213–219.
46. Pastor Isaac in SC50, p. 20.
47. Pastor Ilmari Tammisto and six other pastors of the Synod were the first lecturers; other chief lecturers through the years have been: Dr. Conrad Bergendoff (1939), Dr. Bernhard Christensen (1946), Dr. Eric Wahlstrom (1947), Dr. C. Umhau Wolf (1948), Dr. Jaroslav Pelikan and Dr. Arthur Vööbus (1951), Dr. Jerald Brauer and Dr. Conrad Hoyer (1955), and Dr. Arthur C. Piepkorn (1956).
48. Of course, the goal was fifty thousand dollars for the fiftieth anniversary.
49. As secretary of the Consistory and member of the SSCIR, Pastor Tamminen voted against the resolution (that won 6–3) to cast the lot of the Suomi Synod with JCLU and not with JUC (SSY 1957, p. 163).
50. As a member of the SSCIR, Dr. Hillila voted in favor of the resolution mentioned in note 49.
51. See SSY 1952, p. 80.
52. See SSY 1953, p. 102.
53. See SSY 1954, p. 66.
54. See comments of President Isaac in SSY 1953, p. 104 and SSY 1954, p. 66 and comments of Synod President John Wargelin in SSY 1953, pp. 55f.
55. This movement led to the formation of the ALC in 1960 by the members of the JUC with the exception of the LFC, which later joined the ALC.
56. These two church bodies were joined by the American Evangelical Lutheran Church, and the Suomi Synod and the new Lutheran Church in America was formed June 28, 1962 at Detroit, Michigan.
57. See the many reports contained in SSY 1957, pp. 145–164.

58. MCC 1957, No. 67.
59. SC50, p. 18.
60. Note remarks of President Raymond Wargelin in SSY 1962, p. 108.
61. SSY 1956, p. 77.
62. SSY 1960, pp. 96, 98.
63. SSY 1956, p. 80; the lecturers were Miss Ruth Sievanen and Mr. Ville Repo. See also SSY 1957, p. 88.
64. The student congregation, in existence for only one year (1959–60), was not continued when the position of campus pastor fell vacant. In 1965 Pastor E. Olaf Rankinen was called to that position.
65. MCC 1960, No. 48.
66. WUMM 1966, p. 103.
67. SCSS, p. 40.
68. SCSS, p. 106.

FINNISH-AMERICAN CULTURE

Ruth Esther Hillila

❊ THE MUSIC OF FINLAND[1]

Early Finnish Music

Throughout her Christian history, Finland has been included in the domain of western music. As the chants of the Roman Church spread over the lands of the West, they became the mutual property of the various nations and provided the foundation for the later development of European art music. At the same time, the musical consciousness of individual nations was developed and their aesthetic instincts were directed along similar lines. In Finland, as elsewhere, the church chants influenced folk music, and various characteristics of the chant can be found today not only in folk melodies but in both the vocal and instrumental music of most Finnish composers.

The place of honor among Finnish folk music belongs to the rune melodies to which the *Kalevala* poems were sung. This music forms the ancient traditional music of the peoples of Finland and Estonia. The thousands of rune melodies display a few main characteristics in common. Each moves diatoncially and within a narrow range, often within a fifth. Estonian rune melodies usually have four beats to a measure, whereas, five-beat measures are characteristic in Finland. The extra beat is the result of the lengthening of the last two syllables of each measure. The characteristically

129

lengthened and repeated final notes of each measure of the rune melodies
have penetrated both later folk songs and Finnish art music to the extent
that the device can be considered one of the national musical traits.

At least as old as the runes is the Finnish national instrument, the
kantele, which was used to accompany these melodies. A small "harp,"
held horizontally and plucked with the fingers, the *kantele* possesses a
delicate, lyrical tone, appropriate to a sensitive portrayal of loneliness and
sadness. In its simple, original form it had five strings which were dia-
tonically tuned, corresponding fully with the nature of the rune melodies.
However, more elaborate versions for concert performance have been developed over the years. Because of the *kantele*'s prominent place in the
Kalevala, it has become the national instrument and the symbol, not only
of Finnish music, but of all Finnish culture.

The music of the past is not the only factor in the foundation of
Finland's national music. More important is the entire world of ideas contained in ancient Finnish poetry. When Elias Lönnrot collected and published the *Kalevala,* he revealed the rich spiritual world of Finland's forefathers, a source which has continued to nourish the entire culture of the
nation. Finland's literature and arts experienced an abundant flowering at
the turn of the last century. To be sure, this flowering was not solely the
result of the *Kalevala* tradition; it also received powerful impulses from
international artistic currents. But their unique character, their peculiar
spiritual content, and artistic means of expression are not conceivable without the fruitful soil of antiquity which the *Kalevala* gave to Finland's artists.

In addition to the content of the *Kalevala,* the revival of the Finnish
language itself inspired much of the cultural awakening. And music, particularly the art song, was to receive her share of the inspiration. Just as folk
music and rune-singing throve among the people earlier because it was
based on the vernacular, Finland's art song and music in general could
not blossom until the end of the nineteenth century when Finnish prose and
poetry were in a position to cooperate with it as a result of their cultivation
by the upper classes.

For a long time, Finland took little part in the general development
of European music. The spread of polyphony, larger musical forms, and
purely secular music to the northern European countries came relatively
late, and to Finland, last of all. For some time after the Middle Ages, the
practice of cultivated music in Finland was limited largely to singing in
unison in church and in the church-connected school. There was, however,
some original composition. For instance, some songs in honor of St. Henry
were composed in the Turku diocese around the end of the thirteenth and

the beginning of the fourteenth centuries. One hymn to St. Henry, *Ramus Virens Olivarum,* is sometimes referred to as the Finnish national anthem of the Middle Ages.

Secular music did not flourish in Finland at this time as it did elsewhere, principally because Finland lacked the active court life which supported and encouraged the arts in other countries. Except for records of a small orchestra in the court of John, Duke of Finland, at the Castle of Turku from 1556 until 1563, not much is known about the cultivation of secular music, other than that the various festivals included singers and players of instruments. It is known that the city of Turku as early as the 1600's employed professional trumpet players.

The year 1600, considered an important demarcation point in music history in general, also marks the beginning of a new era in Finnish music. Not only is there more musical activity, but more is known about it; and the founding of the University of Turku in 1640 was the decisive step in establishing the systematic cultivation of music as an art form. Music played an important part in the curriculum of the university, both in theory and practice, and extant academic theses reveal an interest in music research. For more than one hundred and fifty years, the university was the center of musical as well as other learning in Finland.

Eighteenth-century Composers

Johan Helmich Roman (1694–1758), the first great Nordic composer of Finnish origin, was a descendant of Johannes Raumannus, who was born in 1570, in Rauma, Finland, and became a professor at Uppsala in 1598, and later a pastor in Stockholm. Roman studied in London under Ariosti and Pepusch, and knew Handel. When he returned to Stockholm, he became director of court music. Roman is known as the "father of Swedish music," but he remembered the land of his ancestry by donating a valuable collection of musical scores to the University of Turku in 1749.

In 1799, Guiseppe Acerbi, an Italian traveler, writer, and musician, went to Finland. In his book, *Travels Through Sweden, Finland, and Lapland to the North-Cape in the Years 1798 and 1799,* he tells of his musical experiences, especially in Oulu, in northern Finland, where he played clarinet in a quartet which gave a performance every evening for a period of several weeks. Acerbi tells of including, among the usual quartet repertory, an arrangement of a Finnish rune melody, and he relates how moved the Finns were when they heard some of their own music performed. He also describes the *kantele* as being tuned a-b-c'-d'-e'. A result of Acerbi's trip was the first formal instrumental composition using a Finnish folk melody. In a quartet of three movements, Acerbi uses as the main theme in the andante movement a rune melody marked "Runa Finnoise."

In the latter part of the eighteenth century, the newly established custom of public concerts spread to Finland; at the same time, the national cultural awakening headed by Gabriel Porthan gave impetus to the development of inherently Finnish music. First, the Aurora Society, which Porthan founded, and later the Turku Society of Music (*Turun Soitannollinen Seura*), established in 1790, furthered interest in orchestral and chamber music. The Society sponsored private recitals and public concerts of works by Haydn, Mozart, and Beethoven were performed; the Society's music library boasted the scores of over two thousand different works. For some time, Turku remained Finland's musical center. Helsinki went unnoticed until after she became the capital.

During this period, the first Finnish composers of art music emerged. It may be said, therefore, that the history of Finnish music as an art form, considered in its narrow sense, begins at the end of the eighteenth century.

The first significant figure in Finnish creative music is Erik Tulindberg (1761–1814), a public official who practiced music as a hobby. His extant compositions (discovered after one hundred and fifty years) include six string quartets and a violin concerto. Tulindberg was also one of the first to take an interest in Finnish folk music. It was he who supplied information on rune-singing to Bishop Jaakko Tengström, who published, in 1802, a study on early Finnish life including music. Published by the Turku Academy, it was the earliest printed account of Finnish folk music.

Thomas Byström (1772–1839), although he followed a military career, was a composer as well as a performer on the viola, piano, and organ, and taught organ and piano at the Stockholm Music Academy. The brothers, Carl Ludvig Lithander (1773–1843) and Fredrik Ammanuel Lithander (1777–1823), were music teachers, performers, and composers. The latter belonged to the Board of Directors of the Turku Musical Society from 1798 until 1801, part of which time he also served as their librarian.

The talent of Bernhard Henrik Crusell, "The Mozart of the North" (1775–1838), was first discovered through the Suomenlinna Fortress in Helsinki, where he played clarinet in the military band. In 1791, he went to Sweden to continue his studies and later to Paris where he studied with Gossec. In the years that followed, he was to return to Finland only for concert appearances. His last tribute to his fatherland was a set of three solo songs composed to words by Runeberg. Crusell received international recognition as a composer of many forms: an opera, choral music, concertos, chamber music, and songs. An outstanding clarinet virtuoso, he also translated opera librettos into Swedish. It is likely that had Crusell lived in a more centrally located country than Sweden, his name would have been left among the immortals.

The Transition Period

The years between 1835 and 1882, which witnessed the birth of the art song, can be considered a period of transition in Finnish music. Finland was not to have the facilities and faculties for training musicians for several more decades. Therefore, those who had talent and desired training in music for a profession, as Crusell did, turned to Sweden and other countries, where they usually remained.

Most of the professional musicians practicing in Finland were foreigners, and most of the native-born composers practiced music as an avocation. Lacking the proper training, they were limited to working with smaller forms, especially the song. Even later in this period, those few who received musical training abroad, upon their return to Finland, became occupied in other full-time careers, with music remaining more or less a hobby.

A significant step was taken during this time in the development of the solo song. Thus far, only Swedish had been used, but by the end of the era, the first Finnish poems were being set to music. However, the practice did not become general until the time of Sibelius and Merikanto.

During these years, the groundwork for the future was laid in several ways: more significant music was being made available to the public through performances, more and more participants were needed to produce oratorios and operas, there was an increase in amateur interest in music in the homes, and the impact of the *Kalevala* initiated the long line of compositions based on folk-epic materials.

The promising stirrings in Finland's indigenous art music, prodded by the best available talent from abroad, ultimately resulted in a full awakening at the end of the century. Each new development, no matter how small, furthered progress, finally making not only possible but also inevitable the decisive events of the 1880's.

The greatest name of this period is undoubtedly that of the German, Fredrik Pacius (1809–1891). A native of Hamburg and a member of the chamber orchestra of the Swedish court in Stockholm, he was appointed music teacher at the University of Helsinki and remained in Finland to mold her musical future. He arrived in 1835, making his debut with the first appearance of the *Kalevala.* This centuries-old folk material and the newly arrived foreign musician were to effect a miraculous change in the music of Finland during the remainder of the century, with Pacius earning for himself the title of "father of Finnish music." (It is his tune that has become the accepted setting of the national anthem, "Our Land," to the text by Runeberg.) Pacius' significance in Finland can be best expressed in the words of Jean Sibelius to Pacius' grand-daughter, "All that we musicians are now doing here, is built upon the life work of Fredrik Pacius."

Pacius brought with him a Mendelssohn-Spohr variety of gentle German romanticism. This German influence on Finnish music was a necessity rather than a danger. Pacius had to create a musical audience and an interest in great music before truly indigenous Finnish music could develop. Helsinki became a musical center, and he helped create the atmosphere that could inspire and support the cultivation of music in the future.

Pacius' compositions include three operas (*The Hung of King Charles,* performed in 1852, was the first opera composed in Finland), a violin concerto, part of a symphony, overtures, cantatas, and various smaller vocal works. Pacius' best-known songs are "Finland's Song" and "The Soldier Boy." The former played a part comparable to that of Sibelius' tone poem, *Finlandia,* several decades later, in helping the nation live through difficult times.

Finland's "Berliner Schule": Ehrström, Ingelius, and Collan

When Pacius arrived in Finland, the dominant local musical figure was Fredrik August Ehrström (1801–1850), who must be considered the actual pioneer in Finnish art song. Somewhat younger than Ehrström, but belonging to the same stylistic school, were Axel Gabriel Ingelius (1822–1868) and Karl Collan (1828–1871). Their songs were romantically motivated, as was the music of Pacius, and in that sense they are products of their time. However, whereas Pacius belonged to another class as far as technique was concerned, the others were typical native composers whose limited technical facilities related their style to the pre-Schubert song of the *Berliner Schule* composers. Compared with the contemporary German masters of the Lied, these composers in Finland, Pacius included, were, without a doubt, old-fashioned.

Ehrström was known as Finland's "first composer" even before a single song was published, because many of them had been spread around the country in manuscript. The simplicity and melodiousness of his settings, especially of texts by Runeberg, mark the beginning of Finnish lyric song in the last century. Ehrström's best-known songs are "The Swan" and "The Spring."

Ingelius was something of an exception for his time in that he attempted to compose in larger forms, including operas and Finland's first symphony. His symphony's third movement, *Scherzo finnico*, is in 5/4 metre, undoubtedly having been suggested by the rhythm of Finnish epic poetry, and probably the first evidence of nationalism in Finnish orchestral music. Ingelius was an outspoken music critic who did not hesitate to criticize either his teacher Pacius or his teacher Spohr. However, in spite of his critical attitude, he had great faith in the future of the music of Finland.

The third and the most notable member of Finland's *Berliner Schule*, Karl Collan, was a philologist and librarian at Helsinki University. Collan was one of the first Finnish methodical researchers in Finnish folk music, which he sometimes borrowed for his own compositions. He was also the first of the Finnish composers who tried to comply in his art with the exhortation of the national poem, "Listen to the fir tree's sighing, at whose root thy home is founded," and the popularity of his songs lies to a great extent in their faithful reflection of the national temperament. Unfortunately, Collan had been married to Pacius' daughter, Maria, for only a few years, when death cut short his brilliant career.

Foreign-trained Finnish Composers: Von Schantz, Linsen, and Fabritius

The musical life of the country was developing. The change was apparent not only in the increasing number of performances by internationally famous concert artists and in the constantly expanding repertory performed by local individuals and groups, but also in that the names of Finnish composers were now beginning to appear with those from other countries. Music in Finland had reached the stage where the country recognized it as its own and felt obligated to give it its support. In the 1850's, a group of young composers was sent to study at the Leipzig Conservatory; the stipends were from public funds and were awarded for the express purpose of strengthening future native musical endeavors.

In spite of his short life, Johan Filip von Schantz (1835–1865), one of the most gifted and best-trained of the nineteenth-century Finnish composers, had a lasting impact on the music of Finland. Although he became known, as did his contemporaries, chiefly as a composer of songs, he also produced the first large-scale orchestral work based on the *Kalevala*. His overture *Kullervo* (first performed in 1860 at the dedication of the new theater in Helsinki) later inspired Kajanus; and Sibelius based his first great symphonic effort on the same tragic legendary hero, thereby laying the cornerstone of modern Finnish music.

Schantz's overture along with his other works indicates that Finnish music was beginning to set more demanding goals for itself. In the new, nationally awakening Finland of the last century, Schantz was the first native-born composer that could be considered a professional. (He was an orchestral conductor.) Even in his training, he was in a different class from Ehrström, Ingelius, or Collan, and his music shows a more professional touch.

When Selim Gabriel Linsen (1838–1914) returned to Finland after his studies in Leipzig, he taught music. Among his students was Martin Wegelius who was to become one of the most significant names in Finnish music. Linsen composed mostly vocal music, and his fame rests on one song, a setting of Topelius' poem, *Jag gungar i högsta grenen* ("A Summer Day at Kangasala"). Heikki Klemetti says that this song crystallizes much of Finland's cultural history, feeling for nature, and the Finn's love for his country.

Up to this time, it is difficult to isolate any specifically Finnish traits in the music of the solo songs. This may be because the settings were of Swedish texts, and the characteristic rhythms of Finnish folk melodies (especially of the runes) and of the language itself were unable to make an impact on the music. It was only after the *Kalevala* became widely known and the Finnish language was used as a vehicle of expression, especially in the art song, that the music developed an indefinable, intangible, but nevertheless real "Finnish feeling."

Fredrik Fabritius (1842–1899), the third member of the group that studied in Leipzig in the 1850's, was the first composer to set Finnish texts (by Suinio) to music. A concert violinist for a time, his compositions include a violin concerto. However, he became disenchanted with a concert career, went into journalism, and then agriculture. He eventually published a handbook on the care of horses.

After Pacius' arrival, the music of Finland, which had heretofore been connected mainly with that of Sweden, was more strongly influenced by German music. Pacius' successor as instructor of music at the university in Helsinki was Richard Freidrich Faltin (1835–1918), also a German, who had studied at the Leipzig Conservatory. Faltin is more important as a leader than as a composer. His creative work was submerged in an active public musical life. Besides his duties as a teacher at the university, he was an organist at what is now Helsinki Cathedral, and for a time conducted the theatre orchestra. Thus he was in a position to continue the perform-ances of large-scale works as begun by Pacius. Faltin initiated the tradition of Bach performances by first conducting the *St. Matthew Passion.*

By the time Pacius and Faltin had laid the groundwork for a native art, Helsinki had become an active musical center and Finland awaited the developments which would make her musically "of age." Three things were necessary: first, a school in Finland to provide musical training so that students would not have to go abroad; second, a full-time, permanent symphony orchestra to maintain, without interruption, a symphonic tradi-tion; third, works by native composers worthy of performance with inter-national masterpieces. The three men qualified to undertake each of these tasks, respectively, were Martin Wegelius, Robert Kajanus, and Jean Sibelius.

1882—The Turning Point: Kajanus and Wegelius

The year 1882 is one of the most significant dates in the history of Finnish music. It marks the end of the developmental period and the beginning of a new era. In that year were founded the Helsinki Institute of Music (also known later as the Helsinki Conservatory and Sibelius Academy) and the symphony orchestra, designated since 1914 as the Helsinki City Orchestra. They were absolutely necessary for a continuing cultivation of music in the country; that they were established in the same year seemed to emphasize the initiation of a new era. At the same time, two new leaders appeared on the scene. Martin Wegelius and Robert Kajanus, both native Finns, again stressed the advent of a new age. It would no longer be necessary to depend entirely on foreign training and the importing of foreign musicians.

Martin Wegelius (1846–1906) made his impact on the music of Finland more as a teacher than as a composer. His distinguished director-ship of the Music Institute and, particularly, his position as the educator of the rising generation of Finnish composers brought forth a rich harvest in surroundings where there had previously been no opportunities for such a thorough and far-reaching study of music. Equipped with a Master of Arts degree in the humanities from the University of Helsinki and a com-prehensive training in music at Leipzig Conservatory, Wegelius possessed all the qualifications necessary to provide musical education in Finland.

When necessary, Wegelius wrote his own textbooks and he hired competent teachers such as Busoni from abroad. At first, he taught theory and music history himself; thus, along with their musical training, his stu-dents also received the benefit of Wegelius' vast knowledge of literature, aesthetics, history, and philosophy. He was pedantically exacting and a strict disciplinarian. But he had only one aim, to elevate the musical level of the nation to the point where it would both appreciate and eventually produce the best that music had to offer. In 1902, the Senate awarded Wegelius an annual pension for life, the first such grant made to a Finnish musician.

The great life work of Robert Kajanus (1856–1933) was the creation of a Finnish tradition of symphony concerts and the education of a native concert-going public. In 1882, Kajanus organized the Helsinki Symphony Orchestra, which he conducted for half a century. This organization has the distinction of being the oldest orchestra performing on a permanent, professional basis in Northern Europe.

Kajanus studied in Leipzig, Paris, and Dresden; during his student years, his songs and piano pieces were published by Breitkopf and Härtel. In 1880, in Leipzig, his *Death of Kullervo* (inspired by von Schantz's overture composed two decades earlier) was performed; in 1881, his *First Finnish Rhapsody* was played in Dresden. However, as with Wegelius, Kajanus' total creative output remained more limited than it would otherwise have been because of the demands of his position. As a composer, Kajanus was the forerunner of Sibelius, whose talent and potentialities he recognized early. At Sibelius' first concert of his own works in 1892, Kajanus was aware that a new period was beginning in Finnish music. "I sensed that something great had taken place," he said later.

Kajanus was to become the foremost interpreter of Sibelius' music. He first introduced it to the world outside Finland during the orchestra's tour to the World's Fair in Paris in 1900. The trip had far-reaching political implications and was of great significance to the small country suffering under the Russian yoke. A few years later, when there was a danger of the orchestra's having to cease its activity, Kajanus expressed the tremendous significance of music in the life of the people in those trying times: "For when our last constitutional right has been shattered, our culture must remain our last untouched weapon."

As a result of the pioneering work of Wegelius and Kajanus, the musical life of Finland was established sufficiently to take on its greatest task thus far, the responsibility for training Jean Sibelius.

The music of the young Sibelius and the generation of composers that followed received its national stamp mainly from its close connection with Finnish folk melody. Whether following the style of Sibelius or receiving their impressions directly from folk melody, other composers also adopted, among other features, an abundant use of the ecclesiastical modes.

Also, an interest in folk tunes is common to Finnish composers at all times, with the exception of Sibelius who, although he has so obviously fused melodic traits of the rune melodies in his early music, seems to have purposely avoided the use of folk melodies themselves. Finland's younger composers, who have frequently cultivated the newer strata of folk melodies, have appropriated into their work material of a more general, and often of a passing, nature. In any case, there is an undeniable reciprocity between the melodic formation of the art music of the present and that of folk music.

Early twentieth-century Finnish music is also characterized by an abundance of direct impressions from nature. In addition, the music often reflects the particular traits of the Finnish temperament, especially the inclination to a heavy melancholy. At the beginning of the century, these traits, which have not yet disappeared from Finnish music, awakened a warm response in audiences.

Sibelius and Merikanto

Sibelius, the embodiment of Finnish nationalism in music, is so well known, it is unnecessary to go into detail here. He has been referred to often in the foregoing material, but it might be well to add a few more observations. Sibelius was true to the land of his birth throughout his entire life, and his music, especially the early works, always looks to the *Kalevala*. His first great work was the *Kalevala*-based *Kullervo Symphony* for soloists, chorus, and orchestra. Although he did not borrow actual folk music, but received his inspiration directly from nature or literature, Sibelius captured the basic folk feeling in his own style.

Probably no composer has been so well known and loved by the Finns as Oskar Merikanto (1868–1924). There was a time when his name was almost synonymous with song and music. After completing his studies, first in Finland and then in Leipzig and Berlin, Merikanto returned to serve his country's music in many capacities. In addition to composing, he was active as an organist, accompanist, director of the opera, and teacher. Merikanto was a conservative, and his later works especially are deliberate and aesthetically studied. He achieved overwhelming popularity with the people, however, as a result of the spontaneously flowing melodies of his youth, with which he winged the lyrics of the rising generation of Finnish poets. More than anyone else, he converted the masses to a sympathetic attitude toward song as a serious art form. The reason for his success was his use of Finnish texts and the folk-like character of his melodies, which at times cannot be distinguished from folk songs. Veikko Helasvuo has said, "Like the arias of Verdi in Italy and the songs of Stephen Foster in America, the melodies of Merikanto have become the cherished common property of the whole Finnish nation."

Secondary Figures

It would be impossible in such a short account to mention all the composers who made their mark on Finnish music history. The following represent a cross-section of the secondary figures at the turn of the century. The oldest of these, P. J. Hannikainen (1854–1924), produced a great number of simple, patriotic songs, which have enjoyed popularity because of their melodic charm. Many of the texts were by Hannikainen himself. That Hannikainen is sometimes referred to as the Stephen Foster of Finland suggests the general character of his compositions and the part they play in the life of the nation. In the musically eventful year of 1882, he founded the *Ylioppilas Laulajat* (University Singers) Male Chorus, still one of the outstanding performing groups of Finland. Hannikainen was also a music and drama critic and established the first Finnish music periodical, *Säveleitä* (Melodies), in 1887.

The widely performed solo songs of Otto Kotilainen (1868–1936) have many similarities with those of Oskar Merikanto. Although he also wrote orchestral music and large choral works, Kotilainen has always been best known for his melodious, unassuming songs. Wegelius and Sibelius were Kotilainen's teachers, and he himself eventually became a teacher of music in both the public schools and the Conservatory.

Axel von Kothen (1871–1927) was the only Finnish composer who was also a concert singer. Von Kothen's music, which includes over one hundred solo and choral compositions, reveals a decided intellectual approach and shows great thoroughness and workmanship. The songs from von Kothen's late period are his best known, most deeply inspired, and stylistically perfect.

Although the brilliantly promising career of Ernst Mielck (1877–1899) was cut short by an early death, his works had already attracted considerable attention, and his unusual talent as a composer of songs was evident from his early teens. From the age of thirteen, he studied in Berlin with Max Bruch. Adolf Heilborn wrote in the *Berliner Zeitung* of one of Mielck's songs: "The song Fischermädchen seems to speak of a premonition of death, and contains the kind of warmth and devotion found in Schubert's most beautiful songs."

Heino Kaski (1885–1957) "is one of those creative artists in whose works planning and design occupy the background while the melody flows forth as if out of spontaneous inspiration." Kaski's songs number about one hundred, and are, for the most part, simple, sensitive interpretations of their texts.

The songs of Lauri Ikonen (b. 1888) have always been warmly received. Although he studied in Berlin and Paris, he writes in a distinctly Finnish style, refusing more than most other Finnish composers of his age to be swayed by foreign influences. Although he has composed several symphonies, concertos, and other large works, Ikonen is basically a lyricist who composes in a traditional style which has its roots in Finnish soil.

Important Background Figures

No form of art develops in a vacuum. Art needs inspiring leaders, effective teachers, and dedicated researchers whose combined contributions will flow like tributaries into the country's cultural mainstream. The following figures have had a powerful impact on the music of Finland and on the individuals whose lives they have touched.

Three names which are all strongly connected with church music and the choral tradition are those of Nyberg, Klemetti, and Maasalo.

Mikael Nyberg (1871–1940), a cousin of the musicologist Ilmari Krohn and grandson of the great Z. Topelius, was active in folk music research, as a composer of liturgical music, and as a teacher. Of his approximately one hundred songs for solo voice, many of the texts, both in Swedish and in Finnish, are by Nyberg himself.

Heikki Klemetti (1885–1953), "the grand old man of Finnish choral music," was a composer, writer, pedagogue, critic, historian, choral conductor, and a veritable dictator in matters of Finnish voice production. A majority of the country's population until the last decade was directly or indirectly influenced by Klemetti's unique vocal techniques. His choirs were for a long time among the most noteworthy performing groups in the country.

Armas Maasalo (1885–1960) was an organist and choral conductor whose compositions were mainly sacred. However, he also contributed solo songs, which have won him recognition.

The chief importance of Erik Furuhjelm (b. 1883) lies in his pedagogical activities. Carrying on the tradition of Wegelius, Furuhjelm has trained a large number of Finnish composers, the most important being Leevi Madetoja and Yrjö Kilpinen. Furuhjelm was also the first Finnish biographer of Sibelius.

Ilmari Krohn (1867–1960), Finland's first great musicologist, is known to many outside Finland. He was a man of many talents. One of Krohn's chief distinctions was his extensive work in folk music research, especially in the classification of melodies, a system later used by Bartok. He also wrote extensively on the music of such masters as Bach, Beethoven, Schumann, Wagner, and Sibelius, as well as a four-volume treatise on theory. As a teacher of both theory and music history at the University and Music Institute, Krohn's influence extended to many. A composer of stature, mainly in church music, his works include two oratorios, a biblical opera, and a complete setting of the Psalms, in addition to countless smaller works. In some of his youthful, more lyrical compositions, the influence of Finnish folk music is clearly seen, but more often his works follow strictly personal ideals, strongly colored by his deeply religious outlook.

Three Major Composers: Järnefelt, Palmgren, and Melartin

The major composers of Finland, after Sibelius and Merikanto, are Järnefelt, Palmgren, and Melartin followed by the somewhat younger Kuula and Madetoja, with Kilpinen, who specialized in the art song, in a class by himself.

Closest to Sibelius among Finnish composers both in age and education was his brother-in-law, Armas Järnefelt (1869–1958), who was born in Viipuri. He studied first with Wegelius and Busoni in Helsinki, then with Becker in Berlin and Massenet in Paris. Järnefelt at first held conducting posts in Germany and Finland, but he spent most of his life as Court Conductor of the Royal Opera in Stockholm. Although his work as a performing artist necessarily limited his activities as a composer, Järnefelt nevertheless played an important part in shaping the new music of Finland.

Influenced in his youth by national romanticism and Richard Wagner, Järnefelt produced a number of large works, including festive cantatas and a symphonic poem, Korsholma. His international fame rests, however, on his lyrical pieces, the best known of which are the masterful orchestral miniatures, Praeludium and Berceuse. Of Järnefelt's choral music, the male chorus pieces are outstanding and have a permanent place in the repertory of Finnish choirs. Many of his approximately fifty solo songs are concert favorites.

If Sibelius and Järnefelt are considered representative of modern Finnish music in its earliest, nationalistic form, the output of younger composers, beginning with Melartin and Palmgren, reveals glimpses of the temperament of the different sections of the country. Palmgren represents the more rigid formality of western Finland while Melartin reflects the more light-hearted personality of Karelia.

Selim Palmgren (1878–1951), one of the few Finnish composers besides Sibelius known outside his own country, was a concert pianist, whose most original and outstanding contribution was as a composer of piano literature, including five programmatic concertos. Born in Pori, Palmgren grew up in a musical family where he became acquainted with the music of the romantic period. Palmgren's solo songs reveal his lyrical genius and are marked by his characteristic coloring and expressive melody. Especially in his songs, Palmgren is an optimistic portrayer of nature, and his warm harmonies are appropriately descriptive for such scenes. Other compositions include an opera and choral compositions. His songs for male choruses add to the fine repertory of Sibelius and Järnefelt.

Palmgren's studies included piano (with Busoni, among others) and composition, not only in Finland, but later in Berlin, Weimar, and Italy. His extensive travels included a concert tour of the United States in 1921, after which he taught piano and composition for several years at the Eastman School of Music in Rochester, N.Y. After returning to Finland, Palmgren taught at Helsinki Conservatory.

Palmgren's point of departure was romantic nationalism, but his work reveals many Scandinavian and other European influences. His own individualistic impressionism is one of the outstanding features of his music. According to one observer, if Palmgren's music were to be described by one word, it would be, "elegant."

Erkki Melartin (1875–1937) was one of the most productive and versatile figures in Finnish music. In spite of his unusually large output, Melartin's significance as a composer is secondary to his tremendous influence as a teacher and as the director of the Institute of Music.

Melartin studied in Finland with Wegelius, then in Vienna under Robert Fuchs who also taught Sibelius and Madetoja. A few years after Wegelius' death, Melartin became the head of the school of music, a position which he held for a quarter of a century. As a result of his effective organizational ability, the Institute developed into a full conservatory, measuring up to international standards. As a result, the name was changed, in 1924, to the Helsinki Conservatory. As a teacher, Melartin influenced a whole generation of Finnish musicians.

Born in Kakisalmi, Melartin never cast off the childhood impressions made upon him by folk music. While allowances must be made for individual differences (Melartin was melancholic), the Karelians are the most light-hearted of the Finns, and Melartin reflected the vivacious Karelian temperament. The influence of the folk music of that area was always to remain a basic feature of his work no matter how far afield he occasionally went. Melartin, more than any other Finnish composer, com-

posed in a variety of styles and never really developed one that was truly
his own. Composing with extraordinary speed and ease, he also acquired
a highly developed technique in any style he wished to use. This eclecticism
was both his strength and his weakness.

Melartin was many things: a national romanticist (the opera *Aino*
on a *Kalevala* theme), an exponent of contrapuntal technique (the finale
from the *Fifth Symphony*), an impressionist (lyrical piano pieces such as
Rain), and finally, in his *Sixth Symphony* (*The Four Elements*) and his
Book of *Revelation Sonata,* an expressionist. In spite of this variety, Melartin was basically a lyric composer. This is evidenced, among other things,
by his selection of material for treatment from the *Kalevala*.

The Master of the Finnish Lied: Yrjö Kilpinen

Yrjö Kilpinen (1892–1959), considered by many to be the modern representative of the Schubert tradition, has been described by Walter Legge as
the greatest song composer since Hugo Wolf. Like Wolf, Kilpinen is "a
master of psychological nuance, with an uncanny gift for capturing the
essence of a poem." Moreover, although he also wrote some chamber
music, Kilpinen, like Wolf, worked chiefly with the Lied form. Of the
more than seven hundred songs which he composed, approximately one-
half have been published; only about one-quarter of these are in general
use. Those who do use Kilpinen's songs are invariably artists of the highest
intellectual and vocal caliber.

Kilpinen, born in Helsinki, began his studies at the Helsinki Music
Institute, and then continued them in Vienna under Heuberger and in
Berlin under O. Taubmann and Paul Juon. From the beginning, he de-
voted almost all his time to the composition of songs for solo voice.

Yrjö Kilpinen was a highly individualistic composer, who worked
outside the prevailing trends of his time. Though rooted in tradition, Kilpinen's Lied art is nevertheless distinguishable from the romantic Lieder
of the nineteenth century. Furthermore, while it consciously avoids the
features of national romanticism, its musical language remains Finnish,
with recognizable points of contact with the lyricism of Sibelius and
Madetoja. Compared with earlier Finnish art song, the spiritual basis and
point of departure for his art is, to a great extent, new. Although among
his songs there are some isolated lyrical songs of sentiment (but not senti-
mentality) whose appeal lies mainly in their melodic charm, this type of
song does not provide the clearest manifestation of Kilpinen's art. Instead
his songs must be comprehended as belonging to larger artistic units, and

they are often done complete justice only in their original context, as parts of song cycles. That a large portion of Kilpinen's songs were created as cycles was not accidental. One of the most characteristic features of his creative work is the broad vision and monumental artistic totality. He demanded elbow room, and he found this by occupying himself, not with individual poems, but with the entire lyric world of any given poet. This sense of belonging to a larger whole, to a broader artistic vision, is often evident in Kilpinen's songs even if they do not belong either textually or musically to specific cycles. The individual songs themselves cover a wide stylistic range, from simple, strophic, folk-song-like pieces to "spacious, dramatic, expressionistic Lieder of epic grandeur."

Kilpinen's songs can be divided into three major categories based on the language of the poetic texts: Finnish, Swedish, and German. In interpreting the poetry of his own countrymen, Kilpinen proved himself to be a true tone poet of the North. He has captured in his compositions the echo of the national soul and has discovered those tones which transform the white summer nights into music. Kilpinen's last large work, composed in the late 1940's, was the monumental sixty-four-song setting of the folk poetry of the *Kanteletar*. According to Kim Borg, "These songs are probably the greatest master work of art song in our time, almost completely unknown . . . and often not understood even by the Finns."

Toivo Kuula and Leevi Madetoja

The term *Ostrobothnian* is used to describe both Toivo Kuula, who "brought to Finnish concert music the vehemence and brooding passion of his native South Ostrobothnia," and Madetoja, whose loneliness, melancholy, and elegism reflect his North Ostrobothnian background. These two musicians complement each other in several ways. Kuula's musical language, with its pathos and energy tossing about in the cross-currents of emotion, contrasts with Madetoja's lyricism, which leans toward meditative submission and is seldom released into optimistic eloquence. Both composers were involved in the research at the turn of the century which broadened the picture of Finnish folk music.

Leevi Madetoja was an unusually versatile composer. Equally endowed with a talent for composing both vocal and orchestral music, it is difficult to cite his special field. Madetoja's biographer, Kalervo Tuukkanen, remarks that with the same confidence with which Madetoja created a sensitive and fragile miniature, he also drew expansive musical lines. He adds that Madetoja's lyrical, dramatic, and symphonic gifts are linked together in a harmonic whole. Kuula's native genius is evident mainly in his choral compositions. An untimely death prevented him from proving himself in orchestral works. Both Madetoja and Kuula were decidedly influenced by French Impressionism. Finally, national romanticism is the intuitive as well as conscious basis for the work of both composers. Madetoja, however, represents somewhat different musical values from those of his slightly older contemporary, Kuula. Kuula struggled to find his own musical language, and for this reason there is a considerable difference in style between his early and late works. Madetoja, on the other hand, discovered almost in his very first works his own mode of expression to which he was faithful throughout his lifetime.

Toivo Kuula was born in Vaasa on July 7, 1883. From earliest childhood, he showed an interest in music, participated actively in school musical organizations, and finally discontinued his academic schooling to enter the Music Institute in Helsinki. There he studied with Wegelius and later with Ilmari Krohn and Armas Järnefelt. Kuula's early compositions hint at what was later to become central in his life, the question of death. However, in the meantime, his successes encouraged him to apply himself diligently to his composing which began to show the effects of his broadening horizons and deepening artistic sense. Encouraged by Sibelius and other friends, Kuula applied for and was granted a state stipend for two years study abroad. He went first to Italy, but finding the music of that part of Europe lacking, he went to Paris where he studied orchestration with Marcel Labey, a student of d'Indy. Impressionism was in full bloom, and it influenced Kuula's future work, especially the color of his orchestral compositions. Returning to Finland, he became the conductor of the orchestra in Oulu for a time. Performances of his own works in Helsinki were so successful that the music critic, Evert Katila, claimed in his column that only Sibelius ranked above Kuula.

Not satisfied with successes at home, however, Kuula borrowed money to continue his studies in Berlin, during which time Finland granted him a composition prize and a state grant for educational purposes. Upon his return from Berlin, both Kuula and Madetoja (who had also been studying in Berlin) were appointed assistant conductors of the Helsinki Philharmonic, along with Kajanus, for the 1912–1913 season. Kuula also had several students in composition, among them Yrjö Kilpinen. He continued to compose and conduct orchestral concerts; the latter duties took him as far as St. Petersburg.

In the fall of 1916, Kuula accepted a position as conductor of the Friends of Music Orchestra in Viipuri. His musical successes there were overshadowed by the threat of civil war; in the midst of the political turbulence, Kuula began composing his *Stabat Mater,* his musical testament. While working on this composition, Kuula claimed to have been more "detached" from the earth than ever before in his composing. It is an individualistic creation incorporating a variety of styles from ancient polyphony to impressionism. Kuula was not to finish it, however, and it was carried to completion by Leevi Madetoja.

Kuula had always had the premonition that he would die young, and many of his compositions reflect this feeling not only in their music, but in the composer's choice of texts. In the midst of the May Day celebrations in 1918, soon after the city of Viipuri had been liberated by the White Army and two weeks before the end of the war, Kuula was shot. After suffering acutely, he died on May 18, a few months before his thirty-fifth birthday.

Leevi Madetoja was born in Oulu on February 17, 1887. In his home, as in Kuula's, the songs of the Laestadian religious sect were cultivated. From the age of three, Madetoja's outstanding singing voice attracted attention. On his tenth birthday, he was given a choice between a boat and a *kantele;* he selected the latter.

Although the *kantele* was the only instrument which he learned to play with any facility before graduation from high school, he had already made attempts at composing when he was eight. In spite of the haphazardness of his early musical training, Madetoja was not only qualified to enter the Music Institution in Helsinki, but completed in two years the basic courses that usually require four years of study. After completing his high-school education, Madetoja matriculated at the University in Helsinki where Ilmari Krohn was one of his instructors. At the same time he enrolled at the Music Institute where he studied first with Armas Järnefelt and Erik Furuhjelm, and later with Sibelius. Within four years, he had not only completed his Baccalaureate degree at the university, but had also received his diploma from the Music Institution. In addition to these accomplishments, he presented, in his fourth year, the first concert of his own compositions.

Like Kuula and other composers, Madetoja also collected folk songs and in becoming more familiar with the folk material of his own home area, grew closer than ever to the spirit of his people.

Although Madetoja had a late start in his formal musical training, this was counter-balanced by his mature artistic personality. The first concert of his own works created a sensation. Following this, Madetoja, aided by a state grant, went to Paris to continue his studies. D'Indy, with whom he was to have studied, fell ill, however, and rather than locate another teacher, Madetoja studied by himself. After a brief interim in Finland, he studied in Vienna under Robert Fuchs, Sibelius' former teacher, and then in Berlin. In 1914, Madetoja received his Master's degree; the event was all the more memorable because of the performance of the "promotion" cantata which he had composed for the occasion. That fall he preceded Kuula as conductor of the orchestra in Viipuri for two years. During this time, he composed his first symphony and many smaller works. After the first performance of this symphony, Sibelius congratulated Madetoja, extended his hand, and said, "Let us be brothers."

In 1916, Madetoja returned to Helsinki where he became a teacher of music theory and history at the Music Institute and also music critic for the *Helsingin Sanomat* (Helsinki News). In 1928, he was appointed to the music faculty of the university. Madetoja proved an effective teacher who set high standards for his students and was an inspiration to them. The ensuing years witnessed the creation of two of Madetoja's greatest works, his opera, *Pohjalaisia,* and his *Second Symphony.*

Active in teaching and composing during the middle period of his life, Madetoja achieved economic security. His music was being performed outside Finland. However, reverses of various kinds, including declining health, were to plague him, and the last years of his life were spent in relative quietness. Except for the second opera, *Juha,* few works of significance were produced during the last ten to fifteen years of his life. By the age of forty-three, Madetoja had composed his noteworthy song cycle, *Syksy* (Autumn), to texts by his wife, L. Onerva. It could be considered his farewell to the musical life. Madetoja died on October 6, 1948, leaving uncomposed many large works he had planned.

Contemporary Finnish Music

Music continues to be performed and composed in Finland in ever-increasing quantity and, in most instances, quality. Only brief mention can be made here of contemporary Finnish music.

Dean of present-day Finnish composers is Joonas Kokkonen, a member of the esteemed Academy of Finland and professor of composition at the Sibelius Academy. Other prominent names among the older composers include Uuno Klami (*Kalevala Sarja, Karjalainen Rapsodia*), Aaree Merikanto (orchestral and chamber music), Erik Bergman (Finland's first twelve-tone composer), Einar Englund, and Bengt Johansson (electronic music), Tauno Marttinen (television operas), Einari Marvia (mainly a researcher), Ernst Pingoud (symphonic poems, impressionistic), Tauno Pylkkänen (operas, "The Finnish Puccini"), Väinö Raitio, Sulho Ranta (brought first atonal influence to Finland), Ahti Sonninen (ballet, "Pessi ja Illusia"), and Kalervo Tuukanen (prolific output, biographer of Madetoja.)

The most promising of the younger generation are Heininen, Usko Meriläinen, Einojuhani Rautavaara, Aulis Sallinen, Erkki Salemenhaara, and the controversial figures, Henrik Otto Donner and Kari Rydman. The name of Erkki Ala-Könni of the University of Tampere is significant in folk music research today.

In addition to the City Symphony, Helsinki has had for many years an excellent second orchestra, the Radio Symphony. Both orchestras present weekly concerts. The Cantores Minores Boychoir of the Helsinki Cathedral was founded by Ruth-Esther Hillila (also its first director) in 1953. It became instrumental in redirecting the vocal training, particularly of children, of Finland. Under its present director, Heinz Hofmann, the choir won the 1965 BBC European boychoir competition.

The National Opera, founded during the latter part of the last century, not only has contributed to the cultural scene in Finland, but several of her best singers have become known abroad. Most notable of the recent gifts to the international operatic stage is the Wagnerian soprano, Anita Välkki.

More recent directors of the Sibelius Academy, as the Conservatory is now called, have been Ernst Linko and Taneli Kuusisto, both of whom have also composed. The annual Sibelius Festival was supplemented in 1965, the Sibelius centennial year, by the first international Sibelius Violin Concerto competition. It would be impossible to list all the outstanding performing artists of the country, and the names Aulikki Rautavaara, Väinö Sola, and Kim Borg represent only the long line of singers.

Finnish-American Music

Finnish-American composers, performers, researchers, and teachers, numbering in the hundreds, are all leaving their mark on American musical life to a greater or lesser degree. Perhaps a valuable study can be made of the total picture sometime in the future. Here only three names will be mentioned to represent the past and the on-going contribution of American musicians of Finnish descent.

Martti Nisonen, born in Finland on September 12, 1891, was Finland's direct contribution to the cultural life of the United States. Professor

Nisonen, director of music at Suomi College from 1923 to 1946, was also a composer of symphonies, operas, cantatas, vocal and instrumental solos. Upon his death in 1946, Jean Sibelius wrote: "The notable and significant work done by my fellow countryman, Martti Nisonen, for the good of music, especially for the good of Finnish music, will continue increasingly, even now after his departure, to bear rich fruit."

Vaino Mackey, born in Conneaut, Ohio, in 1901, studied at the Cleveland Institute of Music, was a graduate of Western Reserve University, and received a doctorate in music from the University of Berlin. He studied with Roger Sessions and Ernst Bloch, and with the latter conducted performances of Mackey's *Second Symphony* in Brussels, Paris, and Madrid.

Arthur J. Hill was called in 1946 to carry on the work in music at Suomi College, the first American-born musician to fill the position. He has maintained the high standards of instruction and choral work expected at Suomi College and represents the outstanding sense of dedication of his many colleagues of Finnish descent.

NOTE

1. This article is a condensation of the author's doctoral dissertation, "The Solo Songs of Toivo Kuula and Leevi Madetoja and Their Place in Twentieth Century Finnish Art Song" (Boston University, 1964). Detailed references can be procured either from the original copy at Boston University or from a microfilm copy available at the University of Michigan.

Paul Sjöblom

❦ SIBELIUS IN THE AMERICAN ORCHESTRAL REPERTORY

"WHAT A MAN FOR ALL TIME. . . !" He was "born in Finland on December 8, 1865, and died there on September 20, 1957, only to begin a new life in every orchestral repertory of the world." Such was the high praise accorded Jean Sibelius by the veteran music critic, Louis Biancolli, in the *New York World-Telegram* on November 22, 1965. The occasion was a review of the concert commemorating the one hundredth anniversary of the composer's birth played in Carnegie Hall by the American Symphony Orchestra of Leopold Stokowski under the guest direction of Sibelius' son-in-law, Jussi Jalas.

Although his is by no means a lone voice in the wilderness of the contemporary American musical scene, Mr. Biancolli, nevertheless, displayed uncommon independence in unequivocally proclaiming his faith in the Finnish master's immortality, for Mr. Biancolli must have realized that he was challenging the judgment of some of the most influential arbiters of current taste among the American musical intelligentsia, who tend to take a patronizing attitude, at best, toward Sibelius.

To the dyed-in-the-wool Sibelian, of course, there can be no doubt about the Finnish symphonist's being, like his predecessors, Haydn, Mozart, Beethoven, and Brahms, "a man for all time." And what could be more

151

natural and inevitable than that following his death in 1957, Sibelius should "begin a new life in every orchestral repertory of the world!" The regrettable truth, however, is that this is just not so. Ecstatic response to an inspiring performance of great music is one thing; the facts of life in the musical world may be quite another. Mr. Biancolli's fault, in short, is not that he let himself be carried away into poetic transports by Sibelius. His error lies simply in making effusive statements out of line with *fact*. A coldly realistic look at the musical situation reveals that Sibelius never gained even tentative repertory recognition, either during his long lifetime or after, in a number of countries of substantial cultural standing.

While many critics, musicologists, and conductors in the English-speaking world were hailing Sibelius as the foremost symphonist of his generation—and, indeed, of the early twentieth century—their colleagues in much of continental Europe persisted with near unanimity in viewing him as something of an anachronistic curiosity with little claim to serious artistic consideration. Some European orchestras have considered Sibelius unworthy of even an occasional performance. Meanwhile, ever since the Finnish master's magnificent Kalevalian tone poems were composed in the 1890's, the programs of these orchestras have featured a long succession of composers no longer remembered.

It is doubtful whether the annals of music can produce another composer who has been so wildly eulogized by his protagonists and so utterly rejected by his detractors as Sibelius. So-called histories of music have been published, even in the United States, that make not even passing mention of Sibelius. Authors of such literary miscarriages, by totally ignoring a figure as widely recognized among the giants of music as Sibelius, incriminate themselves as incapable of scholarly detachment.

What, then, can be made of the opposite poles of opinion on Sibelius? On the one hand, there are studies like the one published a few years ago in France under the title of "Sibelius, the World's Worst Composer." The originality often cited as the hallmark of Sibelius' musical style is attributed by the French author to unorthodox procedures resulting from "ignorance, incompetence, and impotence." At the opposite extreme are writers like the English composer-conductor, Constant Lambert, who in a popular book entitled *Music Ho!* declared: "Not only is Sibelius the most important writer since Beethoven, but he may even be described as the only writer since Beethoven who has definitely advanced what, after all, is the most complete formal expression of the human spirit (i.e., the symphony)."

Constant Lambert's controversial book was first published shortly before World War II and then re-published after the war in a paperback edition which brought his challenging views to the attention of a new generation of readers. As a practising musician of established reputation, Lambert could hardly be dismissed as a misguided dilettante. This is unpleasant medicine for the anti-Sibelians to swallow—so, characteristically, they turn their backs on it. The accomplished composer and critic, Virgil Thomson, for instance, once conceded that he was aware of the existence of many sincere Sibelius admirers in the world, although he had "never met one among professionally trained musicians." * It should be pointed out that Mr. Thomson lived for many years as an American expatriate in France, a country notoriously hostile to Sibelius.

Constant Lambert has had plenty of prestigious company, notably among British compatriots. Even before Lambert, Cecil Gray made public his conviction that Sibelius was the greatest symphonist since Beethoven, thereby loosing a storm of musical controversy that has not yet altogether subsided. Gray felt that the influence of Sibelius "can only be salutary and beneficial, for his art is based upon the same fundamental, immutable, and ever-fruitful principles that have inspired the great art of the past and are equally destined to inspire that of the future."

Such pronouncements date to the heyday of the prewar Sibelius vogue; as they were made in English, they had a direct impact on American music lovers. The British remained indefatigable champions of the Finnish master even after the war when his vogue was waning in the United States. Sibelius was chosen as the first contemporary composer to be included in the series "Music of the Masters," edited by the prominent English musicologist, Gerald Abraham, on the ground that he was "by almost general consent in Britain and the United States, one of the greatest masters—many would say 'the greatest' without qualification—of twentieth-century music." David Cherniavsky, who contributed the concluding chapter to the volume, declared that Sibelius had in certain works "risen to supreme heights that transcend all comparisons of greatness." Several years later, on the occasion of Sibelius' ninetieth birthday, Ralph Vaughan Williams—a proved professional musician by any standard—wrote in a newspaper article: "Sibelius remains new, just as Bach or Beethoven remain new, like the great melodies of the church and the 'immortal chants of old.' "

By contrast, most continental European critics remain deaf to the Sibelius idiom. As part of the Finnish Government's officially subsidized celebration of the composer's centennial, the Helsinki City Symphony

* This quotation is re-translated from a Finnish translation.

Orchestra went on tour abroad in 1965, giving Sibelius concerts on both sides of the Iron Curtain. On some occasions, notably in Vienna (which has consistently treated Sibelius with indifference), the audience responded enthusiastically to the performances, and some of the concert reviewers deigned to acknowledge certain elements of creative inspiration and artistic interest in the music. From the Sibelian standpoint, however, even the most generously disposed Viennese critics continued to look for and, inevitably, find the wrong things to admire. The *Arbeiterzeitung* described the *Seventh Symphony* as, in essence, a musical scenic guidebook. *Die Presse* warmly welcomed the Sibelius program as an opportunity to hear a composer who is of "great significance in his own provincial area but scarcely ever is accorded a hearing in the international repertory." The *Volksblatt* depicted Sibelius as primarily a patriot and a painter of tonal landscapes, whom Finland has "not ceased to honor even after his death." The reviews in Amsterdam were similar. *De Volksgrant* did not beat around the bush, however: "Sibelius' music is incapable of warming us up, but leaves us cold and indifferent." The Parisian critics' sarcasm was more subtle, though one concert reviewer made no bones about having suffered through an evening of excruciating boredom.

Such then is the state of Sibelius' affairs in the traditional music capitals of continental Europe. Between 1900, when the Helsinki Orchestra made its first continental tour, and 1966, no appreciable change has taken place in the prevailing negative European attitude. In 1955, in an article published in the *Daily Telegraph* of London, Ralph Vaughan Williams attacked this attitude: "I do not count as civilized those mid-Europeans who ignore Sibelius."

The Sibelian might draw comfort from contemplating the fate at the hands of critics of no less a symphonist than Beethoven. The verdict of one Vienna newspaper regarding Beethoven's *Second* was: "A crass monster, a hideously writhing, wounded dragon that refuses to expire, and though bleeding in the finale, furiously beats about with its tail erect." The London *Harmonican* commented on the *Eroica:* "If this symphony is not abridged, it will soon fall into disuse." Another London reviewer wrote of the *Seventh:* "Altogether it seems to have been intended as a kind of an enigma, we had almost said a hoax." And Philip Hale of Boston, America's most famous critic during the early twentieth century, described Beethoven's *Ninth Symphony:* "Oh, the pages of stupid and hopeless vulgar music! The unspeakable cheapness of the chief tune. . . . Do you believe in the bottom of your heart that if this music had been written by John L. Tarbox, now living in Sandom, New Hampshire, any conductor here or in Europe could be persuaded to put it in rehearsal?" "As for these idiots," as Beethoven referred to the critics in 1801, "one can only let them talk. Their prattling will certainly not make anyone immortal, any more than it will serve to immortalize any of those whom Apollo had destined for it." Sibelius, though apparently more sensitive to critical opinion, nevertheless was similarly contemptuous. He once asked, "Who ever heard of a statue being erected in honor of a critic?"

How can one sensibly reconcile totally divergent views on the same artist or the same work of art? The obvious conclusion in its crude simplicity is that there exist no absolute criteria by which to judge art. All values in the arts must rest more or less on the subjective responses of fallible human beings. Individual opinion—which in most cases is the product of random experience—tends to assert the prerogatives of a court of last appeal.

Viewed from this perspective then, the convinced Sibelian will join Vaughan Williams in condemning the critics of continental Europe as victims of stubborn provincial prejudices and complacencies. Cecil Gray shrewdly analyzed this condition: "In Germany, France, Italy, the national art invariably enjoys preferential treatment. They have all established a kind of spiritual *douane,* a tariff wall through which foreign musical imports are only able to penetrate in the form of mere fashionable curiosities, *articles de luxe,* for the delectation of the snobbish few. In the long run, only German music is freely welcomed in Germany, only French music in France, only Italian music in Italy." The British, on the other hand, Gray argued, have been free-traders, musically as well as economically, which would explain the ready British acceptance of imported music like Sibelius'. Enlightened musical opinion in England, he asserted, "is much more alert and discriminating, and actually, though perhaps not apparently, more advanced even, in the conventional sense of the word, than in any other large European country at the present time."

Sibelius' place on the European scene is closely related to his representation in the American orchestral repertory. For one thing, the symphony orchestra is a European invention; all the great symphonies in any repertory have been written by European composers; Sibelius is a European composer and cannot be understood without a European frame of reference. For another thing, until very recently, all the conductors of major American symphony orchestras were European by birth or at least by training. Moreover, many if not most of the players in the major American symphony orchestras were, until very recently, also European by birth and/or training. The American symphonic and orchestral tradition, in short, is a direct offshoot of the European tradition.

Sibelius' representation in the repertory of any given American orchestra depends to a large, sometimes decisive, extent on where the orchestra's music director received his training. If his training was in the mid-European or the Italian or the French sphere of influence, the conductor is likely to grant Sibelius an occasional performance only under public or critical pressure. Where the English sphere of influence has been dominant, Sibelius is likely to be the conductor's choice in close rivalry with Beethoven, Mozart, and Brahms. Leopold Stokowski is a case in point. In spite of his foreign name and assiduously cultivated foreign accent, he is English both by birth and training. And for many decades, with all sorts and conditions of orchestras, he has been playing Sibelius on a par with the masters of the past.

Eugene Ormandy represents a special case. Born in Hungary, he was an accomplished violinist when he arrived in the United States. Whether or not his Hungarian background contributed an element of sympathy for the Finnish culture is a moot question. The circumstances of his career probably explain his predilection for Sibelius far better. Sibelius' popularity in the United States was rising at the same time Ormandy was making his mark as a conductor. Recognizing that Sibelius was what the public wanted, Ormandy mastered the works of the Finnish composer. By the time he was securely established as music director of the Philadelphia Orchestra, Ormandy had played enough Sibelius to have assimilated the composer's highly personal idiom and grown to revere it. And it is to Eugene Ormandy's credit that his allegiance to Sibelius never wavered during the postwar eclipse of the composer's reputation in America.

Serge Koussevitzky, as a product of the Russian school, is another fascinating case for study. In becoming the most ardent champion of Sibelius among conductors in America, he underwent a metamorphosis of taste and training. As with Ormandy, so with Koussevitzky. A growing familiarity with the scores of Sibelius led to a passionate devotion.

The scores of Sibelius do not yield their secrets easily, but once the work of extracting them has been done, the rewards are abundant. It is not hard to imagine, for example, that in the future Zubin Mehta, the gifted young music director of the Los Angeles Philharmonic Orchestra who is not given to conducting Sibelius, might change his attitude. His resistance to Sibelius has a natural enough explanation. Born in India, he is a product of the Viennese school of conducting, which has never been hospitable to Sibelius. Thus, the traditional prejudices of a particular European cultural milieu were transplanted into American soil.

The musical outlook of American-born conductors is conditioned largely by that of their teachers, which, of course, has till the present, meant sharing in various segments of the European tradition. It is hardly a coincidence that Leonard Bernstein, the music director of the New York Philharmonic Orchestra, was a protégé of Koussevitzky's, rather than of a representative of the French, Italian, or mid-European schools. Thor Johnson, who has a legitimate claim as the first American-born conductor to head a major symphony orchestra, was also a Koussevitzky protégé. As music director of the Cincinnati Symphony Orchestra for several years, Johnson gave his audiences an ample diet of Sibelius' works. His Scandinavian parentage must have also contributed a certain predisposition in Sibelius' favor.

Were there more conductors of Finnish and/or Scandinavian birth or extraction active in America, there would probably be a substantial increase in the number of Sibelius performances. It would, in a sense, mean a shift of weights in the balance of traditions and prejudices brought over from Europe. However, these things do not necessarily happen as a matter of course, for Finnish and Scandinavian artists frequently lack confidence in their native cultural heritage.

At present, there is no Finnish conductor at the head of a major American orchestra. The situation has never been conspicuously better in the past. George Schneevoigt was the music director of the Los Angeles Philharmonic Orchestra for a time in the 1920's. When it suited his purposes, he accepted the title of the "world's foremost Sibelius interpreter," but temperamentally he was poorly qualified to live up to such a role. Schneevoigt was basically a virtuoso, at his best in works designed for a brilliant display of histrionics and instrumental effects. As a Sibelius interpreter, he will probably be remembered mainly for "correcting" the conductor's scores for orchestras with arbitrary markings of his own. A couple of decades later, Tauno Hannikainen gave up his post with the Duluth Orchestra to serve the Chicago Orchestra. Some observers considered the move a mistake because he accepted the job of assistant conductor. "Forevermore," one colleague remarked later, "the American public would think of him as assistant conductor." His subsequent promotion to associate conductor did not add substantially to his prestige. Most recently, Boris Sirpo's conductorial and pedagogical activities in the Pacific Northwest have made only a local impression.

The gates to American concert halls were open wide to Martti Similä after his extraordinarily successful Sibelius memorial concert with members of the New York Philharmonic Orchestra at Carnegie Hall a few years ago, but, unfortunately, he died in his sleep without apparent cause a few weeks later. Simon Parmet had conducted a similar all-Sibelius concert

in New York about a decade before. However, the critics' treatment of him
effectively dashed his hopes of building a career on this side of the Atlantic.
Jussi Jalas has made the most frequent guest appearances of any Finnish
conductor in the United States in recent years, but he has apparently not
been offered a regular post at the head of any American orchestra, possibly
because the critical reception has been mixed.

Closest to Finland by way of nativity among conductors of the first
rank presently active in the United States is the Swede, Sixten Ehrling, who
has made quite a reputation as music director of the Detroit Symphony
Orchestra. In guest appearances the last couple of seasons at the Hollywood Bowl, for instance, he surprised the critics with the strength, depth,
and eloquence of his readings. His interpretation of the Sibelius *First* was
a revelation in terms of his growth in skill and interpretative insights since
an ill-starred stint doing the same work at the Sibelius Festival in Helsinki
several years before. Still relatively young, Ehrling could consolidate some
of the substantial gains made for the Sibelius cause during the centennial
celebrations of 1965. Unfortunately, however, Ehrling is haunted by a fear
that his reputation might become too identified with "Scandinavian" music.
He said as much during a radio interview on the popular "Luncheon at the
Music Center" program featured by a Los Angeles broadcasting station.
Ehrling, who owes his breakthrough on the international stage to Sibelius,
via recordings of all seven Sibelius symphonies for an American company,
emphasized his desire to project an image not as a Scandinavian but as a
cosmopolitan artist.

This attitude probably explains Ehrling's failure to fill a conspicu-
ous gap in the program-making of the Los Angeles Philharmonic Orchestra.
The gap was the absence of a single performance of a work by Denmark's
distinguished symphonist Carl Nielsen during the centennial of his birth,
which coincided with that of Sibelius'. Indeed, the records of the Los
Angeles Philharmonic covering its entire history show only one Nielsen
performance—the *Masquerade* overture, played when the Royal Danish
Ballet appeared at the Hollywood Bowl some years ago. On the Bowl
program in the summer of 1965 that gave top billing to the Sibelius *First
Symphony* by way of a centennial tribute, Ehrling offered, to begin with,
an agreeable musical trifle by Kabalevsky. From a strictly musical standpoint, Nielsen would probably be rated by many competent analysts considerably above Kabalevsky. From an enlightened pan-Scandinavian standpoint, the substitution of Nielsen for Kabalevsky would have been a splendid
gesture.

It is conceivable that were Ehrling English or Australian, or Chinese for that matter, it might not have been hard to persuade him to pay tribute to both Sibelius and Nielsen on the same program. That is precisely what Leonard Bernstein did on opening the 1965–66 season of the New York Philharmonic Orchestra. In fact, Bernstein's opening program included music by no other composers than Sibelius and Nielsen.

Ehrling did play Sibelius at the Bowl. And, to his great credit, he played the same *First Symphony* at Tanglewood in the summer of 1966. However, his allergy to his Scandinavian identity could minimize the role in which he has been cast as a specially equipped interpreter of Sibelius. This would be unfortunate considering the rare communicative power of his performance in Hollywood. It is doubtful whether any other conductor presently active in the United States, with the exception of Sir John Barbirolli, could make every bar of Sibelius' romantic *Nordic First Symphony* speak with an equally true accent. If Ehrling's grasp of the other six symphonies of the Finnish master is equally sure, then he would be ready to don Koussevitzky's mantle, if he wished to do so.

The projection of a "cosmopolitan" image has also been the aim of certain Finnish conductors. The late George Schneevoigt, for example, had himself billed as a "Swedish" conductor in Vienna. In the English-speaking world, on the other hand, where being a compatriot of Sibelius' is no handicap and possibly an asset, Schneevoigt did not hesitate to capitalize on his Finnish background. Tauno Hannikainen, during his tenure as assistant and associate conductor of the Chicago Symphony Orchestra, made known to press interviewers his wish to be regarded not as a *Finnish* Sibelius specialist but as an *international* artist with a diversified repertory. To give Hannikainen his due, he did keep Sibelius high on his priority list of composers (along with Heikki Suolahti, a promising Finnish symphonist who died at the age of sixteen). Then there is the case of Jussi Jalas, chief conductor of the National Opera of Finland, who time and again has vented his frustration over being trapped in the vicious circle of publicity as Sibelius' son-in-law. It has been Jalas' aspiration to make his mark not as his father-in-law's anointed apostle but as a self-sufficient artist commanding a broad international repertory of concert and operatic scores.

New pro-Sibelius blood is urgently needed in the American conductoral ranks. Stokowski, for all his miraculous vigor, cannot be very far from retirement. Koussevitzky, of course, is gone. Ormandy has graduated to the lofty eminence of what might diplomatically be called an elder statesman among musicians.

Leonard Bernstein's suddenly re-awakened interest in Sibelius is most encouraging. His readings of some of the symphonies and other works during the 1965–66 season proved, however, overly facile and lacking in depth of insight. His recording of the *Fifth Symphony,* on the other hand, is like an echo of Koussevitzky. Sir John Barbirolli's return to the American scene also bodes well for Sibelius' future in this country. However, Sir John's duties are largely confined to Texas. Barbirolli rates among the several able British conductors who have the mature grasp of the Sibelius idiom that one would heartily wish on the well-meaning American conductors whose interest in the Finnish master has been kindled.

There is little hope of a change of heart among most of the European conductors of established reputation currently in charge of American orchestras. Leinsdorf in Boston, Krips in San Francisco, Abramavel in Salt Lake City, Martinon in Chicago, for example, paid only token tribute, if that, to Sibelius on his centennial. The performance of but a single work or two—in many cases not even a symphony—during the 1965–66 season can scarcely be called doing justice to the memory of a creative genius of Sibelius' stature. Most conductors tend to rest on the laurels they have won with the works they learned as students and as young artists struggling for recognition. In most cases, conductors tackle new or otherwise unfamiliar scores only under special pressures. This is one explanation for the reluctance of established conductors bred in the continental European tradition to expand their repertory. To start performing Sibelius, for them, would be like learning a new language. It is hard work. It is easier to shrug Sibelius off with the specious excuse of temperamental incompatability, as one prominent conductor has done, and keep on merrily soliciting public applause with the old war-horses of the continental repertory.

New vistas occasionally, however, open up to artists who have not shut their eyes or minds. Dr. Leo Arnaud, who arranged the orchestral score for the Academy Award-winning music to the film "Dr. Zhivago," has been performing Sibelius with a vengeance at the head of a couple of community symphony orchestras in the suburban Los Angeles area. A strong contributing factor is his having been commissioned by the Finlandia Foundation (or, to be more precise, its president, Dr. Väinö Hoover) to participate in several events organized to honor the Sibelius centennial. Dr. Arnaud is a Frenchman who received his musical training in France, yet a more ardent Sibelian can hardly be imagined.

The Italian-born violinist and conductor Victor DePinto, who heads a group of semi-professional orchestras in Los Angeles, is another zealous convert to the Sibelian creed. His Metropolitan Symphony Orchestra, which operates in a predominantly Negro neighborhood, is managed by Negroes, and many of the players are Negroes. They gave an all-Sibelius concert to commemorate the composer's centennial. To his great credit, DePinto chose the seldom-heard *Third Symphony*. In studying the Sibelius scores, De-Pinto said, he had gained the impression that there was a greater variety of form and content in Sibelius' seven symphonies than in Beethoven's nine. Be that as it may, the point is that an Italian or French background need not forever keep a musician from recognizing the qualities of originality, beauty, artistic integrity, and nobility of spirit in Sibelius' music.

After all, no less a specialist in the Italian and classical repertories than Arthuro Toscanini was eventually persuaded to try his hand with Sibelius—thanks to the persuasive powers of the critic Olin Downes. Toscanini never displayed a particular flair as a Sibelius interpreter, but he did turn out several performances of *En Saga* and the *Fourth Symphony* that might be described as truly memorable. Charles Munch, the former music director of the Boston Symphony Orchestra, despite his Gallic outlook, has frequently programed the Sibelius *Seventh* in guest appearances around the United States.

The head of the Cleveland Symphony Orchestra, George Szell, is a mid-European conductor who deserves warm commendation for his readings of the most difficult of Sibelius' works, the stark and enigmatic *Fourth Symphony*. Most conductors prefer to sidestep this challenge to their analytic powers and technical skills in favor of less exacting interpretative tasks, such as the *First* and *Second Symphonies*.

Partly for this reason, Sibelius' public image is highly distorted and incomplete. He is usually thought of as the fiery patriot who wrote *Finlandia* and the romantic dreamer who painted the tonal landscapes of the youthful symphonies that have stirred the imaginations of most concert goers and inspired the purple prose of most commentators. The less accessible and greater Sibelius, the Sibelius who has made a distinctive new contribution to symphonic literature, remains for most concert goers and many critics, too, an unknown quantity. Until the opening of the 1966–67 season, the New York Philharmonic Orchestra, for instance, had never played the charming and ingeniously wrought *Sixth Symphony*. Neither had the Los Angeles Philharmonic—nor, indeed, the majority of American symphony orchestras—despite the fact that some dedicated Sibelians would rank it first among the entire seven. The number of performances of Sibelius' symphonies actually seems to be in inverse proportion to their rating by the analysts who know them best.

Some observers have noted that the tide is beginning to turn in Sibelius' favor. In the September 1965 issue of the *Hi Fi/Stereo Review,* Martin Bookspan expressed pleasure over this turn because Sibelius' "heroic and noble style speaks a language that should certainly have meaning for the ages." In the December 1965 issue of the *high fidelity* "magazine for music listeners" (sic), William R. Trotter declared: "At this point in our century, when so much music seems to be written by professionals for the consumption of other professionals, music so much of which is as prickly as a cactus and as cerebral as a UNIVAC, many modern listeners find something enduring, refreshing, and invigorating in the music of Sibelius. It contains the kind of poetry and truth so often lacking in vacuous scores of the type presently flowing from (whisper the black heresy) Stravinsky, who has been playing a practical joke on art for the past thirty years." Ten years before, Ralph Vaughan Williams had championed Sibelius in similar terms, "He never deviated from the strait path that he is truly original and will remain so when the twelve-tone apostles have become mere commonplaces. . . . Sibelius has shown us that the new thought which can be discovered in the old material is inexhaustible."

In the September 1965 issue of *Hi Fi/Stereo Review,* David Hall, now president of Composers Recordings, Inc., wrote:

> The ultimate place of Sibelius and Carl Nielsen in the history of world music hangs at this point . . . on the eventful resolution of some basic problems posed by the communications revolution, which has proceeded at such a dizzying pace since World War II. Not only have its workings created a dominant trend toward a somewhat faceless internationalism in the arts, but there also arises, with increasing frequency, the question as to which works of art— including music—are going to get instant and fashionable exposure worldwide and which are going to be relegated to the archives, there to be experienced only in the form of microfilm, slides, tape recordings, or discs. . . . [For organizations sponsoring live concerts,] the already almost intolerable pressure for a faster turnover in working repertoire will tend to become even greater over the years. Past experience seems to show that the more recently dead an erstwhile major contemporary composer is, the quicker his works will be pushed to one side (a) to make room for the newer livewire novelties by younger composers and (b) to maintain at least a semblance of room for the classical staples dating from before 1880. . . . [The final status of Sibelius] may devolve eventually on the tastes of the individual record buyer rather than on the interest of any institutionalized concert organizations. . . . When [the] time comes, there may arise a renewed and legitimate interest in the

music of Sibelius and Nielsen. It will not be based on a misplaced symphony for a brave and battled little nation or a belatedly recognized master. The music will be revaluated and appreciated for what it is: a part of the meaningful total contribution both to the world music of the past and—hopefully—to a musically creative posterity.

The communications revolution served the Sibelius cause better than well at a juncture when it perhaps counted most. Techniques capable of reproducing the tremendous impact of a symphony orchestra were developed by the recording industry simultaneously with the sudden burgeoning of the vogue for Sibelius' music in America and Great Britain in the early 1930's. In the same decade, the Finnish government subsidized a series of recordings of Sibelius' works in England under the baton of the aged Robert Kajanus. The discs became available on the market just in time to meet the explosive demand created by the crusading articles and lectures of Olin Downes in the United States and the laudatory book on Sibelius by the influential English musicologist, Cecil Gray. It was an amazing coincidence.

More recently, some of the conductors and orchestras that have assiduously avoided Sibelius in concert halls have succumbed to financial inducements and climbed on the Sibelius bandwagon in the recording field. The Vienna Philharmonic, which has otherwise kept the Finnish master under a virtual ban, has made a series of Sibelius recordings directed by the young American conductor, Lorin Maazel. The Berlin Philharmonic, which has also been singularly inhospitable to Sibelius in the concert hall, has evidently found it lucrative to record his music—presumably for the American, British, and Scandinavian markets—under the masterful baton of Herbert von Karajan. Even the Concertgebouw Orchestra of Amsterdam, which could scarcely be pressured to perform any Sibelius score during its guest appearance a few years ago at the Sibelius Festival in Helsinki (insisting on Mendelssohn, instead), has crashed the gates of this market —as has the Prague Philharmonic. A very recent arrival is the Swiss conductor, Ernest Ansermet, a leading exponent of the Stravinskyan school, who has unexpectedly entered the Sibelian fold with commendable recordings of the *Second* and *Fourth Symphonies* and the tone poem *Tapiola*. Unfortunately, however, a large part of the Sibelius output remains either totally unrecorded or out of circulation.

If it were more numerous, wealthier, and more active culturally, the Finnish-American community might make an effective contribution to the incipient revival of the Sibelius vogue. The forces at work could be strengthened and speeded up by various actions: for example, letters to broadcasting stations, orchestra managers, conductors, and newspapers, the purchase of Sibelius discs both for personal enjoyment and as gifts to friends, and systematic attendance at recitals and concerts featuring Sibelius' music. Most Finns are, however, notoriously reticent. As special representative of the Sibelius Centenary Committee of Finland in the U.S., the author had ample opportunity to verify this observation. No matter how urgent, letters addressed to local chapters of the Finlandia Foundation and other Finnish-American organizations repeatedly went unanswered. It was almost impossible to enlist the cooperation of the local Finnish colony in promoting the Sibelius centennial concert at the Hollywood Bowl. (There were, to be fair, some splendid individual exceptions to the rule of indifference.)

The case of the magnificent baritone, Matti Lehtinen, who had been invited to make the trip from Finland to sing at the Hollywood Bowl, is illuminating. At one point, it looked as if his engagement might have to be canceled for lack of funds to pay for his fare. Appeals were addressed to many sources, notably the various local Finnish-American Chambers of Commerce around the country. Not one cent could be raised either in this country or in Finland. (Dr. Hoover was not approached because his financial commitment was already excessive.) The situation was finally saved, however, by a promised donation from a Finnish importer of Finnish woodworking products in New York and a generous concession from the Scandinavian Airlines System.

The Sibelius concert at the Hollywood Bowl gave Arthur Goldberg, music critic emeritus of the *Los Angeles Times,* occasion to take the management of the Los Angeles Philharmonic to task for not having scheduled the complete cycle of Sibelius symphonies. To give the management its due, however, it apparently asked the Czech conductor, Rafael Kubelik, to do an all-Sibelius program in connection with Ruggerio Ricci's appearance at the Bowl as soloist in the Sibelius *Violin Concerto.* But Kubelik, according to an unimpeachable source, had flatly refused. He later fell ill and his substitute, Hans Swarowsky who was hastily summoned from Vienna, found himself obliged to open a Sibelius score for the first time in his long career in accompanying Ricci in the *Violin Concerto.* The performance, incidentally, brought down the house. Ricci was called back to the stage for bows again and again by the cheering audience, which must have given Swarowsky cause to reconsider his estimate of Sibelius' music.

Programming policies are largely the concern of an orchestra's music director; in the case of the Los Angeles Philharmonic, the man in charge wants no part of Sibelius. The new music critic of the *Los Angeles Times,* Martin Bernheimer, found it incumbent on himself to take the matter up with Zubin Mehta. "Why, we wondered," Mr. Bernheimer asked in an interview, "was the Philharmonic ignoring the 100th anniversary of the birth of Sibelius and Carl Nielsen, occasions being currently celebrated with considerable activity by the New York Philharmonic and other organizations all over the world?" Mehta's answer was surprisingly candid and simple, if not wholly satisfying: "The truth of the matter is that I just don't happen to have an affinity for the neo-Romantic composers. I just cannot conduct works that do not move me, and that is the case with Sibelius, Nielsen, Vaughan Williams, et al. This does not mean, however, that I exclude such composers from our repertory. I am happy to say that Charles Munch has agreed to conduct Sibelius' *Seventh Symphony* on February 10 and 11 (3 months after the composer's birth-date)."

The label "neo-Romantic" applied to Sibelius is, of course, silly. On the strength of his last three symphonies, he could just as appropriately be labeled "neo-Classical." The *Fourth Symphony* qualifies Sibelius as a "Modern" or even as an early twentieth-century *avant-garde.* Labels, in other words, mean little or nothing when applied to composers of Sibelius' immense range. As for Mehta's avowed lack of affinity for the neo-Romantics, the programs he chose to conduct himself around the time of Sibelius' birthday included Rachmaninov. The almost aggressive refusal of graduates of the Viennese school to lend Sibelius an ear suggests an instinctive defense mechanism. A provocative line of theorizing is that acceptance of the Sibelian creed of tight concentration of form and material, as exemplified by the composer's mature symphonies, would make it difficult for the Viennese and their disciples to justify the expansiveness and redundancy of their special favorites, notably Bruckner and Mahler.

The musical climate in American cities with orchestras headed by conductors trained in continental Europe is, therefore, less than favorable to the revival of the Sibelius vogue. In the critical and scholarly fields, moreover, opinion is to a considerable extent either indifferent or downright hostile to the Finnish master, largely because of the number of influential American musicians and musicologists conditioned to think along continental European lines.

Forced to leave France during World War II, Virgil Thomson was hired by the *New York Herald-Tribune* as music critic. Gleefully, he challenged his opponent on the rival *New York Times,* Olin Downes, whose authority as arbiter of public taste in the cultural capital of America had been nearly unassailable for the previous decade. Under Downes' aegis, the

Sibelius cult had spread rapidly, thanks no doubt to the public's exposure to the music through recordings and radio broadcasts, media that had just begun to reach artistic standards of reproduction.

In a 1935 radio listeners' poll, Sibelius was voted America's favorite living composer by an overwhelming margin. As intermission commentator for several years for the Sunday New York Philharmonic broadcasts, Olin Downes could claim a good deal of credit for this turn of events. Only a few years before the poll, performances of Sibelius had been rather coolly received by concert audiences. The suddenness of the Finnish composer's breakthrough to popularly recognized greatness introduced the added factor of snob appeal. Present were the thrill of cultural discovery and the gratifying sense of being "in" on a new movement. Jaded palates were refreshed by the "cold spring water" Sibelius had been quoted as offering instead of the highly spiced musical cocktails served by other modern composers. Part of the Sibelius cult of the 1930's consisted of a kind of intellectual return to nature, a reaction to the artificialities of urban civilization.

The situation was tailor-made for an iconoclast with the vigor, will, writing skill, sarcastic wit, and background of Virgil Thomson. Thomson considered Sibelius a "provincial beyond description." The Finn's style reminded him of the music turned out by Hollywood hacks for film soundtracks. (Thomson chose to overlook that some film music may have sounded like Sibelius for the simple reason that the Hollywood hacks borrowed freely from the scores of the Finnish master, as they did from the scores of other masters.) Thomson's antagonism was revealed in such wild assertions as that Sibelius' *Seventh Symphony* was modeled after Tchaikovsky. Thomson found himself riding the crest of a wave of reaction against the Finnish master. Although he was hardly needed to bring about this reaction, Thomson doubtless provided a catalyst. The novelty of discovery had worn off as Sibelius discs made his previously seldom-heard scores readily accessible to record collectors. Familiarity with the Sibelius output was no longer an especially superior achievement; all a person really needed was a pair of ears and the time to listen to records. In short, Sibelius had outlived his value as a status symbol.

Actually, the influence of Thomson, Copland, and other anti-Sibelians would probably have been quickly overcome by the intrinsic values of the Finn's music had it not been for the ironic twist which made the United States a fighting ally of Finland's enemy, the U.S.S.R. At the time Washington decided to support Moscow's war effort, Finland was struggling for survival against the Red Army. Conductors in America, responding to the pressures of patriotic fervor, switched war-horses in their repertory in accordance with switches in the line-up of military powers. The composer of *Finlandia* was banished and replaced by the composer of the *Leningrad Symphony*.

The decisive effect of the changes in American policy toward the Red regime during the war on Sibelius' standing in the repertory has been overlooked by almost all commentators. Yet, the non-musical factors at work in the fluctuations of public taste are far from insignificant. Military and political circumstances have at certain historical junctures, such as the period of World War I, caused a violent revulsion of feeling against, for example, a giant of the stature of Richard Wagner. After Pearl Harbor, even Koussevitzky's ardor for Sibelius seemed to cool and he began to show a special partiality toward Shostakovich.

Olin Downes' loyalty to the Finnish master never faltered, however, in spite of his liberal, slightly left-of-center political leanings (which in the McCarthy era got him in such trouble with the State Department that his passport was invalidated for a trip one summer to Finland to attend the Sibelius Festival). During the war, Downes threw a far-leftist deputation out of his office for asking him to sign a petition designed to pressure the U.S. government to declare war on Finland. The *New York Times* critic's private feelings about Sibelius were even stronger than his public statements. His most laudatory pronouncements were tempered by the realization that his views were vociferously opposed by a formidable segment of the musical intellegentsia. For instance, he qualified some of his laudatory reviews of the first two symphonies by giving grudging lip service to certain supposed technical imperfections in their scoring. And, very much earlier, in 1919, he had tacitly acknowledged his insecurity in a book entitled *The Lure of Music* by including only a couple of short paragraphs on Sibelius, tacked on as a sort of postscript at the end of a whole chapter on Edvard Grieg.

Olin Downes once stated in a private conversation: "The people of Finland idolize Sibelius but even so, they are incapable of realizing his colossal historical importance. In the entire history of music, there are only a handful of men of comparable stature." Downes' immediate reaction to the *Kullervo Symphony,* as played to him on the piano in a private Helsinki home in 1952 from the original manuscript score, was one practically of awe. With Jussi Jalas at the keyboard, it took two afternoons to complete the massive work. After the closing chords, Downes stated: "In later symphonies, Sibelius no doubt made great advances technically, but even Beethoven never scaled greater heights of the spirit than Sibelius did in Kullervo!" Downes never dared, however, commit himself in print to this extent. He did reiterate his pet epithet of Sibelius, "the last of the great heroes of music."

On the walls of Downes' office in the *New York Times,* there were only two pictures: one of Toscanini, the other of Sibelius. "There never will be any other pictures," he once remarked. And he kept his word.

It was Olin Downes who converted Koussevitzky. Before joining the staff of the *New York Times,* Downes had served for many years as a critic in Boston. There he persistently prodded Koussevitzky to play Sibelius. The Russian-Jewish conductor resisted. "Sibelius, ugh!" he would mutter, "he is so cold, so forbidding!" Eventually, however, Koussevitzky agreed to give Sibelius the chance Downes was pleading for. Before long, Koussevitzky underwent a complete change and within a few seasons was performing more Sibelius than any other conductor in America. It was largely due to the services rendered by Downes and Koussevitzky, then, that Sibelius' star rose to its zenith in the United States just before the outbreak of World War II.

Sibelius' star appears to be on the rise again. In the preferential poll of its audiences conducted by the National Symphony Orchestra of Washington, D.C., in the fall of 1964, Sibelius was voted second after Beethoven among the symphonists of all time. It is significant that the poll was held some months before the Sibelius centennial fanfare started. In 1935, it is true, radio listeners gave Sibelius more votes than Beethoven; but what unwary researchers like Harold Johnson have failed to notice is that in the earlier poll, Sibelius was competing among *living* composers. Sibelius' 1964 ranking, therefore, indicated a consolidation of his position in the estimation of American concert goers. Washington cannot, admittedly, be regarded as a cross-section of America; still, the culture-conscious segment of its heterogeneous population should provide a fairly reliable indicator of trends in the country's musical taste.

The Sibelius centennial, powered as it was by the patronage of the presidents of Finland and the United States, might have served as an effective vehicle in breaking down local barriers of resistance such as Los Angeles, San Francisco, Salt Lake City, Chicago, and Boston. The vigorously publicized Sibelius Centennial Concert at the Hollywood Bowl in the fall of 1965 must have projected a vivid Sibelius image to the public in the southern California stronghold of Schönberg and Stravinsky (both of whom established homes there). This event, which drew a larger house than any symphony concert during the regular Hollywood Bowl season, was made possible only by being underwritten by Dr. Väinö Hoover, national president of the Finlandia Foundation.

A plan, endorsed by Dr. Hoover, established a revolving fund to finance a series of all-Sibelius concerts to be held in the major American cities whose orchestras had paid little or no attention to the composer's centennial. Following the impressive Hollywood Bowl event, which had laid down valuable organizational guidelines, another concert was booked for San Francisco around Sibelius' birthday in December 1965. Unlike the Los Angeles Philharmonic, the San Francisco Symphony Orchestra was prepared to participate for the regular fees under its own name. But it proved impossible, either in Finland or from Finnish-American or other interested sources in the United States, to raise the necessary six thousand dollars. The San Francisco concert was canceled and the revolving fund project scrapped.

The potential donors in Finland, notably the government, had evidently become disillusioned by the critical setbacks suffered by the Helsinki City Symphony Orchestra during its costly concert tour of North America. The situation in America is far different. The Sibelius centennial year should have been the starting point of a systematic, long-range campaign to break down the existing barriers to general recognition of Sibelius.

Unfortunately, however, Sibelius is now strictly on his own. The revolving fund project, given much enthusiastic lip service but no material support whatsoever, could have added considerable momentum to a Sibelius revival. There is consolation, at any rate, in the thought that his survival in American orchestral repertories is assured by the persistent devotion of conductors like Stokowski, Ormandy, and Barbirolli and the return to the Sibelian fold of a public idol like Leonard Bernstein.

Thomas A. Sebeok

✳ THE STUDY OF FINNISH IN THE UNITED STATES

TWO OF THE EARLY AIDS to the study of Finnish in the United States may be recommended. The first by Clemens Niemi, *A Finnish Grammar* (Duluth, Minnesota: Finnish Daily Publishing Company, 1917, and several later editions), is no longer very useful. The work was not conceived as a scientific enterprise, and even its pedagogy may be subject to question. On the other hand, there is Severi Alanne's *Finnish-English Dictionary* (Superior, Wisconsin: Työmies Publishing Company, 1919), which is still without a peer in the United States. It is remarkably usable in spite of having been superseded in several respects by Aino Wuolle's excellent little dictionaries (*Finnish-English* and *English-Finnish*) and P. E. Halme's *Finnish-English Dictionary* (Helsinki, 1957).

"Finglish," the name given by Nisonen to the Finnish dialect as spoken in America, received its first public attention from that tireless monitor of American English, H. L. Mencken, in *The American Language* (New York: Alfred A. Knopf, 1936), pp. 675–680.

Selma Siiri Sahlman presents a survey of the entire matter in "The Finnish Language in the United States," *American Speech*, 24 (1949), 14–24. She fails to mention, however, four earlier studies by the political scientist, John Ilmari Kolehmainen: "The Finnicization of English in America," *American Sociological Review*, 2 (1937), 62–67; "The Retreat of Finnish," *ibid.*, 887–889; "Finnish Surnames in America," *American Speech*, 12 (1939), 33–38; and "A Note On Finnish Given Names in America," *The Modern Language Journal*, 24 (1939), 179–180.

"Finglish" still awaits a definitive, full-scale study (perhaps something of the nature of Witold J. Doroszewski's study of Polish as spoken in the United States), although Meri Lehtinen's "An Analysis of a Finnish-English Bilingual Corpus" (Doctoral dissertation, Indiana University, 1966) is a long step in the right direction.

A fascinating special problem, which has often been cited but never actually subjected to research, is the influence on spoken Finnish by the English and Chippewa Indian languages near Sugar Island.

The first American linguist to attack the phenomenon of Finnish as such was John Kepke ("The Finnish Declensional e-Stems," *Language*, 17 [1941], 139–142; see also, "Note on the Finnish Allative-Illative Opposition," *Studies in Linguistics*, 6 [1948], 95–97).

The Second World War accelerated interest in teaching the Finnish language in America. The writer was commissioned to prepare a handbook for teaching Finnish to the armed services which appeared later in a public edition, *Spoken Finnish* (New York: Henry Holt & Company, 1947). The book was accompanied by a phonograph record with the Finnish spoken by the Finnish Ambassador to the United States, K. T. Jutila. Other papers appeared as an adjunct to the author's research in Finnish, several being published abroad as well as in the United States. The latter include "The Imperative in Spoken Finnish," *Language*, 20 (1944), 240–242; and "Finnish Adverbial Nonce Forms," *Word*, 1 (1945), 281–283.

The production of a proposed Finnish-English and English-Finnish dictionary for the armed services was also a consequence of the war. A large group of native Finns performed this work in the Language Division of the War Department under the supervision of John Kepke. Although both dictionaries were completed, the ending of the war prevented their publication. The entire subject matter is still on card file, in a form unfortunately not usable by the general public.

Suomi College, at Hancock, Michigan, was the main center for the study of Finnish before the war. During the war, the Army Specialized Training Program maintained two centers for instruction in Finnish to American soldiers. The first was located at the University of Minnesota; the second, at Indiana University. Miss Kyllikka Järvi, a former assistant in course instruction at the latter institution, described the program at

Indiana in an article for the Finnish illustrated monthly for women, *Eeva*, 12 (1946), 8–9, 22.

After the war, the University of Minnesota discontinued its instruction in Finnish. However, in 1947, Indiana University introduced instruction in Finno-Ugric Studies into its curriculum. Then the only one of its kind in the United States, the program was initially assisted by the Rockefeller Foundation.

Björn Collinder, of the University of Upsala, lectured at Indiana University on the *Kalevala* during 1947–48. At the same time, the writer offered a course in introductory Finnish. In 1948–49, Lauri Posti, of the University of Helsinki, offered a course in intermediate Finnish. Indiana University has also offered related courses: An Introduction to Finno-Ugric Linguistics (Collinder 1947–48, Posti 1948–49, Knut Bergsland, of the University of Oslo, 1949–50), Estonian (Posti), Lapp (Bergsland), Cheremis (Sebeok) and Samoyed (Bergsland). Since 1947, the library of Indiana University has obtained a vast number of the basic documents and materials essential for the study of the Finnish language.

Columbia University (John B. Olli) and Harvard University (the late Julius Mark) have regularly or intermittently offered instruction in Finnish.

The foregoing is a shortened English version of my article, "Suomen kielen harrastus Yhdysvaltoissa," published in the 1950 volume of *Virittäjä* (pp. 337–338). By 1958, Columbia and Indiana Universities were offering Finnish on the graduate level, along with related languages such as Hungarian and Estonian; Georgetown University and Suomi College were offering practical language courses in Finnish. A systematic development of library facilities ensued, especially at Indiana University. The Library of Congress also continued to increase its extensive holdings in Finnish. Indiana University contributed fourteen monographs on Uralic peoples for the Human Relations Area Files, including Eeva Kangasmaa Minn's four-hundred page book on Finland.

Between 1959 and 1963, the American Council of Learned Societies sponsored an extensive program of compilation and research in twenty-six major Uralic and Altaic languages, supported by the United States Office of Education under Title VI of the National Defense Education Act. This program, described by its Director, John Lotz, in the ACLS *Newsletter,* 14 (1963) 1–11, included the following projects concerned with the Finnish language or Finland:

Basic Course in Finnish, by Meri Lehtinen, supervised by Thomas A. Sebeok.

Finnish Tapes, by Elli-Kaija Köngäs.

Finnish Reader and Glossary, by Robert Austerlitz.

Finnish Literary Reader and Notes, by Paavo Ravila.

Finnish Folklore Reader with Glossary, by Elli-Kaija Köngäs.

Finnish Grammar, by Robert Austerlitz.

Finnish Structural Sketch, by Robert T. Harms.

Karelain Survey, by Alo Raun.

The Structure and Development of the Finnish Language, by Lauri Hakulainen.

Finnish Social and Cultural History, by John Wuorinen.

In 1960, Indiana University created a *Uralic and Altaic Series,* under the editorship of Thomas A. Sebeok. Of the seventy volumes published to date, the following deal with the Finnish language or culture:

Vol. I, *American Studies in Uralic Linguistics* (1960), including "Two Nascent Affective Suffixes in Finnish?" by Robert Austerlitz, and "Stress and Juncture in Finnish," by Robert T. Harms.

Vol. III, *The Structure and Development of the Finnish Language* (1961), by Lauri Hakulainen.

Vol. IX, *Latvian and Finnic Linguistic Convergences* (1962), by Valdis J. Zeps.

Vol. XV, *Finnish Reader and Glossary* (1963), by Robert Austerlitz.

Vol. XXVII, *Basic Course in Finnish* (1964), by Meri Lehtinen (supervised and edited by Thomas A. Sebeok).

Vol. XXXIX, *The Finno-Ugric Peoples* (1964), by Toivo Vuorela, including a chapter on the Finns (pp. 16–46).

Vol. XXXXI, *Morphemic and Semantic Analysis of the Word Families: Finnish ETE- and Hungarian EL- 'fore',* by Kálmán Keresztes.

Vol. XXXXII, *Finnish Structural Sketch,* by Robert T. Harms.

Vol. XXXXIV, *Finnish Literary Reader,* by Paavo Ravila.

Sebeok's report on *Hungarian and Finnish Teaching Materials,* available through Xerography from the Micro Photo Division of the Bell & Howell Company, presents further details concerning materials developed for Finnish-language instruction at the Army Language School, the National Security Agency, and the Foreign Service Institute and those used at various U.S. academic institutions over the past decade.

Finnish is among the "critical languages" currently offered at NDEA language and area centers at two sponsoring institutions, Columbia and Indiana Universities (see Donald N. Bigelow and Lyman H. Legters,

NDEA Language and Area Centers: A Report on the First Five Years [Washington, 1964], p. 122). In 1963, with the active cooperation of the Finnish government, Indiana University created a chair in Finnish Studies; the first incumbent, for 1964–66, was Jaako A. Ahokas.

RELIGIOUS LIFE IN THE FINNISH COMMUNITY

Taito A. Kantonen

❋ FINNISH THEOLOGY ON THE AMERICAN SCENE

BEFORE DISCUSSING Finnish theology in America, it is necessary to present a brief survey of the distinctive emphases and outstanding exponents of theology in Finland.

As in other Lutheran lands, theology in Finland in the seventeenth century was marked by orthodoxy and in the eighteenth by the tension between rationalism and pietism. Modern systematic theology finds its first representative in A. F. Granfelt (1815–1892), professor at Helsinki for two decades and author of both a *Christian Dogmatics* and a *Christian Ethics*. With Martensen and Dorner he belonged to the school of "mediating" theologians. He accepted the Bible as the source of divine revelation and the confessions as witnesses to revelation, but rejected orthodox biblicism and mechanical conformity to the confessions. While making the atonement his central theme, he spurned a purely forensic approach and sought to interpret the ethical significance of the atoning death of Christ. Opposed to a pseudopietistic withdrawal from the world, he endeavored to place Christian ethics in the context of cultural life.

The man most influential in shaping Finnish theology at the turn of the century was Gustaf Johansson (1844–1930), Granfelt's successor to the chair of systematic theology at Helsinki, later bishop and archbishop.

177

Johansson introduced into Finland the "Biblical realism" of J. T. Beck of Tuebingen, combining with it his own heritage from the main line of Finnish pietism. On this ground he took a firm stand against the rationalism of Hegel, the emotionalism of Schleiermacher, the moralism of Ritchl, and the syncretistic ecumenism of Söderblom. But as a staunch churchman and biblical scholar, he was also critical of sectarian pietism. An enlightened loyalty to the Scriptures, a direct appeal to conscience, and a vital eschatological perspective characterize this outstanding spokesman of Finnish Christianity.

The leading twentieth-century Finnish theologian was Antti J. Pietilä (1878–1932), professor of systematic theology at Helsinki from 1919 until his death. Influenced by Beck, Wilhelm Herrman, and the Erlangen school, he gave conceptual expression to the vital depths of Finnish piety. His three-volume *Christian Dogmatics* (1930–1932), the most creative work of Finnish theology, combines objective revelation and personal faith into a living synthesis. Well-versed in philosophy and the sciences of religion, he grapples in original and vivid style with the central issues of theology—God and the word, sin and grace, justification and regeneration, eschatology and ethics. He seeks constantly to relate faith and life, convinced that "in the history of theology no bigger mistake has ever been made than when the new life has been separated from faith and justification." Pietilä not only wrote a comprehensive *Christian Social Ethics,* but he was also a fiery prophet of social righteousness.

The influence of Johansson and Pietilä, as well as of Karl Heim, is evident in the theology of Osmo Tiililä, professor of dogmatics at Helsinki for the past quarter of a century. Using his own "theoteletic" method, in which the revealed will of God is the dominant motif, he has written a two-volume *Dogmatics* and numerous other works. His latest interests have been the theology of pietism, eschatology, and a prophetic critique of the institutional church.

During the past three decades, Finnish theologians have participated actively in the new Luther research initiated by Karl Holl. The Finnish pioneer in this field is Eino Sormunen, a professor who soon became bishop. His major work is *The Grace of God,* the second volume of which is a study of Luther's thought on this central theme. His concise *History of Dogma* traces Christian thought from apostolic origins to the Reformation. A prolific writer, Sormunen has not only applied Luther's "simul iustus et peccator" to ethics and religious education, but has entertained a variety of cultural interests, roaming over the fields of world literature, art, and philosophy. Another early participant in Luther research, Yrjö J. E. Alanen (1890–1960), professor of Christian ethics, analyzed the reformer's concept of conscience and wrote an extensive work on the atonement, in which he takes issue with Aulén. Like Sormunen, Alanen extended his investigations into the general area of culture, exploring the spiritual values in both classical and modern literature and their relation to Christianity. Finland's leading Luther scholar today is Lennart Pinomaa, who has concentrated on thorough research in the field and won an international reputation. He has written in both German and Finnish on such themes as Luther's concept of divine wrath, the existential nature of Luther's theology, the incompatibility of the "third use of the law" with Luther's basic thinking, and Luther's doctrine of sanctification. Outstanding among the many younger investigators of Reformation theology is Lauri Haikola, Alanen's successor in the chair of Christian ethics, with his studies of Flacius and of the uses of the law.

As befits "the world's most Lutheran country," the central theme of modern theology in Finland has been the doctrine of salvation. Leading theologians have drawn heavily upon their heritage of the sturdy Finnish pietism manifest in the revival movements of the eighteenth and nineteenth centuries. But while the watchword is living faith, Finnish pietism, by and large, is quite free from subjective sentimentalism and moralistic casuistry. Although it has shared to some extent pietism's general tendency to look with suspicion upon "worldliness," the result has been a quickening of spiritual life within rather than a withdrawal from the church. A wholesome objectivity is provided by reverence for the Word and adherence to the radical Christ-centeredness of Luther's soteriology. The Lutheran confessions are studied seriously even among the common people.

These emphases are reflected in the theological constructs. The Beckian types of "Biblical realism" have been more congenial to the Finnish theologians than the lines of thought initiated by Kant, Schleiermacher, or Kitschl. The influence of Swedish theology has been felt, but strong opposition was aroused by Aulén's conception of theology as an academic science in which neither the church's confessions nor the personal faith of the theologian play an essential part. The Lundensian method of "motive research" has been suspected of endangering the autonomy of theology and reducing it to a general science of religion. Barth's view of theology as a churchly science grounded in objective revelation and his uncompromising Christocentrism, as well as Brunner's "believing-thinking," have struck a more responsive chord. But it is in Luther that Finnish theology has found its principal guide and inspiration. Fidelity to the reformer has kept theology anchored in the Word and occupied with the central issues of evangelical faith. But Luther's own vigorous participation in social and cultural affairs has also been duplicated. From Granfelt to the present day, theologians have not only studied the relations of Christianity and culture, but have also played a prominent role in the corporate life of the nation. It is significant that Alanen, the scholarly professor of ethics and author of *Christian Ethics* and *Christianity and Culture,* was also the moral and spiritual leader of the Social Democratic party. Finland's progressive social legislation is indeed a true test of the dynamism of Lutheran social ethics.

This brief survey of Finnish theology would not be complete without a brief notice of the branches other than systematic theology. Since the Bible has been the center of Finnish theology, it is not surprising that Finland has produced outstanding exegitical scholars. The research of Edward Stenij, Arthur Hjelt, and A. F. Puukko in the Old Testament and Elis Gulin, Rafael Gyllenberg, and Aimo Nikolainen in the New Testament is known far beyond their native land. In the field of church history, the most prominent names are Herman Rabergh, Jaakko Gummerus, Martti Ruuth, Ilmari Salomies, and Aarno Maliniemi. Although much of the research has centered on Finland's own past, Maliniemi's studies in medieval literature and liturgy have won him an international reputation. Mikko Juva, a Finnish church historian, is the present chairman of the theological commission of the Lutheran World Federation. The occupants of the chair of practical theology at Helsinki have provided significant leadership for both the church and the nation. The first incumbent, F. L. Schauman (1810–1877), "the father of Finland's church law," mapped the course of Finnish policy on the relations of church and state. Lauri J. Ingman (1868–1934) not only pioneered in new teaching methods, but also served as minister of education, president of the Parliament, and prime minister, and finally became archbishop. Of similar stature as an educational and political leader was Paavo Virkkunen (1874–1959), who served as parish pastor rather than as university professor. Ingman's successor as archbishop, Erkki Kaila (1867–1944), a theologian and philosopher with wide cultural interests who began his career as an instructor in the University, made a significant contribution to religious education in the public schools. Aleksi Lehtonen (1891–1951), another professor of practical theology who became archbishop, was a leading ecumenist. Least involved in political or ecclesiastical affairs was Aarni Voipio (1891–1964), whose research included psychology of religion, hymnology, and homiletics. The present archbishop, Martti Simojoki, formerly Voipio's assistant in practical theology, is a widely known ecumenical leader and an interpreter of the Christian message.

The first representative of the Church of Finland in America was one of Finland's greatest educators, Uno Cygnaeus (1810–1888), who served from 1840 until 1845 as Lutheran pastor to the Finns, Swedes, and Germans in Alaska. Returning to his homeland, he became the founder of its public school system and teacher-training program, but understandably, he left hardly a trace upon American life.

The first lasting impact of Finnish theology upon America resulted from the work of Juho Kustaa Nikander (1855–1919), the founder and first president of Suomi College and Theological Seminary. Among the varied labors of the patriarch of Finnish Lutheranism in America, theological education had top priority. At first almost single-handed, he devoted himself for over two decades to the task of training pastors for Suomi Synod. His theology bore the stamp of the scholarly biblicism of Gustaf Johansson, and he was well versed in the biblical languages. He taught his students to avoid sectarian preconceptions and to cultivate an attitude of reverent sensitivity to what the Word itself had to say. Chief among his writings is a book on the life and work of Martin Luther. He also wrote a *Bible History* for use in parish education.

Many other Helsinki-trained pastors have taught at Suomi Seminary and helped to maintain the bridge between Helsinki and Hancock. Some of them, including Rafael Hartman, M. I. Kuusi, K. H. Mannerhorpi, and Ilmari Tammisto, returned to continue their ministry in the Church of Finland. Tammisto, an outstanding scholar in theology and philosophy and an expert in religious education, did much to promote a high standard of scholarship. Others, including Alfred Gröning, Isaac Katajamaa, Kaarlo Huotari, John Beck, and Viljami Rautanen, gave courses in the Seminary, but their primary service was as pastors in Suomi Synod parishes. Rautanen's book, *The Finnish Church in America,* is a valuable source of information on church life during the early years of Finnish immigration.

More recently, two Church of Finland clergymen, engaged for many years in training ministers for American churches, have made original contributions to Lutheran theology in America. Uuras Saarnivaara, who returned to Finland after teaching at Suomi during the 1940's and 1950's, has returned to the United States to teach in the newly founded seminary of the Association of Free Lutheran Churches. His career as a teacher in all the main branches of theology is matched by a prolific literary production covering such a variety of subjects as baptism, the Sunday School, absolution, Laestadianism, the Lundensian theology, and the origin of the universe. Saarnivaara's principal contribution to theology has been in Luther research, the subject of his doctoral dissertations at both Chicago and

Helsinki Universities. His book, *Luther Discovers the Gospel,* is an important product of this research. Among his other works are *The Power of the Keys* and *The History of the Apostolic Lutheran Movement in America,* both of which have been published in English. Armas Holmio, who came to the United States in 1930, has taught continuously at Suomi College for the past two decades, principally in history and philosophy. Dean of Suomi Theological Seminary when it merged with Chicago Lutheran Theological Seminary in 1958, Holmio preferred to continue his teaching at Suomi College. Having devoted the early years of his ministry to the Finnish Missionary Society, he has written on the world mission of the church. However, the special field of his theological scholarship is indicated by the titles of his doctoral dissertation at Boston University, *The Lutheran Reformation and the Jews,* and his book, *Martin Luther, Friend or Foe of the Jews?* Holmio's present research is in the cultural history of the Finns in America.

Another clergyman trained at Helsinki and now teaching theology in America is Toivo Harjunpää, professor of church history at Pacific Lutheran Seminary. With a background as parish minister in Finland and in the United States, head of the Finnish Seamen's Mission in London, and secretary to Archbishop Lehtonen, his main academic interest has been historical research. The most recent of his scholarly articles deals with Uno Cygnaeus. He has also studied and taught in the field of liturgics and is one of the leading Lutheran scholars in the theology of worship.

The newest theologian to arrive on the American scene from Finland is Aarne Siirala, professor of systematic theology at Waterloo Lutheran Seminary in Canada since 1963 and a leading representative of the new Finnish Lutheran research. While serving as director of the Parish Institute at Järvenpää, he completed his doctoral studies at Helsinki with a dissertation in German on *The Law of God According to Luther.* He has also made a careful original study of the relations of theology and psychotherapy, the results of which are contained in his book, *The Voice of Illness.*

Alvar Rautalahti (1882–1966), a scholarly pastor and church administrator rather than professional theologian, must also be mentioned. He served parishes in Finland and the United States and was for some years president of Suomi Synod. Throughout his long ministry, he showed an ardent interest in interpreting Finnish theology in America and American Lutheranism in Finland. His writings include *Lutheran Home Mission Work in America.*

Finnish theology in America is represented today not solely by men from Finland, but also by a generation of American theologians of Finnish background. Since the writer of this article is the pioneer in this category, objectivity demands that I give some account of my career as a theologian. Upon graduation from Suomi Seminary and ordination by Suomi Synod at the age of twenty, I continued my studies in philosophy and theology while serving as the pastor of small congregations in Minnesota and Massachusetts. My doctoral dissertation at Boston University was *The Influence of Descartes on Berkeley*. In 1932, I was called from an assistantship in philosophy under E. S. Brightman of Boston University to be L. S. Keyser's successor as professor of systematic theology in Hamma School of Theology, a position which I continue to hold. During my early years, I also taught philosophy and psychology at Wittenberg University. In the transition from philosophy to theology, my thinking has gravitated from personalism to the Kierkegaardian existentialism of one of my former teachers, D. F. Swenson of Minnesota. The theologians to whom I owe most are A. J. Pietilä and Karl Heim, both of whom were my personal friends. Although the influence of such teachers as Whitehead, Hocking, Knudson, and Brightman is ineradicable, I have considered it my mission to communicate in my lectures and writings the little-known riches of Finnish theology. To the hundreds of pastors who have sat in my classroom and now serve American churches, the Finnish theologians reviewed above are not complete strangers. On the other hand, in a series of eight lectures delivered at the University of Helsinki on "Lutheran Theology and American Culture" and published in Finland under the title *Risti ja Tähtilippu* (*The Cross and the Stars and Stripes*) I sought to interpret American thought and life to the Finns. *Resurgences of the Gospel* is one of the first efforts to introduce the new Reformation research to America. *The Message of the Church to the World of Today* has the Second World War as its background. *The Christian Hope* contains the 1954 Knubel-Miller lectures on the Evanston theme, while *Life after Death* is a brief eschatology for laymen. *Theology of Evangelism* and *A Theology for Christian Stewardship* are pioneering attempts to ground the practical work of the church in evangelical theology. Three of my books have been translated into Japanese, two into German, two into Spanish, and one into Portuguese. Of contributions to theological journals, symposia, and encyclopedias in the United States, Germany, and Finland, it may be relevant to mention thirty biographical articles on the history of Finland in the new *Encyclopedia of the Lutheran Church*. As a member of the Commission on Theology of the Lutheran World Federation and of the Faith and Order Commission of the World Council of Churches, I have been privileged to engage in theological labors on an international level with many of the leading theologians of our day.

The next Suomi Synod pastor to become a theological professor outside the Synod was Jacob W. Heikkinen, professor of the New Testament at Lutheran Theological Seminary in Gettysburg, Pennsylvania. He is well known in Finland, for following the Second World War, he served as administrator of American aid to the Church of Finland and later returned for a year of research and teaching at the University of Helsinki. Heikkinen earned his doctorate at Princeton, and his scholarship in the New Testament is precise and up-to-date. In the best Finnish tradition, he is a theologian with broad cultural interests, especially in music. He is also an ecumenist and serves at present on the Faith and Order Committee of the National Council of Churches.

Walter J. Kukkonen, professor of systematic theology in the Lutheran School of Theology at Chicago and a former pastor of Suomi Synod parishes and professor at Suomi Seminary, has pursued graduate studies at Chicago and Helsinki and holds a doctorate from the institution he now serves. His special field of research has been Finnish pietism; he has recently spent a year at Tuebingen investigating the roots of the theology of pietism. In addition to his articles in theological journals and his book, *The Faith of our Fathers,* he has also translated Lennart Pinomaa's *Faith Victorious.* Kukkonen, Karl Mattson, Axel Kildegaard, and I prepared the doctrinal article for the constitution of the Lutheran Church in America.

Other Suomi Synod pastors who have engaged in theological and religious education are Karlo Keljo, who has taught New Testament and other subjects at Suomi, at Lutheran School of Theology at Chicago, and at Hartwick College; Robert Hetico, a leader in parish education who teaches courses in that field at Hamma School of Theology; and David Hartman, teacher of religion at Wittenberg University.

An account of Finnish theology in America would not be complete without reference to three former presidents of Suomi College, all primarily educators rather than theologians, but all ordained by Suomi Synod and contributors to theological education. John Wargelin has served as educational administrator both at Suomi and in public schools; his academic research has dealt with the Americanization of Finnish immigrants. But as the spiritual and cultural leader of the American Finns for many decades, he has always been primarily a churchman. He has presided over Suomi Synod, taught in Suomi Seminary, and among other literary labors translated Nikander's *Bible History.* V. K. Nikander, son of the founder, holds a doctorate in philosophy from Harvard and is professor of philosophy and chairman of the department of religion and philosophy at Wagner College. During his presidency of Suomi, he translated the catechism of the Church of Finland for use in Suomi Synod churches. He is the co-author of a college text, *Religion in Life, a Christian Interpretation*. Bernhard Hillila, now the dean of California Lutheran College, served for a few years as the dean of Hamma School of Theology. A skilled professional educator with a doctorate from Columbia, he has been an advocate of progressive ideas in theological education.

In addition to the main line of the Finnish heritage represented by Suomi Seminary, the Finnish National Lutheran Church had at one time a seminary of its own with two clergymen from Finland as instructors, K. E. Salonen and A. Vasunta. This group has now merged with the Missouri Synod, where Finnish-born Alex Monto and his successor, Gerhard Aho, taught in the seminary at Springfield, Illinois. During the years of heavy immigration to the United States from Finland, American Congregationalists promoted a revivalistic religion among the Finns with K. F. Hendrickson in charge of training pastors for the Finnish churches of this denomination.

Since the main wave of Finnish immigration to America coincided with the rise of nationalism in Finland, most of the immigrants brought with them an intense loyalty to the spiritual and cultural values of their native land. The founding of Suomi College and Theological Seminary was motivated both by the desire to train pastors for Suomi Synod in the Finnish tradition and by the determination to preserve the Finnish cultural heritage. A close relationship has thus existed from the beginning between Finnish Lutheranism in America and the Church of Finland. Not only have most of the teachers in the Seminary been clergymen of that Church, but the curriculum of the Seminary was originally patterned on that of Helsinki and Finnish continued to be the main language of instruction. As recently as two decades ago when American-born students were fighting a losing battle with the intricacies of the language of their fathers, they had to obtain their knowledge of Christian doctrine by struggling with the elegant Finnish of Pietilä's *Dogmatics*. Knowledge of Finnish has indeed been the key to the treasure house of Finnish theology. The only American theologians with access to this theology have been the few who are at home with this beautiful but difficult language. The theologians of Finland are keenly aware of the language barrier which separates them from the English-speaking world. Some of them, for example, Pinomaa, Nikolainen, and Gulin, have lectured here, but regrettably few of the writings of Finnish theologians are available in English. They are better known in Europe for an increasing number of their scholarly works are being published in German. Through these translations professional theologians everywhere now know something of the work of the Finns. However, had the *Dogmatics* of Pietilä and Tiililä been published in English, they would undoubtedly have had a strong influence upon theological thought both in America and the rest of the world.

In recent years, the Finnish Theological Literature Society has published in English seven issues of an occasional journal entitled *Theologia Fennica*. It contains summaries of books and surveys of the various fields of Finnish theological research. The latest issue is in the form of a book, *Finnish Theology Past and Present,* edited by Lennart Pinomaa, and published in connection with the Fourth Lutheran World Assembly held in Helsinki in 1963. In this work, the best introduction in English to modern Finnish theology, each of the main branches of theological study is reviewed in its historical setting by an outstanding authority, and the reader is given a bibliography of the principal publications by Finnish theologians in languages other than Finnish between 1959 and 1963. The Assembly itself served both to focus world attention upon Finland and to promote an ecumenical outlook in Finland.

It is obvious that Finnish theology in America presents no unified school of thought. Theologians have reflected influences derived from a variety of academic backgrounds and have responded, each in his own way, to the progress of scholarship in their respective fields. Yet, the theologians who have drawn upon Finnish theological scholarship to relate the Christian message to the American scene manifest an underlying coherence based primarily upon a conscientious but not slavish fidelity to the fundamental doctrines of the Lutheran Reformation and its confessions. Today, the lively Reformation research, in which theologians on both sides of the Atlantic have participated, furnishes the principal guidelines. But the true spirit of the Reformation is not to concentrate attention upon itself nor upon any denominational or national structures of thought, but upon the Word of divine revelation. Finnish theology is a theology of the Word, not in the sense of fundamentalistic biblicism, but of listening with Luther to the "God who speaks" and making constructive use of biblical scholarship to interpret the meaning of the divine speech. Another distinctive trait of Finnish theology is the creative appropriation of the legacy of the pietistic revival movements in Finland. To the Finnish understanding of the Christian faith, Finnish pietism in its various forms has given a depth and vitality which have prevented it from becoming a mere academic exercise. Paavo Ruotsalainen's concern for an awakened conscience, F. G. Hedberg's interest in personal assurance of salvation, and L. L. Laestadius' stress on "the power of the keys" have all had their exponents on the American scene. Tensions have existed in the past between these varying emphases, but in the historical and ecumenical perspective of today, they may be seen to complement one another, each serving in its own way to drive the church and its theology closer to the living Word. As Lutherans in America move toward a united front and as Christendom as a whole seeks a unified witness to the world, it is to be hoped that the heritage of Finnish theology will play a constructive role in the fulfillment of the church's mission.

Douglas J. Ollila, Jr.

❖ THE SUOMI SYNOD
IN PERSPECTIVE:
AN INDIGENOUS INSTITUTION

ONE HUNDRED YEARS OF Finnish life in America is, from a historical perspective, a brief period of time. Yet in only one century, the Finns in America moved from a hesitating, fledgling community to highly articulate, self-conscious associations of divergent ideals, and finally, to a loss of identity through acculturation, intermarriage, merger, or the loss of faith in once vibrant ideologies.

Today, third and fourth generation Americans of Finnish descent look back to their heritage with great interest, occasionally with amazement, or a touch of humor, and sometimes with great admiration. Four brands of socialism, eight branches of Lutheranism, several "sects," temperance advocates, cooperative movements, and an infinite variety of lesser organizations, ranging from anti-socialist leagues to mutual benefit societies, were clear signs of vitality. The spirit of association and fellowship, even if it led to bitterness and hatred, nevertheless, assisted the new immigrant in adjusting to his environment and gave him endless opportunity for self-expression.

Most of this immigrant vitality has now disappeared. The socialist and conservative press hang on by threads which grow thinner every week. The temperance movement lies on its deathbed, while church bodies have given expression to their Americanization through amalgamation with others of like mind. Suomi College in the mid-sixties is an entirely different institution from the *Opisto* of her founders, and she must dream ambitious dreams in order to take her rightful place in American education. Historical societies write the obituary of the immigrant era.

Contemporary historians of the Finnish movements in America place them into the broader context of American history. It is likewise appropriate to interpret the history of the Suomi Synod as an immigrant institution heavily influenced by her American environment, which, in fact, moved to become an indigenous church in the earliest days of her history. It is patently false to view the Synod merely as a cluster of Finnish Pietists transplanted into an insulated ghetto, dreaming of the glories of faith and life in the motherland.

The moment a Finnish newcomer stepped off the steerage deck, he was thrust into an entirely new set of circumstances, which created a revolution in his outlook and patterns of life. He brought with him the faith of his fathers, but this soon began to bear the image and stamp of Anglo-Saxon Protestantism. In the English section of the *Siionin Laulukirja* were British and American hymns rather than transpositions of the plaintive melodies and translations of the moody lyrics of his native land. His ethical patterns reflected the morality code of nineteenth-century American revival Christianity as much as Vaasanlääni morality. He sent his children to a modern variation of the revivalist camp meeting called Bible Camp, where Gospel songs were as vigorous as personal testimonies of religious experience. J. K. Nikander's Beckian biblicism influenced a generation of pastors, but it was really not radically different from the prevailing patterns of American pietism, especially that generated by the Fundamentalist-Modernist controversy.

Democracy in Finnish church life had theological continuity with the European mother church. The revival movements were essentially lay-centered, and they produced a peasant-clergy closely attuned to the needs and expressions of the people. The state church lost the support of intellectuals who adopted a scientific world-view. Further alienation was created through Beckian biblicism, which sought no conversation with philosophy and science. The Lutheran Church of Finland then moved to its own source of strength, the peasant classes, by turning from dependence on the government and the pillars of society to the believing people. This was the "folk church." [1] Mikko Jurva suggested that this movement can be regarded as an emancipation.

Legal recognition of the rights of the people was pronounced in a law in 1887, which allowed sectarian groups to found congregations and to organize national church bodies. This symbolized complete recognition of the freedom of the revival movements to form *ecclesiolae in ecclesia*.

Thus the development of the Finnish Folk Church with its vigorous, pietistic lay-movements provides the context for the development of the Suomi Synod. Nikander, who provided the most important leadership during the formative years of the church, came from a tradition which emphasized the role of the laity rather than that of the ecclesiastical hierarchy. Faithful to the Beckian principles of his teacher, Gustaf Johansson, he accentuated the importance of the "true congregation" within the broad, national church. This meant a church of the people rather than a church of the clerics. One of Nikander's favorite phrases was *kansan suosio* (the favor of the people), which came directly from the Pietists and Beckians.

It appears almost providential, then, that Nikander assumed leadership in the early Synod. He came to America with a democratic bias. This enabled him to wait patiently for movements to gain momentum through popular sanction before he assumed leadership and the articulation of the spirit of the people; it also explains his usual slowness in making decisions and public statements. Furthermore, he mediated between the enigmatic J. W. Eloheimo, who imagined himself bishop of all the Finns in North America, and the spirited J. J. Hoikka, who urged rapid and immediate change most often in the direction of the synodical polity of his own Swedish Augustana Lutheran Church.

If European Finnish Lutheranism provided a context for the democratization of institutions in America, it was, nevertheless, the American experience itself which created representative democracy in the Synod. To begin with, congregations were usually organized apart from the direction of national church bodies, often by laymen alone without the benefit of the clergy. Finnish Lutheranism was a people's movement served by a painfully small number of clergymen, who had to depend heavily on articulate laymen to maintain congregational life. The Suomi Synod was more a merger of previously formed congregations than a church which directly organized congregational life, though home mission activity was certainly not lacking.

Careful examination of the early records shows quite clearly that the Synod moved inexorably in a democratic direction, often because of the pressure of popular movements among fellow clergymen. The original decision to found an ecclesiastical body was made in 1886 in Minneapolis, and it was decided to pattern the movement as a democratic synod, if the meager sources available are accurate.[2] No immediate action on the proposal was taken until 1888, when J. W. Eloheimo began to press for organized church activity. His new proposals were strangely different. The Hoikka correspondence and the Finnish-American press, especially the *Yhdysvaltain Sanomat,* reveal that Eloheimo envisioned grandiose schemes of an episcopal church with himself as chief bishop. Even before consulting his fellow pastors, he announced a financial drive for constituting a church and appointing a bishop.

Eloheimo's proposal was greeted coldly by the press, and Hoikka refused his support because Eloheimo confided to him that the clergy would work completely independent of congregations and popular opinion.³ Two other schemes, a proposal by the Astoria, Oregon congregation to found an association called the "American Finnish Church," ⁴ and an organization called the Finnish Evangelical Missionary Society of the United States of America ⁵ both proved abortive because no support could be found among the scattered Finnish population.

Once Eloheimo had been silenced by popular opinion, the three pastors in Upper Michigan, Nikander, Hoikka, and Kaarlo Tolonen, moved independently to determine the patterns of future church activity. A series of mission festivals in 1889 culminated in an image of a new church. It would be Lutheran, though even this was not entirely a foregone conclusion since the immigrant press urged a broader basis for ecclesiastical activity. Further, the church would be orderly, inclusive of saints and sinners (similar to Johansson's national church with a circle of true believers) and not Laestadian.⁶ On November 7, it was decided that a church body would be organized along the lines of synodical polity.⁷

Unfortunately, the authoritarian hand of the would-be bishop intruded itself into the new series of proposals. When the consistory was organized as a *pro tem* governing body for the proposed church, Eloheimo was elected temporary chairman. Exactly why he received the chairmanship is not clear. Hoikka, now Eloheimo's sworn enemy, was not at the meeting to contest his election. Nikander had a reputation for modesty, and it may have been that he humbly stepped aside to give honor to the aggressive "bishop," whose aspirations were only too well known.

More important, however, Eloheimo was given the task of writing the constitution for the proposed Synod. This nearly proved the undoing of the infant church. Incorporated into the governing instrument, the 1890 *Perustuslaki,* were several episcopally oriented provisions. It was determined, for example, that the ratio of clergymen to the total number of representatives at the annual convention "shall never be less than one to three or more than one to two." ⁸ Clerical privilege was further revealed in the provision that the congregation would never lower a pastor's salary from that stipulated in the letter of call notifying him of his election.[9]

Violent opposition to the proposed constitution developed quickly. The *Kansan Lehti* and its inflammatory editor, Ino Ekman, hurled repeated charges of authoritarianism against the constitution, and Eloheimo was compared with the Shah of Persia. Even the seemingly innocent reversionary property clause, which provided for synodical ownership of property in the event a congregation disbanded, was interpreted by Ekman to mean that local congregations had no control over their own property.

More important was the schism in the Calumet congregations. On March 17, 1890, Eloheimo excommunicated five hundred members from his flock because they opposed joining the proposed Synod. This resulted in the formation of a "People's Church," which became the nucleus of another Lutheran movement among American Finns, the Evangelical Lutheran Church. This movement counted seventy-nine congregations by 1923, and served sixty independent congregations by providing itinerant pastors. Originally it bore the image of a completely democratic church, but later it identified itself with the tradition of the evangelical revival movement of Finland.

There is no real evidence that the beginning of the National Church can be traced to a theological controversy between Beckian Pietists and Evangelical Pietists. The Calumet People's congregation was for a time served by two men of Laestadian background, A. L. Heideman and W. A. Mandellof. The journalist, Kalle Haapakoski, prompted independent congregations to join together to found a national body, but such calls for organization were never founded on a theological basis; rather, the problem was church polity and the rights of the people.[10] It was only after 1900 that there was specific identification with the Gospel Society of Finland.[11]

While Eloheimo's efforts created great dissent, the constituting convention of the Synod, held on March 25, 1890, accepted the governing instrument with hardly a murmur. No traces of weakness were found. It must be remembered, however, that the delegate list included the decidedly conservative elements of the Finns in America which were prone to accept powerful clerical leadership. Nikander expressed his discontent with the constitution, but wanted to proceed slowly with major changes.

If these earliest days of the Synod exhibited some traces of clerical authoritarianism, such vestiges of feudal paternalism were destined to die quickly because of the clamor of the powerful Finnish-American press as well as the problem of schism in local congregations. Hoikka, now a pastor in Sweden, gave his own sharp but perceptive criticism in Fred Karinen's temperance newspaper, the *Tyomies*.[12] Haapakoski of the *Amerikan*

Uutiset was a sworn enemy of the Synod, and the *Yhdysvaltain Sanomat* continued a heated dialogue with Nikander's and Tolonen's *Paimen Sanomia*. New congregations continued to appear, even in Hancock. Independent congregations were also founded; they usually publicly vowed never to be a part of the hated Synod.

But the air cleared quickly. Eloheimo began to have mystical paroxysms in the form of a revelation of a Universal Kingdom, in which he, "minister Elohim," would be supreme governor. This led to his release from the Synod. He then founded his own "Fenno-American Church," which was a fiasco from its beginning. After that, he accepted the presidency of the National Church, which was founded in 1898.

Freed from the bishop, the 1893 convention changed the troublesome reversionary property clause to a trusteeship arrangement in the event a congregation dissolved.[13] The 1896 convention thoroughly revised the constitution in the direction of synodical polity with a highly democratic flavor. For example, the consistory, as the executive board of the church, was given fairly broad powers; but the annual church convention was the final court of appeal, and the consistory was directly responsible to it.[14] The proportion of laymen to pastors was not even mentioned in the revised constitution, and subsequent conventions of the church were splendid examples of representative democracy at work. The Suomi Synod emerged with a strong tradition of clerical strength and leadership, but laymen were no less powerful.

Equally important was the strength of the congregation as spelled out in the constitution. Congregations themselves elected representatives to the annual conventions, selected their own pastors and managed their own activities. In fact, the 1896 constitution had a strongly congregational flavor.[15]

Thus, from 1893 until 1896, the church underwent her most decisive change, at least, from an institutional perspective. This period saw the triumph of synodical polity, which maintained a careful balance between the power of the clergy and that of the laity, provided the framework for thoroughly democratic procedures, and emphasized the role of the local congregation.

A final factor in the indigenous development of the Synod was her relationship to the Church of Finland. One of the earliest concerns of the infant church was to obtain official recognition from the mother church. Thirty years passed before any official "blessing" was pronounced; by that time it was a somewhat meaningless gesture, since the Synod had learned to walk on her own feet, though somewhat haltingly.

Before the Synod was founded, the Bishop of Kuopio, Gustaf

Johansson, privately suggested that the Finns should join the Augustana Synod.[16] However, once founded, the Suomi Synod was given tacit approval by numerous Church of Finland officials, including Johansson, who became Archbishop. But no official recognition was given, partly because Finland was a Grand Duchy of Imperial Russia. A special convention of the Synod was called on October 17, 1894, to discuss the problem of unity with the mother church. This involved points of canon law such as the legality of pastoral acts performed in the United States. Specific recognition of pastoral acts apparently could not be given because of legal technicalities such as the requirement of a *kuulutus,* or hearing, before a wedding.[17]

Official recognition of the Synod was not given until 1923, after the visit of Bishop Juho Koskimies.[18] However, whether early official recognition would have greatly assisted the Synod is debatable. The people's movement probably would have continued, but non-recognition did force the Synod to depend on itself rather than wait for the protection of a kindly mother. She did claim that she was the American representative of the mother church, but immigrants, nearly intoxicated with their newly-found freedom of choice, joined Synod congregations for other reasons.

The Synod did depend on the Church of Finland for clergymen. Between 1890 and 1930, fifty-one Church of Finland pastors came to the United States. However, thirty-four returned, usually after serving two to four years. Thus the church had to train her own clergymen and again depend on her own resources.

It can be concluded then that the Suomi Synod moved in the direction of an indigenous institution, sensitive to its American environment and reflecting American democracy in her life. It was not overly difficult for her to blend into the American scene as symbolized by her merger into the Lutheran Church of America.

Obviously this study in Americanization and accommodation is not the whole story of the Synod. Differentiation is also characteristic of her growing church life and from 1910 to 1950, the intensity of her self-image grew. The language controversy revealed the growth of Finnish nationalism among all American Finns, especially after 1917, when Finland became an independent nation. From 1940 to 1955, some pastors began asking about the sources of the faith of the church, concluding that the Synod was truly Finnish in theological spirit. There is ample evidence that Finnish nationalism was stronger after the formative period of the Synod. Tolonen, Nikander, and Hoikka were keenly aware that the Finns would be rapidly assimilated into their environment, but after 1920, the appeal for the Finnish language and Finnish culture grew ever stronger.

While it is true that differentiation—"we are special"—is an important factor in the history of the Synod, it developed along with an almost inevitable assimilation. Self-definition was necessary for the Synod's survival. The immigrant church, according to Oscar Handlin, was the only institution to be transplanted intact from Europe because Christianity was a psychological necessity for the uprooted peasant who had no other supports for his unhappy life in America.[19] Conservative Finnish peasants in America constructed church buildings at great sacrifice because the church was central in their lives.

From an institutional perspective, self-definition and differentiation occur because of the tenacity of organizations to persist rather than to merge or to die. The failure of the 1913–1915 negotiations for merger with the Evangelical Lutheran National Church is a clear indication of this tendency. The Americanization process, however, was finally victorious.

NOTES

1. Mikko Jurva, *Valtiokirkosta kansankirkoksi* (Porvoo, Finland: Werner Soderstrom, 1960), pp. 359–60.
2. J. J. Hoikka, "Sananen Ameriikan Suomalaisten ev. Lutherilaisten kirkollista yhdistyspuuhista," *New Yorkin Lehti*, February 20, 1894, p. 4. See also, *Kirkollinen Kalenteri*, 1903, pp. 33–54.
3. Letter of J. W. Eloheimo to J. J. Hoikka, Republic, Michigan, April 18, 1888.
4. Excerpt from the Minutes, Evangelical Lutheran Congregation of Astoria, August 12, 1888.
5. Articles of Incorporation and Minutes of the Finnish Evangelical Missionary Society of the United States of America.
6. *Paimen Sanomia*, August 21, 28; November 13, 20, 1889.
7. Amerikan-Suom.-Ev. Luth. Kirkkokunta eli Suomi-Synodi Kirkko-kunta-historia, p. 3.
8. *Amerikan Suomalaisen Evankelis-Lutherilaisen Kirkkokunnan eli Suomi-Synodin Perustuslaki* (Hancock, Michigan: Paimen Sanomain Kirjapainossa, 1890), Chapter 5, Article 30.
9. *Ibid.*, Chapter 2, Article 23.
10. *Amerikan Uutiset* (Calumet), January, 1898; May 26, 1898.
11. G. A. Aho and J. E. Nopola, *Evankelis-Luterilainen Kansalliskirkko* (Ironwood, Michigan: National Publishing Co., 1949), pp. 31–105.
12. *Tyomies* (Ishpeming), April 23; November 5, 1890; January 12, 1891.
13. Kirkolliskokouksen Pöytäkirja, Negaunee, Michigan, June 6, 1893.
14. *Amerikan Suomalaisen Evankelis-Lutherilaisen Kirkkokunnan eli Suomi-Synodin Perustuslaki ja Sivulait* (Hancock, Michigan: Paimen Sanomain Kirjapainossa, 1897), By-laws, Articles 34–40.

15. *Ibid.*, Articles 3–31.
16. Letter of Gustaf Johansson to J. J. Hoikka, Republic, Michigan, August 10, 1889.
17. Juho R. Koskimies, *Piispa J. R. Koskimiehen Yhdeksannelle Yeeiselle Kirkolliskokoukselle Amerikan Suomalaisiin Seurkuntiin Suomen Kirkon Edustajana Vuonna 1921, Matkasta Antama Kertomus* (Turku, Finland: Uuden Auran Kirjapaino, 1923), pp. 1–3.
18. *Amerikan Suometar*, July 7, 1923, p. 1.
19. Oscar Handlin, *The Uprooted* (New York: Grosset and Dunlap, 1951), pp. 117–43.

ON THE
CHARACTERISTICS OF
AN ETHNIC GROUP

Carl E. Waisanen

❧ THE SOCIAL PROBLEMS OF THE FINNS IN AMERICA

IT IS STILL CUSTOMARY to identify certain social problems by referring to the groups primarily affected, for example, the Negro problem or the Indian problem. While such labeling is often a matter of linguistic convenience, it tends to perpetuate the notion that these problems derive from the peculiar and often undesirable characteristics of those so designated. The matter is not so simply explained; the title of this article is used only for the sake of convenience.

Another point in this regard may need some elaboration. It is obvious that all people, singly or collectively, suffer at least some of the problems which beset mankind. The term, social problem, does not necessarily encompass all of the difficulties of the human race. A given society may not, for example, consider a high rate of infant mortality a social problem. Another society may insist that thumb-sucking is a social problem of serious dimensions. For the purposes of this article, a social problem is defined as any social condition which has become a matter of serious public concern.

It is questionable that the social conditions relating to the *Finnish* immigrant in America became a matter of general public concern. Nevertheless, the Finns who migrated to the United States did have difficulty adjusting to their new country. Certainly, the Finnish immigrants were part of the immigrant problem, and consequently fit within the above definition.

From a sociological point of view, the general problem of the immigrant to the United States can be reduced to his social and economic status. The immigrant generally possessed neither wealth nor education. The majority came from the lower social classes. Thus the immigrant was destined to begin his new life at the bottom of the social and economic ladder.

The salable skill of the immigrant was his bodily strength, and it was the need for manpower which swelled the flow of immigration to North America. Being at the bottom of the social and economic ladder, the immigrant was given the least desirable employment. Except for jobs which were highly dangerous or physically demanding, he was poorly paid. He was often the first to be fired and the last to be hired.

The economics of the immigrant's situation, which was abetted by his usually larger than average family, dictated that he adopt the general living standards of his wage-earning class. His home, if not in the slums, was in the cheaper residential districts. He was often caught in the credit game when his unwary mind or financial situation lured him to emulate the native or to ease a pressing financial burden. His style of living was focused on the everyday needs of existence. His life situation and, perhaps, past inclination led the immigrant to a feast-or-famine psychology. Impulses to behavior were gratified when he received his paycheck, and there was little concern for the more distant tomorrows. When faced with circumstances which did not permit impulse gratification, he was stoical or worked out his frustrations in less acceptable and more aggressive ways.

Complicating the immigrant's adjustment to his new society was his proclivity to settle among his own ethnic group. This tendency was natural for it afforded him social and psychological security and some practical advantages. However, it also retarded the acculturative and assimilative processes. The concern here is not whether the immigrant should or should not have established "Little Italys" and "Little Finlands," but to emphasize that the ethnic community, once established, became a contributing factor to the immigrant's problems.

The consequences of the ethnic communities were many. The immigrant was retarded in learning the language of his new country. In his own neighborhood, with his own social affairs, he was more easily persuaded to see himself as essentially different from those who were not of his kind. This typical in group-out group phenomenon, with its biases, stereotypes, and emotional currents, further decreased intergroup contact. In effect, the immigrant became more visible. He could be identified geographically as well as culturally. His foreignness acquired a physical dimension, and he was more easily placed in the social class system.

The essence of social class determination is categorical evaluation. An individual is located in a more or less broad grouping of people who are assumed to have a somewhat similar social worth. Although an individual's virtues, or absences of them, may be taken into account, other criteria, such as his occupation, income, and family background, are more influential. Further impersonalizing the evaluative process is the tendency to blanket evaluation, in which some common denominator is ascribed to a visible group. The common denominator, in turn, determines the social position of a member in the group. He is stereotyped as "good-natured but lazy," "hardworking but clannish," or "hot-tempered but honest." Such was often the fate of the immigrant.

Caught in the vortex of forces which he little understood and appreciated, the immigrant reacted in understandable ways. Militantly or passively, he exaggerated the differences between his own kind and those of the dominant native groups. Analogously, the latter exaggerated the immigrant's "foreignness." As one feared and distrusted the other, so the other distrusted and feared him. The net consequence was the immigrant's further withdrawal from the larger community which may have fostered a disquieting sense of social isolation, a doubt as to whether he really belonged in this new country. It was perhaps at this stage that more than a few immigrants decided that the new country was not all it was claimed to be, and packed their bags to return to their native country or to a different environment. Some hastened to pioneer isolated communities, the names of which still recall the ethnic origins of their founders.

The social history of the immigrant in the early decade of his American life, was, therefore, a process in which barriers, both real and imaginary, were created between him and the larger society. These barriers perpetuated his foreignness, inhibited his Americanization, and maintained his low social and economic status. In the context of a public policy, such as existed in the late nineteenth and early twentieth centuries, which strongly urged the rapid Americanization of the immigrant, the situation may well have reached the proportions of a serious social problem. As mentioned before, the social situation gave rise to anxieties, stereotypes, and other negative feelings. Both the minority immigrant groups and the dominant native groups succeeded in communicating these feelings to the rising generations who fought the same battles on more or less the same battlefields, although not necessarily with the same outcomes.

A final note regarding the immigrant's participation in the political and power structure of his community seems in order. While this aspect may have general relevance to the second wave of immigrants, it seems to be particularly relevant to the situation of the Finnish immigrant.

Coming to America without the benefits of education or wealth and without the skills which might have given him more remunerative occupations, the immigrant's social and political power was almost nonexistent. While this would be the expected condition of the newly arrived immigrant for perhaps the first decade of his stay in America, its continuance must be considered unusual. Why did these immigrants, especially when they were located in a community in which they were at least a strong minority, not manage to use their political power to gain a voice, and thus attempt to better their social conditions?

This question poses interesting problems. Were the practical difficulties of naturalization and learning the mechanics of politics significant obstacles? Was it a further symptom of the immigrant's tendency to withdraw? Could it have been that he was inhibited by the occasional radical and schismatic political expression of some segments of his group? Perhaps the best answer is indicated by the personality of the immigrant.

Most of the immigrants came from countries in which they were peasants. Whether they considered themselves, or actually were, oppressed is not the crucial issue here. The point is that these people were the product of a long period of social conditioning which made them psychologically incapable of active political participation in the American democratic context. Although the concept of democracy may not have been totally unknown to the immigrant, his arena was the more formal and polite elections of minor officials of village and church offices. To him, American politics was a strange and bewildering activity. It was as if it lacked the proper decorum; it was not the place for the grave and careful deliberation which the immigrant may have expected and appreciated. The immigrant considered the spirit of American politics wrong and somehow not in the nature of things.

To understand his reaction to the American political scene, one must see the immigrant's personality as a mixture of idealism, rigidity, and humility. He was a kind of Puritan who preferred the world in black and white. He was more comfortable with absolutes and statics than with relativities and dynamics. He had, unsophisticated and limited as it may have been, a sense of the proper order of things, and even though he may have been enthralled with his new freedom, he was not yet psychologically free to reject his past and participate freely in the American context. Thus, the immigrant was inhibited in his political participation. Such an inhibition dies hard; it is still found, in some degree, among the immigrant's children and grandchildren.

Available data place the number of Finnish emigrants to the United States at approximately three hundred thousand, at least eighty percent of whom arrived after 1900. Of the total number of emigrants to the United States up to 1920, the Finns make up less than one percent.

The Finnish immigrant was part of what is known as the second, or "new," immigration, largely composed of people from the southern, central, and eastern areas of Europe. Americans tended to characterize the Finn, not as Nordic or Scandinavian, but as "eastern" or Slavic, even Mongolian as some earlier racial classifications had described him.

The reception accorded the Finnish immigrant by America was not a friendly one. The height of Finnish immigration to the United States coincided with a growing public fear of and hostility toward the foreigner. That the Finnish immigrants were predominantly Protestant and tended to settle in the more isolated areas did not, apparently, affect the image. He was rated as a foreigner, sharing the rather low social esteem accorded the "new" immigrants, and was barely tolerated as a resident of the country.

The analysis of the general immigrant problem already given fits the Finnish immigrant. He was poor, his occupations were manual, and, though literate in his native language, was uneducated. He lacked the confidence and poise of the more acculturated groups. He was in the lower social strata; his social and political influence was minimal. He, like most of the ethnic groups the second wave, was trapped by the social conditions of the day.

A number of writers, both Finnish and non-Finnish, have written about the Finnish immigrant. He has been described as phlegmatic and unimaginative, hardworking and persevering. Another has seen him as temperamental, jealous, and inclined to unpredictable behavior. One writer considered him moderate, thrifty, and mechanically inclined; yet another believed him addicted to strong drink. The Finnish immigrant has been characterized as individualistic and clannish, religious and superstitious, radical and conservative. He is also, according to one writer, loyal to his friends and generous to strangers. Whatever cautious conclusions may be drawn from this listing of characteristics, the most obvious is that the

Finnish immigrant was many things. It may also be inferred that he was sufficiently different from the native American to be recognized as a foreigner.

Less impressionistic information shows that the Finnish immigrant generally conformed to the common social patterns of American life. He married at the usual age, had a larger than average family, but an average life expectancy. He educated his children in the public schools, and was in the main law-abiding. There is little evidence to indicate that he was more, or less, prone to poverty, mental illness, or disease than any other of the immigrant groups of his time. That he tended to marry within his ethnic group, to attend and support his own church and other social organizations, and to live among those of his own kind is abundantly clear. In these respects, he followed the pattern of most, if not all, ethnic groups during their earlier years in their new country. On the other hand, it seems plausible that certain characteristics of the Finnish immigrant did affect his adjustment to the American way of life. These, in the main, involve his withdrawal from the larger community and his ineffective participation in the American democratic process of social and political decision-making.

The immigrant's disinclination to participate in the rough aspects of American political life has already been mentioned. The Finnish immigrant was psychologically incapable of active participation in the American context. He tended to accept the idea that his future was intimately related to his own character, virtues, and conduct. His emphasis was on moral growth, on the development of self-control and the will to resist the evils of the world. While this may be taken as a religious influence, it was also characteristic of the so-called radical and non-church Finnish immigrant. The left-wing Finnish immigrant leader, for example, did not usually condemn the economic structure of capitalism, but rather the capitalist himself. It was the capitalist who was evil, who lacked the virtues of human decency, and thus brought on the suffering of people. This view of human behavior produced a rigidity which the Finnish immigrant did not easily overcome. The author remembers many instances of Finnish immigrants' remarks on some aspects of political life: "You should vote for J——, he is a *good* man." Or when the results of an election were in, "Well, that is the way it goes, the good man was beat again." The goodness of a man was not deduced from his actual or presumed effectiveness in political office.

The Finnish immigrant was frank in his self-conception. Not only were there good and bad people, there were also the *herrat* and *meikäläiset* (roughly, aristocrat and commoner). Even though he saw the social structure in terms of an aristocrat-commoner dichotomy, he was not self-conscious about his own position. He admitted his lower status, not reluctantly nor with regretful humility, but as a statement of fact. This was in the order of things and, therefore, to be accepted. There was no stronger criticism of a *meikäläinen* than to say that he pretended a *herra* status. On the other hand, high praise of the *herra* was to say that he was like us *meikäläinens*. The Finnish immigrant usually regarded those matters outside of his immediate concerns as the province of the *herrat*. Aspiration to a more important political or business position was often defined as an undesirable pretension. If an immigrant's son or younger brother advanced economically or socially through, for example, his occupation, his achievements were regarded with awe, and almost disbelief that it could have happened. When asked for advice by his son or daughter regarding a position denoting a higher status, the father's advice may have ranged from indignant opposition to a cautious and worried condonation.

There was an unusual type of ethnocentrism in the Finnish immigrant, that of a man of simpler manners and taste from a rural and peasant background, who saw life and its demands as intimately connected with his willingness and ability to work manually and diligently to produce the basic necessities. Although this ethos finds a more natural expression in a rural setting, it was extended to the urban environment when the Finn's livelihood was dependent thereon. There was pride in his strength and endurance, but there was also hate and sullenness when he felt he was being taken advantage of. This was followed by a tendency to define his condition, which may have been the result of impersonal factors, in particular and personal terms. The enemy was not the system, it was the outsider, the *herra* or the group who was represented by him. At the same time, he believed that he could not overcome them; indeed, they too may have been in the order of things. There was little to do but withdraw, either to his native country or to another, preferably rural, environment. If these were not possible, then he retreated to a more intense ethnic fellowship or sometimes, unfortunately, into the recesses of his own mind. It is of interest to note the not uncommon case of a Finnish immigrant who crossed the ocean eight times before he finally decided to settle permanently.

Withdrawal was not interpreted as a setback or defeat. From the Finn's point of view, honor had not been at stake. Unable to conceive of himself as a competitor in an impersonal social structure, the Finn's

rationalization was that the native American was different from him. For
example, it is doubtful whether the Finnish immigrant worked hard in order
to keep someone else from getting his job. He worked hard because it was
his duty to do so; it was a matter of self-expectation and an inner com-
pulsion. On the other hand, the Finnish immigrant did understand and
participate in a *conflict* situation in which a personal enemy could be
identified. That was the time to step in, as of old, and "throw the rascals
out." This syndrome of extreme behavior is also illustrated by the typical
Finnish immigrant father. He was aloof and disinterested in the tolerable
peccadilloes of his offspring, but if they went beyond his point of tolerance,
he was apt to react severely.

In one sense, the Finnish immigrant's withdrawal from the larger
society was an attempt to avoid conflict. However, complete withdrawal
was not possible, nor perhaps desired; some involvement was inescapable.
When he became involved with bitter consequences, the Finn created,
perhaps unconsciously, a personal enemy. While this preserved his own
integrity, it blinded him to the integrity of the outsider.

Moreover, the Finnish immigrant was not comfortable in a situation of compromise. He was not at ease with the sins of the world, for
he was too much of an idealist to accept the imperfection of man and
to work within the realm of the possible. Socially, he was not future-
oriented, and the concept of social betterment was either beyond his understanding or considered nonsense. It was as if there were too many day-to-
day matters to contend with, and any ideology which spoke of systems,
processes, and consequences was either beyond the pale, or devised to
confuse or corrupt an honest, simple man.

Finally, leadership which would have given the Finnish immigrant
group a collective focus was conspicuously absent. Although it cannot
be maintained that the Finnish immigrants lacked a sense of collective
unity, this sense often had unpredictable effects. While there seemed to
have been a collective pride or guilt whenever a Finnish person attained
public attention, it seldom united the immigrants in a common cause.
Undoubtedly, the very heterogeneity of the Finnish immigrants' social and
political activity was a factor. Other hypotheses such as intra-group jealousy
seem less defensible. A more acceptable explanation of the absence of a
collective political and social expression was that the Finn did not have
the social and cultural experience for assuming the role of a leader in an
impersonal and competitive culture. While a kind of *gemeinschaft* leadership may have arisen, as indeed it did within his own church and social
organizations, this leadership was charismatic and unless the charisma was

unusually strong, it was influential only in a limited situation. It was only much later that the Finnish immigrant or his progeny understood the possibilities of leadership and the value of the practical politician.

In conclusion, it is necessary to reiterate that this analysis is chiefly speculative. The empirical studies which may or may not support the numerous contentions made here have not yet been undertaken. There has been no intention to make any final judgments as to the character, conduct, or worth of the Finnish immigrant.

or worth of the Finnish immigrant.

Ralph J. Jalkanen

❧ THE POSSIBILITIES FOR PRESERVING A PARTICULAR ETHNIC HERITAGE

ARCHIBALD MACLEISH once commented that "Our period is unique
for the great number of middle-aged individuals who have knowledge of the
future and are eager to share that knowledge with others." The kind of
prescience referred to by MacLeish is not responsible for this contribution
which makes no claim to a special knowledge of what the future may
bring to an ethnic heritage. However, there are developments which seem
highly improbable in the immediate future and others that appear rather
more likely.

Because the Finnish immigrants came relatively late to America,
they were among the last of the ethnic groups to establish themselves in
small colonies, usually near a major body of water.[1] They took their places
in the lower economic classes as carpenters, lumberjacks, masons, ma-
chinists, miners, operatives in mills, fishermen, domestics, janitors, common
laborers, farmers, and storekeepers. They tended to live in isolation from
other groups, with a clear recognition of differences in status and social
composition. The Finns and the Irish, who often lived in the same communities and worked in the same industries, for example, maintained
separate neighborhoods. Generally, the Finns were content with their lot,

208

though the norms of the higher classes did cause restiveness, especially among radical groups and their leaders.

Such factors as low rentals, easy accessibility to work, the influence of the church, and social pressure enforced segregation in the early period and helped to keep the immigrants from attaining much mobility. That workers, middle, and upper class people tended in each community to live in isolation from one another delayed assimilation. In addition, the Finnish immigrants may have, in part, elected to live together or to isolate themselves from other groups, especially in the early years, in reaction to discrimination and pressure against them as they moved out from their residential areas.

Lacking the Irish immigrants' mastery of the English language, faith in the superiority of their church, and ethnic militancy and cohesiveness, all of which helped them to press for social and religious leadership, the Finns did not drive for leadership and upward social mobility in the first generation. Rather, recognizing their peasant background, they became laborers—and the common people. Their stolid temperament and acceptance of work conditions made them easily acceptable to employers. The motto of many early immigrants may well be stated: "work, save money, have children, and return to the old country."

Although there were at one time over three hundred and eighty thousand foreign-born Finns in America,[2] almost equal to the number of several other immigrant groups at the turn of the century, they apparently had little impact on the American culture in the early days. One reason for this may be sought in the divisive proclivities of the Finn. The many newspapers published in the Finnish language at the time represent political, social and economic views in a continuum from the extreme left to the right. The immigrants were avid subscribers to the *Tyomies* (The Worker), the *Raivaja* (The Pioneer), the *Industrialisti* (The Industrialist), or the *Suometar,* along with numerous denominational newspapers and a number of middle-of-the-road papers. Even the churched Finns were divided among various Lutheran, Methodist, Congregationalist, and Unitarian churches.

There was in America no regularly established church for the immigrant. There existed only individual mission-spirited ministers who had come to America after their countrymen had arrived in large numbers. The lack of an established church may have contributed to the disorganization and lack of solidarity among the early Finnish immigrants as well as to their apparently slight impact upon the socio-cultural life about them.

Durkheim saw the chief function of religion as that of representing

those collective beliefs and rites which provide the integration and solidarity of a society. For him, religion symbolized the dominant values in
society. Thus, social life without communal and devotional affirmations
of universally accepted values is characterized by *anomie*—disorganization,
normlessness, apathy—in short, the loss of society. For the early Finnish
immigrant, the dominant values were not religious ones, and so he lacked
adequate norms of behavior and probably suffered from anomie.[3]

Ernest Troelsch posed the "ultimate problem" in the study of religion and culture as, given a civilization in which there are decisive forces
such as state, economic organization, and innumerable other formative
powers, how do religious institutions harmonize these forces in such a way
that together they will form a unity of civilization? It appears that the
immigrant church because of its dependence upon individual clergymen
rather than on strong organization was seldom able to weld together the
masses by creating an integrated and meaningful view of the world and
of the social forces surrounding the immigrant.

As the established church of the homeland, Lutheranism provided
by far the strongest religious community in the new land. However, even
Lutheranism suffered from fragmentation and during this period probably
never mustered more than one-third or one-fourth of the total number of
immigrants into its fold. If we consider that the church which regarded
the Church of Finland as her mother church never attained a membership
larger than thirty-six thousand,[4] one-tenth of the total number of immigrants, we have a measure of the formal religious strength of the community. If an approximately equal membership is postulated for each of the
two major branches of Apostolic Lutheranism [5] and several thousand sec-
tarians are included, the number of "religious" Finnish immigrants approxi-
mates one hundred thousand, or less than one-third of the immigrant
population.

This does not mean that the Finns were irreligious. If anything,
the opposite was true. But the immigrant seldom saw adequate cause for
"joining" a church into which he was born and which had been given him
as a birthright in the old country. Also, in many cases he was antagonistic
not to religion per se but to an institution which had coerced him to pay
"church taxes" in kind or in labor back home. Moreover, he had other
business to attend to for the moment, such as earning a livelihood, and
was perhaps avowed to care for his religious concerns when age was upon
him. Will Durant perhaps sums up the matter best: "Only when man has
had enough bread to eat and has satisfied his passion, does he have a little
time to set aside for the religious function."

After the early days, especially when a new generation of clergy trained in America came into its own in the Lutheran church, church leaders differed as to whether support of the national language and traditions strengthened the church or not. The clergy trained in Finland, as well as many who spoke only Finnish, sought to use the resources of the church to maintain national mores and manners within the parish and community, since it was more difficult for them to adjust to the host culture than for the second-generation clergy. Many lamented the decrease of church-centered activities which accompanied Americanization and appealed poignantly for the simultaneous preservation of Lutheranism and Finnish culture:

> We desire to be Lutherans of the Finnish language. Why do we become Americanized so rapidly when our Finnish culture, so abundant and rich, can contribute to the cultural enrichment of the United States? The founders earned their daily bread by hard toil. Why should we who are the beneficiaries of their toil and battles, neglect our beautiful language?

But American Finns typically sought their social life through organizations separate from the churches, even when the churches sponsored their own parish-centered adult and youth organizations. The Kaleva Lodge, temperance societies of various kinds, and political groups representing the left (as the church groups were *ipso facto* defined as representatives of the political right), each with its own "hall," sprang up while numerous sub-groups bore witness to various traditions and loyalties through separate organizations and activities. Perhaps only the Finnish Midsummer festivities centering about *Juhannus* (St. John's Day), a national Finnish holiday from which the religious stamp had long since disappeared, were able to unite the various sub-groups.

In spite of strong efforts and commitments by many groups to the contrary, the process of assimilation prevailed. In fact, the very culture which the Finns brought with them from Europe subtly served to accelerate the Americanization of the second and third generations of Finnish Americans. Although language had originally prevented the process in the first generation,[6] to the Finns, race, nationality, and religion, even at the beginning, constituted no overwhelming barriers to the acculturation process. Many second-generation Finnish Americans maintain that assimilation of the Finn into American society was, if anything, too rapid, not affording him time to recognize and accept the values in the culture from which his progenitors had come. Generally, however, the second-generation Finn, except in the most isolated areas, took on the American way as though accelerated assimilation had been encouraged by some divine command. The third generation typically had lost the language of his immigrant forebearers and was altogether out of touch with the ethnic culture.

Like every immigrant group, early Finnish immigrants were subject to discrimination and were the objects of prejudice. Second- or third-generation Finnish Americans, however, would scarcely recognize the discrimination their immigrant fathers once felt. The vast majority of the third generation, in fact, no longer think of themselves as the children of immigrants. At most, they consider themselves "Americans of Finnish descent."

Given the background of the Finns in Europe, it should not be considered strange that they did, in fact, show evidence of some unusual features with regard to assimilation.

Since the Middle Ages, a majority of Finland's population have spoken Finnish; a minority, Swedish. Although the Swedish-speaking minority was concentrated on the west coast, they were, nevertheless, sufficiently dispersed throughout the southern part of the country to pose a problem in intergroup relations. There was a great deal of mutual discrimination, and feelings between the two groups often ran high. The Swedes tended to be merchants while the Finns were mostly farmers; when industrialization began, the Swedes generally became the entrepreneurs while the Finns became the workers. Because of the language advantage, the Swedes tended to be better educated. Consequently, the conflict was one of class, with the numerical minority occupying the dominant position. Finland did not attain independence until World War I; only then did the federal government set about equalizing the position of the two language groups. With the democratization of privilege, the status differences between the two groups quickly diminished, and higher cultural opportunities and economic leadership became available to Finnish-speaking persons. Today the conflict is hardly discernible, although memories of the past are kept alive by the older generation.[7]

If one bears in mind then that both the early (1880–1900) and later (1900–1920) waves of Finnish immigrants were born and reared in a country in which they had never possessed independence and never constituted a dominant cultural group with its attendant prerogatives, it is not surprising that they put an inordinate stress upon liberty, justice, and freedom.

Love of freedom may well be the most striking characteristic of the Finn. He possesses a kind of instinctive love for freedom which is revealed in his love for the homeland, love of independence, and a self-respect based upon them. He hates slavery and resents domineering attitudes. Self-esteem begets in him a basic honesty and integrity. The Finn appears to dislike authority of any kind and has a great deal of difficulty in obeying and subjecting himself to rigid discipline.

Second, in spite of its small size, Finland has always lived in relative ease with both political and religious pluralism. The Communist Party has inevitably been accepted as one among the many political parties where a coalition is sought only after elections, not before them as in America. Pluralism in religion has existed for centuries, the Eastern Orthodox faith living side-by-side with Western Lutheranism.

Finns have an unusually profound respect for knowledge, for the abilities which a trained intellect can bring to bear on a situation, for *syntyja syvia* (penetrating insights and inspiration). Literacy is universal and few countries can boast such a well-rounded reading public. The peasant in the north may possess a modest home library of basic works in theology, philosophy, literature, and history. Even scientific works are read in a land where the typical university professor takes it upon himself to write semi-popular works in his field. The largest bookstore in all of northern Europe supplies the literary needs of the Finns. Cultural and educational activities made possible by many agencies and institutions produce a well-developed citizenry.

The Finn is typically of a meditative, philosophical nature. His folk wisdom has been clothed in proverbs, several volumes of which exist in print. He is prone to introspection and evaluation of his own attitudes, characteristics conducive to the production of a self-analytic meditative poetry which is read with great interest.

Certainly among the Finn's best-known attributes are his ambition and perseverance. Without them, he would never have succeeded in cultivating the unyielding land of the north without modern equipment. Finnish *sisu,* for which no exact equivalent exists in other languages, consists of the Finn's ability to outlast and outperform, to exert himself beyond ordinary human limitations. At labor, at war, and in sports, this spirit has achieved worldwide recognition.

It might appear unusual that a high degree of literacy should exist in a land where the monarchy forced a minority rule, using a tongue unknown to the majority. But when independence was won and the long language struggle was resolved in favor of the language of the people, the

Finnish language was not only well known and read among the populace, but was available in such a sophisticated form as to make it a suitable vehicle for the arts, the sciences, and the humanities. This was possible because of the theretofore unnoticed contribution which the church had made to the welfare and edification of the people since the Reformation. The church had labored long in teaching all the inhabitants to read and write. Because of her efforts, there had existed since the middle of the sixteenth century a written language which she, in lieu of an adequate system of public education and sometimes against the will of the ruling powers, had taught to all comers. Confirmation was compulsory, and to be confirmed one had to learn to read.

Four factors—race, nationality, religion and group status—are keys to understanding an immigrant cultural group, its place in the community, and its dynamics. In addition, there are socio-economic factors— the predominant family pattern, the language used daily, the degree of education and vocational goals, avocational interests, political and religious affiliations, and attitudes toward other groups—which influence and give distinctiveness to any sub-culture group. A minority group's length of residence in America and its acceptance by the dominant group bear upon the pattern. Generally, members of the first, second, and third generation increasingly adopt the American way of life. The original immigrant inculcates personal attitudes, folkways, skills, and ideas, as well as group behavior in his children with varying degrees of consistency. The third generation commonly continues the process of social assimilation, though many groups retain certain traditions indefinitely.[8]

On the basis of the above determinants, we shall attempt a brief sketch of some traits which characterize the Finnish American while at the same time recognizing the dangers of oversimplification.[9]

Finnish immigrants to the United States came chiefly from northern Finland. The first generation, now aged and swiftly disappearing from the scene, still use their native language, name their children on the basis of the names appearing in the almanac, and are retiring and modest in their social communication. In speech, their use of intonation and understatement convey qualities of meaning that cannot be easily understood by outsiders.

Leisure-time activities are engaged in by men and women separately, the men having their own meeting places. Drinking, mostly by men, is done outside the home, if anywhere, since the church has traditionally frowned upon liquor, which was frequently associated with other sins such as card-playing, gambling, and dancing. Finnish women are typically closely tied to the home and have few recreational interests. Singing and acting were popular among the first generation, with a melancholy minor folk idiom used in popular songs as well as the dance.

Finnish-American families were not especially closely knit. The husband dominated the wife and maintained family discipline. Children were taught to be seen and not heard and were often sent to another room when visitors arrived. They were sent to work while still young, although those with a "school-head" were encouraged to attend school. Wages were usually kept by the working youth although he may have been expected to pay for his upkeep at home. The members of the family developed fairly strong patterns of mutual interest and protection, though overt manifestations of affection were frowned upon. The tradition of a large family has tended to die out with the immigrant Finn. People of Finnish extraction are considered restrained and inhibited in their social relations although they may engage in heated arguments among themselves.

Though Americans enunciate principles with respect to the democratic treatment of immigrant groups in the United States, a gap has existed between the concepts espoused and the authoritarian beliefs of many communities and individuals. Immigrants to America have been received under the auspices of three separate historic principles: Anglo-conformity, the "melting pot," and cultural pluralism based upon social tolerance. These were, of course, never given official approbation, but operated as informal opinions and unconscious presuppositions.

Every society regards strangers as outsiders. In America, white Anglo-Protestants established the dominant cultural pattern, and, after the early nineteenth century, regarded immigrant peoples from continental Europe as an out-group. Economically deprived or politically dissatisfied with conditions in their homelands, immigrants began to arrive in significant numbers. They brought with them the only folkways they knew—those of the old world.

Immigration grew so rapidly that the established Anglo-Americans became concerned that their manner of life would be destroyed by the impingement of "foreign" groups. Naturally, they sought to defend their supremacy, using their prestige to preserve social control and to define what was to be the American pattern of life. The minority patterns were all regarded as inferior because "foreign," a condition which made adaptation to the social environment difficult. But as the homogeneous groups of immigrants increased, they held to their customs, organized their own clubs, linguistic newspapers and churches, and by accepting the pressure toward Anglification, tended to become second-class minorities. Immigration quota systems were passed to give preference to northern and western Europeans who fitted the American scene more easily.

The early efforts of the Americanization movement attempted to bring the foreign-born to accept the anglicized version of what constituted good citizenship. Patriotic groups looked down on non-acculturated people who perpetuated old ways and used a foreign language, quite unconcerned about the fact that this was the only means of communication open to them. Some immigrant groups reacted to this process by maintaining their own ways against all persuasion to the contrary. Others made heroic efforts to cast off their old ways and become accepted by the Anglos, with a subsequent loss of considerable folk-art, customs, skills, and, more tragically, their children's respect. Consequently, authoritarianism worked badly in building democratic peoples, denying what it purported to convey.

The melting-pot concept sought to appeal to common elements existing underneath the different customs and language. It was based upon the immigrant's need to belong and to be accepted in his newly adopted land. Although in rural areas immigrants withstood the erosion against their heritage for as much as seventy-five years, most groups found it impossible to live only within themselves. However, a review of the melting-pot period indicates that while assimilation indeed took place, many people did not "melt" freely into the main body of American life. Strong minorities maintained their separate ways, and new blood perpetuated old customs.

Hence, the principle of amalgamation did not funtion rapidly enough, nor did it fuse people into a unity. The process was incapable of producing a democracy, as many an individual wished to retain an identification with his ethnic group and found therein profound satisfaction. It was considered non-American to encourage cultural differences in the plan of building a uniform society.

The third idea developed when it was recognized that it was more acceptable to build human relations based upon cultural heterogeneity sought through pluralism and tolerance than in any other way. It recognized that many peoples have a deep pride in their heritages, and by maintaining their loyalty to them, they can be better Americans. This concept considers the domination of minorities a thing of the past as no ethnic group requires the tutelage of some other in the field of Americanism. E. George Payne describes this viewpoint:

No culture contains all favorable elements, but each group that makes up a total American population has unique values, and the nation will be richer and finer in its cultural make-up if it conserves the best that each group has brought. The theory assumes, furthermore, that the minority groups have been so thoroughly conditioned by their heritages that the historic past could not be sacrificed even if they chose to forget the past experiences. Their natures, characters, and personalities are built out of cultures different from our own, and the method of effective cultural transmission requires that the fundamentals of their heritage be preserved for generations. The only other option is cultural deterioration, the disintegration of family life, and the maladjustments in our social life.

Tolerance is based upon acceptance or an attempt to understand the beliefs, habits, and practices of another without sharing them or making them one's own. However, many today consider tolerance undesirable and patronizing: to tolerate is not to assimilate and may even express duplicity.

As none of the three principles has been found without a weakness in building a foundation for a united civilization, in practice if not in precept, it is thought today that a more comprehensive precept for a multicultural society may be one in which the individual discovers his cultural role under the basic democratic values of freedom, responsibility, and their balance.

A good citizen is considered to be practicing cultural freedom if he respects human differences in society. Cultural heterogeneity is a uniquely American expression of freedom, in which every constituent group of people is encouraged to be itself and to nurture its own traditions, whether brought from the old country or developed indigenously in America.

The United States has reached a point in her national life where we may look with tolerance upon our ethnic pluralism; it may well be at this point also that our national purposes can be rediscovered, redirected, and sustained by some minority which has a significant contribution to make in this regard. The present is as fortunate a time as any for an ethnic group to make a singular contribution, if it has one to make, to abate the decay, apathy, rigidity, and moral emptiness which surrounds us and to communicate whatever spirit of dynamism it may possess. However, any contribution must be made in the spirit of American culture and further its goals. Any "foreign" view which is at variance with the cultural base would certainly gain little hearing, and with good cause.

Significant insights from Finnish culture can be brought to bear upon the American scene. Consider that America has, in one sense at least, exchanged positions with Finland in being the Soviet Union's "neighbor to the west." Small nations in an age of missiles and nuclear power are no longer viable enemies of large nations. The only real contestants are the large nations which may have something to learn from a country and culture which has co-existed for centuries alongside of Russia. How does it happen that only Finland of all the European countries lying on the eastern border of Western Europe still has its independence? Is it possible to transfer the commitment and attitude which have made it possible?

Americans want freedom and espouse it as a prime national objective. But we cannot achieve it unless it becomes the business of every individual in our society. We must become capable of maintaining the idea of freedom in a world, by and large, hostile to the concept. History reveals that free societies survive only when they are worthy of freedom. They must deliver what they promise by keeping alive cherished values and practicing a disciplined life. An enlightened people must be quick to recognize the kinds of effort required to keep a society vital and strong. If a given ethnic heritage, joined in a common purpose with others, can keep alive the aim of freedom, that would be contribution enough.

But it need not be all. Tradition also has something to say about religious values and moral decay. The people who have made the best contribution to the welfare of mankind on earth have had a vision and lived by a firm faith in still another kingdom. Finnish Christianity seeks the sensitive ethic of the attitude of man, not in some outward ostentation but in humility of heart of the individual standing before his God.

Finnish Christianity bears evidence of the meditative and philosophical bent of the individual believer. It blends sensitivity with rigor; it seeks out the immovable One with a quiet persistence. The revival movements within the church express a sensitivity of soul responding to the grace of God. There is a basic humility about the faith which searches out the ways of God and seeks contentment therein. Struggling and striving are more elemental to this position than are peace and joy. It seeks to penetrate beyond the logical and rational schemata of a scientific world view. The depth of meditation found here is the mark of a kind of primitive creativity. Man becomes small when compared to God's majesty and goodness. He despises nothing quite so much as self-made goodness and a fake concept of high spiritual attainment as a result of one's experiences.

No set of laws can prevent chaos in a society which lacks moral commitment, a higher fealty. In fact, even the concept of freedom must be rooted in man's philosophical and religious views. Everyone, of course, does not need to agree in order to have a consensus on values, but a substantial portion of the population, especially those who shape the national purposes, must do so. Those values are the religious beliefs from which man gains his deepest views on the life of man in the light of God.

It will be no easy thing to espouse religious values in a society where the majority have come to believe that the intelligent thing to do is to assume a "scientific" neutrality or agnosticism toward these values. It is true that both natural and social scientists have found that neutrality with respect to certain values is essential to their work. Social scientists have achieved the relativist point of view at the cost of a great struggle; the legitimate benefits resulting from their effort must be respected. Nevertheless, the notion that neutrality with regard to all values can be adapted to all of life is absurd. Even the scientist accepting and living only by the concept of moral relativism is in danger of being an "absolute relativist." However, when great numbers of people in a given society take up the toleration of all values in a moralistic laissez faire, the result is a belief in nothing in particular except to stand aside and act the part of an interested observer.

Many moderns find it embarrassing to talk about moral concern. But to be embarrassed about moral seriousness is a disease of a society in the process of decay. Those without affectation will consider consultation with their deepest values natural. It is not that faith will give ready answers to all the problems which beset modern man, but it does afford the strength to face the problems. Religious commitment has been at the root of all civilizations during their apogee. Whether a civilization can survive and be renewed without it remains a moot question.

Finnish culture differs from most in that its heroes are poets, musicians, artists, architects, and sculptors. Only during a national emergency does attention shift to the military service of a Mannerheim. Otherwise, this society is lifted above its internal conflicts by leaders who have achieved excellence: Aleksis Kivi, Lönnrot, Snellman, Runeberg, Sibelius, Aalton, Saarinen, or Paavo Nurmi.

Lyman Bryson once said, "The purpose of a democratic society is to make great persons. . . ." A society becomes that which it admires; a free nation and its institutions exist to keep and develop the intrinsic powers of men. We may learn something about ourselves and the possibility for the maintenance of a free society if we look at the kind of men we have made our heroes. It speaks well for a society not to divide its people into two categories, those who achieve and create and those who do not. A nation's heroes should say rather that each man can achieve a measure of greatness for himself; the difference is one of degree.

Our society must ask itself if it honors the excellencies which will, in the end, most fructify its own vitality. What do our heroes imply as to the tone and texture of our life and purpose? Each individual should be afforded the possibility of working out his own potential in the rich possibilities available to him. There is hope for a society which sees the necessity of high standards and the striving required to achieve those standards within the limits of each person. We must encourage a sense of self-fulfillment for every degree of ability and all acceptable activities. But it cannot be done without adequate models.

Finally we may learn of still another kind of equality from this heritage, that of equal political suffrage. Historically, women in Finland gained political suffrage before those in America. However, political equality and equality before the law must be followed by equality of opportunity.

One of the gravest losses in our society has been a lack of concern for the education of women. Equality of opportunity requires that females, as well as males, be encouraged to strive for individual excellence in all its forms, whether in political life, in education, or in industry.

In summary, it appears that there exists a need in American society for the preservation of the best concepts and ideals of ethnic heritages. However, the preservation of the best of any given heritage can be accomplished only insofar as it fructifies the new culture from within.

In order to accomplish anything in this vein, we must learn to know, understand and genuinely accept our past and believe that there are values and attitudes inherent therein which are worthy of inculcation into American life. We must select those ideals which will be the most appropriate for the society in which we exist as a minority and maintain a certain optimism concerning the possibility for their acceptance.

NOTES

1. Only the exceptional Finnish immigrants settled as far inland as North and South Dakota. They are found in larger numbers in upper Michigan, northern Minnesota, along Lake Erie in Ohio, upper Illinois, on the East Coast from Boston to New York, California and the Northwest.
2. See Reino Kero, "Emigration from Finland."
3. The deep sense of anomie suffered by some may be grasped from the case of an immigrant who, as soon as he had earned passage, returned to Finland

only to find himself miserable in both his former homeland and America. After having crossed the ocean several times by ship, he came to the conclusion that the only place in the world in which he could find contentment was aboard a ship bound for either Finland or America.

4. *Kirkollinen Kalenteri* reports this as the apogee for the immigration period. As baptized children were normally included in the membership statistics, this figure may represent as few as ten to fifteen adults.

5. Apostolic Lutherans have no known published figures of membership from this period, but if one allows that the two dominant groups of Laestadians (the term used in Finland for persons of this persuasion) each had as many members as the Finnish Evangelical Lutheran Church in America, the figures may be regarded as an educated guess as to the number of immigrants actually related to a church.

6. One reason for this lay in the fact that the Finnish language has no common root words with English, nor with any of the Teutonic languages. Hence, it was more difficult for the Finnish immigrant to learn English than it was, for example, for the immigrant from the Scandinavian countries. When a Finn did learn English, it was as a distinctly new language. Many did learn English, but such factors as age of emigration, intelligence, proximity to other Finnish-speaking Finns, nature and place of employment, isolation, etc., were all related to the outcome.

7. See Eino Sormunen, *Omalla Pohjalla* (Upon our Foundations) (Helsinki: Werner Söderström Osakeyhtiö, 1944). It may be that many of the second-generation Finns—as well as others—did not teach their children the language of their immigrant parents because they were aware of studies in bilingualism and intelligence since the early 1920's which attempted to determine whether monolingual and bilingual young people differ in intelligence as measured by standard tests. Many of these studies concluded that bilingualism had had a detrimental effect on intellectual functioning. Because of the recent emphasis on second language learning, a revival of interest in this problem has occurred. Studies made since 1960 have not sustained the conclusion drawn earlier. Peal and Lambert [The Relationship of Bilingualism to Intelligence, Psychological Monograph 174 (16), 36 pp. (1962)] studied monolinguals and bilinguals in Montreal French schools, and, contrary to prevalent findings, report that bilinguals performed better than monolinguals on both verbal and non-verbal intelligence tests. They argue that bilinguals are more facile at concept formation and have greater mental flexibility. They also found that bilinguals have a more diversified set of mental abilities than monolinguals. Another study investigated the hypothesis that exposure is one form of enrichment of the environment which results in the development of different patterns of cognitive abilities. This study demonstrated the superiority of bilinguals on tests of cognitive flexibility. Another recent study concludes that bilinguals received lower scores on verbal intelligence tests but not on non-verbal tests. The inconsistent results of investigations are pointed out. It appears that little of a really substantive nature is known about the way in which second language learning affects cognitive ability.

8. Child's classification of the responses of second-generation southern Italians

to the family may be helpful in conceptualizing the reactions of second-generation Finnish Americans as well. He separated the "in-group" reaction, the rebel reaction, and the apathetic reaction. The in-group shows greater adherence to the Italian marriage pattern than the rebel group. The rebels break with Italian ideals by selecting a wife of non-Italian descent who tends to be totally Americanized. He seeks a high standard of living, social mobility for his children and a democratic household. Moreover, he projects his drive for acceptance as an American to his children and provides incentives for acceptance through the patterns of his family life. The apathetic group conforms to Italian ideals. They are influenced more by American culture than the in-group, but less than the rebels. I. L. Child, *Italian or American?* (New Haven: Yale University Press, 1943), p. 110.

9. The stages of adjustment to American life through which most immigrants pass is shown by Campisi in his analysis of the Italian family in the initial contact, the conflict, and the accommodation stages.
The first stage covers the first few years of American life when the family is still highly integrated, although a different physical environment, new equipment, new types of work, attendance of children in public and parochial schools, recognition that the Italian way of life means low status, perhaps work outside the home for the wife, and pressure from American economic and political institutions mean that considerable modification has to be made in the peasant family pattern. The conflict stage begins about ten years after the family's arrival in the United States and when the children begin to acquire American ways while their parents attempt to enforce Old World patterns. During this stage there is much frustration and misunderstanding as the father loses his importance, the daughters acquire a "shocking" independence, and the parents give ground on accepting an American way of life. The accommodation stage is reached when parents and children realize that further hostility will bring about the complete deterioration of the family. This period begins when offspring reach adulthood and establish families of their own. The children are more tolerant of their parents, but they tend to work out their family destinies along the lines of the contemporary urban American family. Campisi says that the adjustment of the American-born parents to the American culture takes three forms:

(a) Complete abandonment of the Old World way of life. Individual changes his name, moves away from Italian neighborhood and has little to do with his parents and relatives. This type of family usually passes for an American family. A rare form. [Corresponds to Child's "rebel" reaction.]
(b) Strong desire to become Americanized and to pattern the family after the contemporary American family. Parental way of life not wholly repudiated, although there is some degree of rejection. Likely to move out of Italian neighborhood and to communicate less and less with first-generation Italians, but family ties are not completely broken. Relationships with parents and immigrant relatives are affectionate and understanding.

(c) Second-generation family oriented inward toward an Italian way of life. This type of family prefers to remain in the Italian neighborhood, close to a parental home. Interaction with the non-Italian world is at a minimum. [Corresponds to Child's "in-group" reaction.]

Campisi states that the second form is the most representative second-generation Italian family in the United States. P. J. Campisi, "Ethnic Family Patterns: The Italian Family in the United States," *American Journal of Sociology* (May 1948), p. 447. See also, G. E. Simpson, *Racial and Cultural Minorities* (New York: Harper and Brothers, 1953), pp. 475–76.

NOTES ON CONTRIBUTORS

Tauri Aaltio is executive secretary of Suomi-Seura, Helsinki, the organization presently responsible for maintaining and furthering Finland's relations with her emigrants everywhere.

David T. Halkola is professor of History, Michigan Technological University, Houghton, Michigan, and is a former president of Suomi College.

Ruth Esther Hillila is on the faculty of the Chinese University of Hong Kong. She received her Ph.D. in Musicology from Boston University, and also did graduate work in Finland.

Lauri Honko is professor of Comparative Religion and Folk Poetry, University of Turku, Finland.

Ralph J. Jalkanen is president of Suomi College, Hancock, Michigan.

A. J. Joki is professor of Finno-Ugric Linguistics, University of Helsinki, Finland.

Eino Jutikkala is professor of History, University of Helsinki, Finland. He has published several books on the agrarian and industrial history of Finland.

T. A. Kantonen is professor of Systematic Theology, Hamma Divinity School, Wittenberg University, Springfield, Ohio.

Reino Kero is a research assistant in the Department of History, University of Turku, Finland.

Francis Peabody Magoun, Jr. is professor emeritus, Harvard University. The article in this volume is taken from his translation of *The Kalevala,* or Poems of the Kaleva District by Elias Lönnrot.

Douglas J. Ollila, Jr. is professor of Religion, Augsburg College, Minnesota.

Thomas A. Sebeok is professor of Linguistics, Indiana University, Bloomington, Indiana. He is Director of the Research Center in Anthropology, Folklore & Linguistics, as well as editor of the Uralic-Altaic Series.

Paul Sjöblom was the special representative of the Sibelius Centenary Committee of Finland in the United States in 1965, and is also Helsinki correspondent for the *Christian Science Monitor* and other newspapers.

Arnold Stadius is professor of Finnish and Religion, Suomi College, Hancock, Michigan.

Carl E. Waisanen is a social-psychologist and Academic Dean, Suomi College.

224